Published by:

Wiley Publishing, Inc.

111 River St.
Hoboken, NJ 07030-5774

ISBN-13: 978-0-7645-7983-7
ISBN-10: 0-7645-7983-5

Editor: Caroline Sieg
Special thanks to Aliyah Vinikoor and Stephen Bassman
Production Editor: Ian Skinnari
Photo Editor: Richard Fox
Cartographer: Elizabeth Puhl
Production by Wiley Indianapolis Composition Services
Chapter 1 illustration by Mary J. Gillot

For information on our other products and services or to obtain technical
support, please contact our Customer Care Department within the U.S.
at 800/762-2974, outside the U.S. at 317/572-3993 or fax 317/572-4002.

Wiley also publishes its books in a variety of electronic formats. Some
content that appears in print may not be available in electronic formats.

Manufactured in China

5   4   3   2   1

A Note from the Publisher

Organizing your time. That's what this guide is all about.

Other guides give you long lists of things to see and do and then expect you to fit the pieces together. The Day by Day guides are different. These guides tell you the best of everything, and then they show you how to see it *in the smartest, most time-efficient way*. Our authors have designed detailed itineraries organized by time, neighborhood or special interest. And each tour comes with a bulleted map that takes you from stop to stop.

Hoping to relive the Summer of Love, or to hop on a cable car to the Fisherman's Wharf? Planning a drive across the Golden Gate Bridge, a hike up Telegraph Hill to Coit Tower, or a jaunt over to the best vineyards in the Napa Valley? Whatever your interest or schedule, the Day by Days give you the smartest route to follow. Not only do we take you to the top sights and attractions, but we introduce you to those special moments that only locals know about—those "finds" that turn tourists into travelers.

The Day by Days are also your top choice if you're looking for one complete guide for all your travel needs. The best hotels and restaurants for every budget, the greatest shopping values, the wildest nightlife—it's all here.

Why should you trust our judgment? Because our authors personally visit each place they write about. They're an independent lot who say what they think and would never include places they wouldn't recommend to their best friends. They're also open to suggestions from readers. If you'd like to contact them, please send your comments my way at mspring@wiley.com, and I'll pass them on.

Enjoy your Day by Day guide—the most helpful travel companion you can buy. And have the trip of a lifetime.

Warm regards,

Michael Spring, Publisher
Frommer's Travel Guides

About the Author

Noelle Salmi was born in the San Francisco Bay Area and lived there as a young child until moving with her family to South America. She returned to the area as a student at Stanford University, before heading to Columbia University in New York to earn a masters degree in international journalism. She worked at a major daily newspaper and at CNN in Rio de Janeiro, Brazil; at Associated Press in Berlin, Germany; and in public relations in both New York City and Seattle, Washington, before moving back to the Bay Area in 2001. Her articles have appeared in numerous US and international publications, including *Jornal do Brasil*, *The West Side Spirit*, *Emerging Markets*, *USA Today*, and *Bay Area Parent*. She is the author of *Frommer's San Francisco with Kids*, 2nd edition, and lives in San Francisco with her husband Mika and daughters Annika and Natasha.

Acknowledgements

For my husband, Mika Salmi, and my daughters, Annika and Natasha.

Thank you to Nina Thompson for her diligent research assistance and her ever-upbeat attitude. Thanks also to Raili Salmi for her help on the home front, which made writing this book possible; to my father William Veale for his proofreading skills; and to everyone in my family for their patience and support. Very many people provided their thoughts and insights into the best places to explore, sleep, shop, dine, and stroll in San Francisco, and I am grateful to all them. My appreciation extends also to my editor Caroline Sieg, whose guidance and expertise were invaluable. Above all, thanks to my husband Mika for his unfailing encouragement and enthusiasm.

An Additional Note

Please be advised that travel information is subject to change at any time—and this is especially true of prices. We therefore suggest that you write or call ahead for confirmation when making your travel plans. The authors, editors, and publisher cannot be held responsible for the experiences of readers while traveling. Your safety is important to us, however, so we encourage you to stay alert and be aware of your surroundings.

An Invitation to the Reader

In researching this book, we discovered many wonderful places—hotels, restaurants, shops, and more. We're sure you'll find others. Please tell us about them, so we can share the information with your fellow travelers in upcoming editions. If you were disappointed with a recommendation, we'd love to know that, too. Please write to:

Frommer's San Francisco Day by Day, 1st Edition
Wiley Publishing, Inc. • 111 River St. • Hoboken, NJ 07030

Frommers.com

Now that you have the guidebook to a great trip, visit our website at
www.frommers.com for travel information on more than 3,000 destinations. With features updated regularly, we give you instant access to the most current trip-planning information available. At Frommers.com, you'll also find the best prices on airfares, accommodations, and car rentals—and you can even book travel online through our travel booking partners.

Star Ratings, Icons & Abbreviations

Every hotel, restaurant, and attraction listing in this guide has been ranked for quality, value, service, amenities, and special features using a **star-rating system.** Hotels, restaurants, attractions, shopping, and nightlife are rated on a scale of zero stars (recommended) to three stars (exceptional). In addition to the star-rating system, we also use a **kids icon** to point out the best bets for families.

The following **abbreviations** are used for credit cards:

AE	American Express	DISC	Discover	V	Visa
DC	Diners Club	MC	MasterCard		

A Note on Prices

In the Take a Break and Best Bets section of this book, we have used a system of dollar signs to show a range of costs for one night in a hotel (the price of a double-occupancy room) or the cost of an entrée at a restaurant. Use the following table to decipher the dollar signs:

Cost	Hotels	Restaurants
$	under $100	under $10
$$	$100–$200	$10–$20
$$$	$200–$300	$20–$30
$$$$	$300–$400	$30–$40
$$$$$	over $400	over $40

15 Favorite
Moments

15 Favorite **Moments**

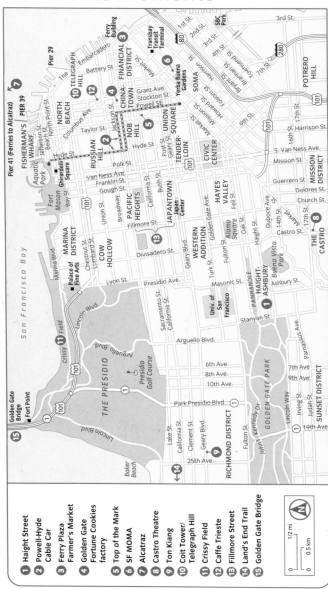

Pier 41 (Ferries to Alcatraz)

0 — 1/2 mi
0 — 0.5 km

Shop for eclectic clothing and accessories on funky Haight Street.

peeled as it crests Russian Hill — you'll catch your first breathtaking glimpse of the San Francisco Bay and Alcatraz Island. See p 7.

❸ Stroll through the Ferry Plaza Farmers Market on a Saturday morning. Taste samples of farm-fresh fruit, handcrafted cheeses, and roasted nuts. Buy breakfast from a restaurant trailer car and enjoy your morning meal by the bay. See p 15.

❹ Eat a fortune cookie with no fortune at the Golden Gate Fortune Cookies factory in Chinatown. Have a still-hot, round wafer right off the machine that makes it. Then watch fortunes be hand-folded into other wafers. See p 80.

❺ Make a toast at the Top of the Mark, the Mark Hopkins InterContinental's panoramic penthouse bar. Wives and girlfriends of World War II servicemen once watched loved ones' ships sail off below the Golden Gate Bridge from the northwest "Weepers' Corner." See p 124.

❶ Hunt for vintage clothing on Haight Street, the one-time epicenter of the 1967 "Summer of Love." See p 32 & 73.

❷ Ride the Powell-Hyde Cable Car. Catch a northbound car to Fisherman's Wharf. Keep your eyes

❻ Behold Henri Matisse's Woman with the Hat. Visit the San Francisco Museum of Modern Art and admire the outstanding collection of 20th-century art. See p 18.

A row of isolation cells inside Alcatraz. Between 1933 & 1963, this infamous island prison (aka "The Rock") housed some of the country's most toughened criminals, including famous gangsters Al Capone & "Machine Gun" Kelly.

The Castro Theatre is a popular, one-of-a-kind moviegoing experience.

7 Contemplate an isolation cell on Alcatraz Island during the audio tour of the former prison. Step inside one of the unlit cells, which were sealed by solid metal doors, and close your eyes to sense the eerie loneliness. *See p 11.*

8 Watch a flick at the Castro Theatre, a 1992 Art Deco movie house in one of the city's most unique neighborhoods. A restored Wurlitzer organ provides musical accompaniment. *See p 66 & 135.*

9 Savor dim sum at Ton Kiang. Drink hot tea as servers bring a procession of tasty Chinese morsels. The options keep changing as the kitchen whips up new batches of shrimp dumplings, pork buns, and other delicacies. *See p 115.*

10 Climb to the top of Coit Tower on Telegraph Hill. Ascend the 210-foot San Francisco landmark for sweeping city views. Inside the base of the tower are impressive murals (titled *Life in California*) painted by more than 25 artists, many of whom studied under Mexican artist Diego Rivera. *See p 9 & 53.*

11 Have a picnic at Crissy Field, the Bay Area's youngest national park. Buy sandwiches at the Warming Hut, sit at a picnic table, and watch ships sail under the Golden Gate Bridge. *See p 85.*

12 Order a cappuccino at Caffé Trieste, the first espresso house on the West Coast and a favored hangout of beatniks, including Jack Kerouac and Allen Ginsberg. *See p 30.*

13 Window-shop on Fillmore Street. Have coffee at a sidewalk cafe before exploring the many boutiques that clothe San Francisco's sophisticated young urbanites. *See p 44.*

14 Walk the Land's End Trail, on San Francisco's northwestern corner. Take in the splendor of the Pacific Ocean, the Marin Headlands, and the Golden Gate Bridge's less-viewed western side. *See p 87.*

15 Cross the Golden Gate Bridge by Bike. Riding across this San Francisco icon on a bike is an awesome experience. The views of the Marin Headlands to the north and the city to the south are awe-inspiring. *See p 40.*

Stand on the Golden Gate Bridge and look up—its bright red steel arches seem to touch the sky.

The Best **in One Day**

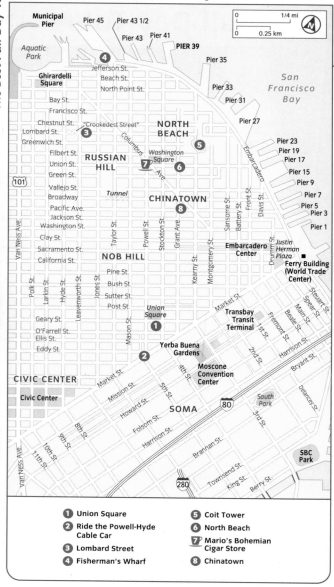

| 0 | 1/4 mi |
| 0 | 0.25 km |

Municipal Pier

Pier 45 Pier 43 1/2

Pier 43 Pier 41

PIER 39

Aquatic Park

4 Jefferson St.

Pier 35

San Francisco Bay

Beach St.

North Point St.

Pier 33

Ghirardelli Square

Bay St.

Pier 31

Francisco St.

Pier 27

Chestnut St. "Crookedest Street"

NORTH BEACH

Lombard St. **3**

Pier 23

Greenwich St.

Pier 19

Filbert St.

Columbus Ave.

5

Pier 17

RUSSIAN HILL

Washington Square

Pier 15

Union St. **7** **6**

Embarcadero

Pier 9

Green St.

101

Pier 7

Vallejo St.

Tunnel

Broadway

CHINATOWN

Sansome St.

Front St.

Davis St.

Pier 5

Pacific Ave. **8**

Pier 3

Jackson St.

Battery St.

Pier 1

Washington St.

Taylor St.

Powell St.

Stockton St.

Grant Ave.

Clay St.

Montgomery St.

Embarcadero Center

Justin Herman Plaza

Sacramento St.

Kearny St.

Drumm St.

Ferry Building (World Trade Center)

California St.

NOB HILL

Pine St.

Polk St.

Larkin St.

Hyde St.

Leavenworth St.

Jones St.

Mason St.

Bush St.

Sutter St.

Market St.

Steuart St.

Post St.

Transbay Transit Terminal

Spear St.

Main St.

Beale St.

Fremont St.

1st St.

Geary St.

Union Square

1

Van Ness Ave.

O'Farrell St.

Ellis St.

Harrison St.

Bryant St.

Eddy St.

2

2nd St.

Yerba Buena Gardens

CIVIC CENTER

Market St.

Moscone Convention Center

Delancey St.

Civic Center

Mission St.

4th St.

5th St.

South Park

3rd St.

Howard St.

SOMA

Folsom St.

80

8th St.

9th St.

Harrison St.

10th St.

11th St.

Brannan St.

SBC Park

Van Ness Ave.

280

Townsend St.

King St.

Berry St.

1 Union Square

2 Ride the Powell-Hyde Cable Car

3 Lombard Street

4 Fisherman's Wharf

5 Coit Tower

6 North Beach

7 Mario's Bohemian Cigar Store

8 Chinatown

This **full-day tour** introduces you to San Francisco's best-known neighborhoods—Union Square to scenic Fisherman's Wharf, historic North Beach, and vibrant Chinatown. Once you arrive at Fisherman's Wharf, the rest can be done on foot, but public transportation options are listed just in case. START: **BART/Muni: Powell or Montgomery. Bus: 2, 3, 4, or 38 to Powell St.; 30 or 45 to Geary St. Cable Car: Powell lines.**

1 Union Square. Start your tour at the shopping and commercial hub of San Francisco. The square itself (named for a series of violent pro-union mass demonstrations staged here on the eve of the Civil War) reopened in 2002 after a $25-million restoration that replaced stretches of lawn with a 245-foot-long (76m) floor of granite and scattered greenery—turning it from a resting spot for the homeless into a welcoming plaza and exhibition space. All that remains from the old square is the 90-foot (27m) *Victory* tower, dedicated by Theodore Roosevelt after the Spanish-American War. ◷ *30 min.; best before 9am. Union Sq. is between Post, Geary, Stockton & Powell sts. BART: Powell or Montgomery. Bus: 2, 3, 4, or 38 to Powell St.; 30 or 45 to Geary St. Cable car: Powell lines.*

2 ★★ kids Ride the Powell-Hyde Cable Car. Head to the cable-car turnaround at Powell and Market streets and await the Powell-Hyde line. The first of these engineless cars made its maiden voyage in 1873. The cable car will take you over Russian Hill. Pay attention as you crest Hyde Street at Greenwich Street—you'll catch your first breathtaking glimpse of the San Francisco Bay and Alcatraz Island. For details on how these cars work, *see p 12.* ◷ *30 min.; best before 9:30am. Powell & Market sts. $3 per ride.*

3 ★ Lombard Street. "The crookedest street in the world" is in fact not even the crookedest street in San Francisco (Vermont St. between 20th and 22nd sts. in Potrero Hill is more crooked!). The zigzags were added in the 1920s, as the street's 27-degree pitch was too steep for cars. Cars are only permitted to descend, but pedestrians can take the stairs up or down on either side. The street is loveliest in spring, when the hydrangeas are in bloom. ◷ *30 min.; best: weekday mornings. Lombard St. (between Hyde & Leavenworth sts.). Cable Car: Powell-Hyde line.*

Riding a cable car is one of San Francisco's most entertaining activities.

4 ★★ **Fisherman's Wharf.** San Francisco's most visited destination is filled with history and a multitude of activities. Although most of the wharf is rife with tacky souvenir shops and overpriced restaurants, this is still a must-see for any tour of San Francisco. Consider the following minitour—it points you to the wharf's most scenic aspects and keeps time near the throngs to a minimum. *Hyde & Beach sts . www.fishermanswharf. org. Cable Car: Powell-Hyde line to Fisherman's Wharf, Powell-Mason line to Taylor & Bay sts; F streetcar to Jones & Beach sts. Bus 10, 30, or 47 to Van Ness Ave. & N. Point St.; 19 to Polk & Beach sts.*

Fisherman's Wharf

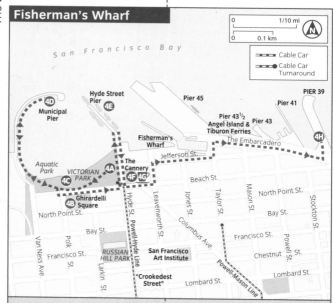

4A **Victorian Park** is where you'll alight from the cable car. You'll see arts and crafts for sale as you walk towards **4B** **Ghirardelli Square,** built in 1893 as Domingo Ghirardelli's chocolate factory. When the factory moved in the 1960s, the building became a National Historic Landmark and now houses a mall. **4C** **The Maritime Museum** (p 23, bullet **7**), a three-story Art Deco structure shaped like an ocean liner, offers a free look at the city's seafaring past. A walk along the **4D** **Municipal Pier** affords views of the Golden Gate Bridge. The **4E** **Hyde Street Pier** (p 22, bullet **4**) holds refurbished antique ships, including a 19th-century square-rigger. **4F** **The Cannery,** once a fruit-canning facility, now houses shops, restaurants, and the National Maritime Visitors Center. **4G** **Order a crepe** from the cart in the Cannery courtyard. Now fortified, you can brave the crowds at **4H** **PIER 39.** Look for the infamous sea lions that have lived by the pier since 1989. ⏱ *2–3 hr.; go in the morning to beat the crowds and bring a jacket—it can be chilly year-round.*

Pier 39's sea lions bathe, bark, and splash about—all around heart-melting fun.

5 ★ Coit Tower. The 210-foot (64m) landmark atop Telegraph Hill was erected in 1933 with $125,000 bequeathed by local character Lillie Hitchcock Coit, who wished to add beauty to the city. Inside the tower's base are murals by several artists, many of whom studied under Diego Rivera. Commissioned as part of the New Deal's WPA, the murals have a pro-worker motif that caused a stir in their day. The fee to climb the tower is worth it: a 360-degree city view awaits you.

While on Telegraph Hill, look out for the flock of wild green parrots, descendents of escapee pets. ⏱ *45 min. From Fisherman's wharf walk or take bus 39 to Coit Tower.* ☎ *415/ 362-0808. Admission to the top $3.75, $2.50 seniors, $1.50 kids 6–12. Daily 10am–6pm.*

6 ★★ North Beach. The immigrants from Genoa and Sicily who founded the Bay Area's fishing industry settled into North Beach in the 1870s—establishing a plethora of Italian restaurants, cafes, and bakeries. In the 1950s, the area's cafes and bars became a haven for writers and artists from the **Beat Generation** (p 30). Today the neighborhood is a combination of Mediterranean warmth and bohemian spirit. For more on this area, see p 52. ⏱ *1–2 hr. From Coit Tower walk; or take bus 39 to Washington Sq. Best Mon-Sat from 11am-4pm. Sundays and early mornings shops are closed.*

7 Mario's Bohemian Cigar Store. Pick up sandwiches and enjoy them in **Washington Square Park** (p 54, bullet **5**) across the street. *566 Columbus Ave. (at Union St.).* ☎ *415/362-0536.* $

8 Chinatown. The most densely populated neighborhood in San Francisco, Chinatown is home to over 14,000 residents. Take a walk down Grant Street to find shops filled with creative, eclectic knick-knacks. Chinatown locals shop on Stockton Street, which is teeming with grocery stores, herb shops, and vendors of ceremonial items. (See p 58 for a complete tour of this colorful neighborhood.) ⏱ *1–2 hr.*

Coit Tower crowns Telegraph Hill.

The Best in **Two Days**

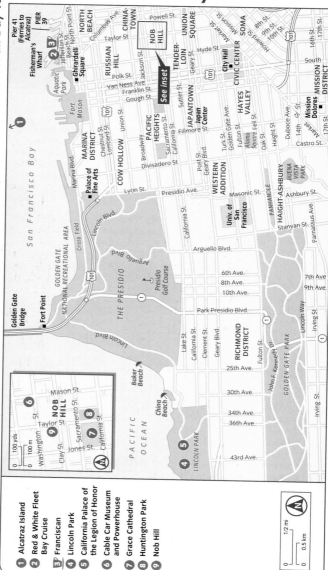

If you have two days, plan your first day as detailed on p 6. For your second day, I recommend you start by going to jail! For many, a visit to Alcatraz is a major highlight—however, pre-reserved tickets are required. If you are unable to get tickets ahead of time, I've listed an alternative bay cruise. Following Alcatraz (or the cruise), you'll visit Lincoln Park, a less-visited but striking corner of San Francisco, and get a taste of 19th-century San Francisco on Nob Hill. START: **Pier 41, Fisherman's Wharf. Cable Car: Powell-Mason. Bus: 30. Streetcar: F.**

1 ★★★ **Alcatraz Island.** Spanish for "pelican," Alcatraz was so named in 1775 by Juan Manuel Ayala for the birds that nested on its rocky shores. From the 1850s to 1933, the U.S. military used Alcatraz as a fort, protecting the bay's shoreline. In 1934, the government converted it into a maximum-security prison to house the country's most hardened criminals, including Al Capone, "Machine Gun" Kelly, and Robert Stroud (the Birdman). Given its sheer cliffs, frigid waters, and treacherous currents, Alcatraz was considered inescapable. However, the prison's upkeep cost a fortune; all supplies had to come by boat. After a 1963 prison escape, the prison was shut down. The island remained unoccupied until 1969, when Native Americans seized it to publicize American Indian rights' issues. They were expelled in 1971. Today, the National Park Service manages Alcatraz. Once inside, you'll receive a headset which plays an audio tour, including stories from former guards and inmates, and riveting tales of escape attempts. From October to mid-February, you can tour the island itself on a walking path. Evenings, the more expensive "Alcatraz After Hours" tour is especially eerie. ⏱ *2–3 hr., including ferry ride. Take the 1st ferry of the day, if possible. Wear a jacket & walking shoes; it's an uphill walk from the ferry landing to the cellblock (motorized carts carry visitors with disabilities). The ferry sells snacks, but there's no food on the island. Pier 41, Fisherman's Wharf.* ☎ *415/773-1188 for information, or 415/705-5555 to reserve tickets. www.nps.gov/alcatraz.* **Note:** *I highly recommend purchasing the ticket that includes the informative audio tour. Admission (ferry & audio tour): $16, $14 seniors 62+, $11 kids 5–11. Without audio tour: $12, $9.75 seniors, $8.25 kids 5–11. Winter daily 9:30am–2:15pm; summer daily 9:30am–4:15pm. Ferries run every half hour. Arrive 30 min. before departure in summer (45 min. in winter). After-hours tours depart at 6:15 & 7pm in summer & 4:20 & 5:10pm in winter. Bus: 30. Cable Car: Powell-Mason line. Streetcar: F.*

Take a tour of Alcatraz, a former prison located on an island in the San Francisco Bay.

2 ★ **Red & White Fleet Bay Cruise.** If you were unable to pre-reserve Alcatraz tickets, take a 1-hour bay cruise with audio narration. You'll travel under the Golden Gate Bridge and around Alcatraz. 🕐 *1 hr. Pier 43½* ☎ *415/673-2900. www.redandwhite.com. Ferry ride & audio tour: $20, $16 seniors 62+ & kids 12–18, $12 kids 5–11, kids under 5 free. Check the website for discount fares. Transport: see bullet* **1***.*

3 For a light lunch, the Fisherman's Wharf seafood counters sell fresh Dungeness crab from November to May. $ (**Note:** If you don't see crates of live crabs, the crab is frozen and precooked.) For a sit-down meal with a view, try the **Franciscan** (p 105) at Pier 43½ ☎ *415/362-7733. $$$*

4 ★ **Lincoln Park.** This lovely park in the northwest corner of San Francisco boasts expansive lawns, eucalyptus trees, an 18-hole golf course, and breathtaking views. Walk north to the Land's End trailhead for a closer look at the Marin Headlands and western profile of the Golden Gate Bridge. 🕐 *30 min.; best in the afternoon, when fog has burned off & the sun turns the Marin hills a golden color. Clement Ave. & 33rd Ave. Powell-Hyde Cable Car to Geary St., transfer to bus 38 to Geary Blvd. & 33rd Ave.; then walk or take bus 18 to Legion of Honor.*

5 ★★★ **California Palace of the Legion of Honor.** Adding to Lincoln Park's splendor is this neo-classical memorial to California's soldiers lost in World War I, which opened on Armistice Day in 1924. An exact replica of the Legion of Honor Palace in Paris, it houses a fine collection of 4,000 years of art, with European paintings by Monet and

Rembrandt, among others, and international tapestries, prints, and drawings. It boasts one of the world's best collections of Rodin's sculptures, including an original cast of *The Thinker.* 🕐 *1 hr. Clement St. & 34th Ave.* ☎ *415/863-3330. www.thinker. org. Admission $15, $13 seniors 65+, $12 youths 12–17, $3 kids 5–11; free to all every Tues. Tues–Sun 9:30am–5pm. Transport: see bullet* **4***.*

6 **Cable Car Museum and Powerhouse.** When British-born engineer Andrew Hallidie saw a horse and its heavy carriage fall backward down a steep San Francisco hill, he vowed to create a mechanical transportation device for the city. By 1873 the first cable car traversed Clay Street. Cable cars have no engines; instead, they are attached to an electrically powered cable that runs at a constant 9½-mph (15kph) rate through an underground rail. When it's time to stop, the car's conductor, or "gripper," pulls a lever to release the car's grip on the cable. Inside this free, fascinating museum, you'll see the cables that carry the cars. Once running over 600 cars, the system today operates only three lines. 🕐 *20 minutes. 1201 Mason St. (at Washington St.)* ☎ *415/474-1887.*

Grab a bite of fresh dungeness crab at the Fisherman's Wharf.

A view of the Transamerica building from the top of Nob Hill.

www.cablecarmuseum.com. Free admission. Daily 10am–5pm; until 6pm Apr–Oct. Closed major holidays. Cable car: Powell lines.

7 ★ **Grace Cathedral.** Following the destruction of the Crocker mansion, Crocker's family donated the land to the Episcopal Church to build Grace Cathedral. Completed in 1964, Grace Cathedral is built from reinforced concrete beaten to achieve a stonelike effect. Some features to look for include the main doors (stunning replicas of Ghiberti's bronze *Doors of Paradise* in the Baptistry of Florence) and the Singing Tower to the right of the main entrance, which has a 44-bell carillon. Inside, note the organ dating from 1840 and the impressive stained-glass windows, some of which depict such modern figures as Justice Thurgood Marshall, San Francisco native poet Robert Frost,

and Albert Einstein. ⏲ *25 min. 1100 California St. (at Taylor St.) www. gracecathedral.org.* ☎ *415/749-6300. Free admission. Mon-Fri 7am–6pm, Sat 8am-6pm, Sun 7am-7pm. Bus: 1. Cable car: All lines.*

8 **kids** **Huntington Park.** David Colton, who also participated in building the Southern Pacific Railroad, had his mansion here until he sold it to Collis Huntington in 1892. The mansion burned following the 1906 quake, and the lot lay empty for 9 years until Huntington donated it to the city. Framed by the granite walls that were once part of the Colton estate, the park is a lovely oasis in a very urban section of town. ⏲ *15 min. Taylor & California sts. Bus: 1. Cable car: All lines.*

9 **Nob Hill.** This famous hillcrest neighborhood is named for its once wealthy residents, or "nabobs" as the elite of San Francisco were known. The "Big Four" railroad barons of the Southern Pacific Railroad—Leland Stanford, Mark Hopkins, Charles Crocker, and Collis Huntington—built their ostentatious mansions here in the late 1870s. They were all destroyed in the fire following the 1906 quake. Today some of the city's most prestigious hotels occupy Nob Hill. ⏲ *20 min. Taylor & Sacramento sts. Bus: 1 from Clement St. & 33rd Ave. to Taylor & Sacramento sts. Visit any day during daylight hours, although the view from the Top of the Mark (see p 124), a fancy penthouse-level lounge, can also be appreciated at night.*

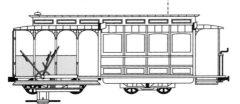

Learn how a cable car actually works at the Cable Car Museum.

The Best **in Three Days**

The Best **Full Day Tours**

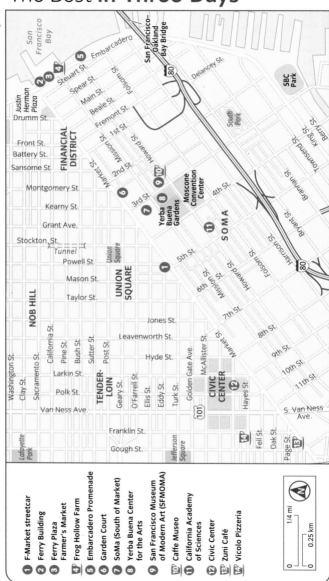

1 F-Market streetcar
2 Ferry Building
3 Ferry Plaza Farmer's Market
4 Frog Hollow Farm
5 Embarcadero Promenade
6 Garden Court
7 SoMa (South of Market)
8 Yerba Buena Center for the Arts
9 San Francisco Museum of Modern Art (SFMOMA)
10 Caffe Museo
11 California Academy of Sciences
12 Civic Center
13 Zuni Café
14 Vicolo Pizzeria

0   1/4 mi
0   0.25 km

If you've already made your way through "The Best in Two Days" you'll find your third full-day tour gives you a taste of the city's epicurean underpinnings, as well as its rich artistic and cultural life. You'll want the whole day for this tour. It can be done on foot, but the F-Market streetcar is an attraction in itself. *Note:* although the Civic Center is just a few blocks from SoMa, the east-west blocks are quite long. START: **From Union Sq., hop on the F-Market streetcar at the Powell St. station; exit at the Ferry Terminal loop.**

① ★ **F-Market streetcar.** Several streetcars travel along Market Street, but the F line also heads along the scenic waterfront. Its streetcars are imported from around the world, including vintage cars from Europe and turn-of-the-20th-century trolleys from other U.S. cities. ⏱ *15 min. From Union Sq., enter at the Powell St. station; exit at the Ferry Terminal loop. Fare $1.25, 35¢ seniors & kids 5–17. Avoid rush hour (M-F, before 9:30am & 4:30–6:30pm).*

② ★★ **Ferry Building.** This 1898 building reopened in 2003 after a 4-year, multimillion-dollar renovation. Outside, you'll see a 240-foot (73m) clock tower. Inside is a collection of restaurants and gourmet-food stores offering artisan cheese, handcrafted chocolates, and other specialty foods. Make your way to the back of the building for a view of the Bay Bridge. If you are lucky, you'll visit on a day the **Farmer's Market** is being held. ⏱ *1 hr. 1 Ferry Building (at the Embarcadero & Market St.).*

Mon–Fri 10am–6pm; Sat 9am–6pm; Sun 11am–5pm. www.ferrybuilding marketplace.com. F or any Market St. streetcar to the Ferry Bldg. or Embarcadero; bus 2, 7, 14, 21, 66, or 71 to Steuart & Market sts.

③ ★★★ **Ferry Plaza Farmers Market.** Four days a week (Tues, Thurs, Sat, and Sun), local farmers and food producers set up booths around the Ferry Building. Saturday mornings are busiest, as San Francisco residents make their regular market trek to stock up on organic fruits and vegetables, naturally raised meats, fresh-baked goods, and so on. Saturdays also feature trailor cars out back, from which city restaurants serve gourmet breakfasts. Given the penchant for using local, organic, and naturally raised produce and meats at many San Francisco restaurants—not to mention homes—this market is a hallmark of city life. ⏱ *1 hr. 1 Ferry Building (at the Embarcadero & Market St.). Tues, Thurs & Sun 10am–2pm; Sat 8am–2pm.*

Take a ride on a vintage F-market line streetcar.

4 **Frog Hollow Farm.** Grab a coffee and a fruit-filled pastry here, before strolling along the scenic waterfront. *Ferry Building Marketplace.* ☎ *415/445-0990. $.*

5 ★★ **Embarcadero Promenade.** The 1989 earthquake destroyed the ugly elevated freeway that once obscured this lovely stretch of waterfront extending from SBC Park to Fisherman's Wharf. The wide sidewalk and scenic views make this a favored destination for pedestrians, bikers, and runners. Notice the Embarcadero Ribbon, a 2½-mile (4km) continuous line of glass encased in concrete, as well as the 13-foot-(3.9m-) tall metal pylons and bronze plaques embedded in the sidewalk, which are imprinted with photographs, drawings, poetry, and historical facts about the waterfront. ⏲ *30 min.–1 hr.; a walk in either direction is pleasant at any time of day, but avoid the traffic on weekday afternoons 4–6pm. Return to Market St. to catch the F-Market streetcar to the Montgomery St. station, or walk.*

6 **Garden Court.** The extravagant Palace Hotel astounded San Franciscans and bankrupted its owner, who allegedly committed suicide a day before the grand opening in 1875. Three decades later the hotel was ravaged by one of the many fires that swept through San Francisco following the 1906 earthquake. The hotel was restored and reopened in 1909, unveiling the magnificent Garden Court with a domed ceiling made from 80,000 panes of glass. Regard this impressive room (which includes the dining room of the Garden Court Restaurant) and absorb its grandeur, then step into the Pied Piper to glimpse the $2.5-million Maxfield Parrish painting of the same name. ⏲ *20 min. 2 New Montgomery St. (at Market St.).* ☎ *415/546-5089. www.gardencourt-restaurant.com. Mon–Fri 6:30am–2pm; Sat 6:30–10am; Sun 10am–2pm; tea Sat 2–4pm. BART/Muni: Powell or Montgomery.*

7 ★★★ **SoMa (South of Market).** This former industrial area south of Market Street has become a major center for art and entertainment, museums, and galleries. ⏲ *to stroll through the neighborhood: 2–4 hr. Visit any time during daylight hours. Note: SFMOMA (see bullet* **9** *) is closed Wednesdays.*

The ceiling of the Garden Court is a glittering masterpiece of glass.

8 ★★★ kids **Yerba Buena Center for the Arts** is the cultural anchor of SoMa. It serves as a major arts-and-entertainment center, with cultural programs for adults, educational and recreational facilities for kids, and lovely gardens that serve as an oasis in a very urban neighborhood. *Best time: daylight hours. Weekdays you'll see office workers taking a lunch break in its lovely grounds, while on weekends families with kids enjoy the slides and play areas.*

Yerba Buena Center for the Arts/Yerba Buena Gardens

8A ★★★ kids **Yerba Buena Center for the Arts** contains three galleries for high-tech and traditional exhibitions, plus a dance space. The **8B** **Center for the Arts Theater** hosts dance, music, and theater performances. An architect, sculptor, and poet came together to design the **8C** **Martin Luther King Jr. Memorial** and its 50-foot waterfall. From May through October, the Yerba Buena Festival brings world-class musicians to the **8D** **Esplanade** for free concerts. The **8E** **Sony Metreon Entertainment Center** is a massive complex with movie theaters, shopping, and attractions like Maurice Sendak's

Where the Wild Things Are. ⏱ 1 hr. 101 4th St. ☎ 800/638-7366. www.metreon.com. Free admission. Attractions $6–$12. Daily 10am–10pm. **8F** **Zeum** is a hands-on science museum for older kids. *701 Mission St.* ☎ 415/777-2800. www.zeum.com. Admission $7, $5 kids 4–18. Wed–Sun 11am–5pm. The **8G** **Children's Center** has bowling, ice-skating, a carousel, and an outdoor playground. *Ice-skating & bowling: 750 Folsom St.* ☎ 415/777-3727. Skating $7, $5.50 kids under 13. Bowling Sun–Thurs 10am–10pm, to midnight Fri–Sat. $3.50/game or $20/hr. ⏱ 1–3 hr. Between 3rd, 4th, Mission & Folsom sts.

⑨ ★★★ San Francisco Museum of Modern Art (SFMOMA). In 1995, SFMOMA moved in to its $62-million home, designed by Swiss architect Mario Botta. The permanent collection includes over 15,000 works by the likes of Henri Matisse, Jackson Pollock, and Georgia O'Keeffe. The first major museum to recognize photography as art form, SFMOMA also has numerous excellent examples by Ansel Adams, Man Ray, and others. Not enough of the permanent collection is on display at any one time, but temporary exhibits are usually excellent. ⏱ 1½ hr. 151 3rd St. (between Mission & Howard sts.). ☎ 415/357-4000. www.sfmoma. org. Admission $10, $7 seniors 62+, $6 students with ID, free for kids under 13. Half price Thurs 6–9pm. Free to all 1st Tues of the month. Thurs 11am–9pm; Fri–Tues 11am–6pm. Closed Wed & major holidays. Opens at 10am in summer. Bus: 15, 30, 45. BART/Muni: Montgomery St. Best time: weekdays.

SFMOMA's skylight is just one of the museum's architectural highlights.

⑩ Caffe Museo. SFMOMA's on-site cafe sells excellent soups, sandwiches, and salads (151 3rd St.; ☎ 415/357-4500; $).

⑪ ★ kids California Academy of Sciences. The country's fourth-largest natural-history museum will be in SoMa until 2008, while a new facility is built in Golden Gate Park. The temporary location is not as expansive as its old home, but does include terrific temporary exhibits, fascinating animal life in the Steinhart Aquarium, and twice-daily, narrated penguin feedings. ⏱ 1–2 hr. weekday afternoons are best, as mornings are full with school tours. 875 Howard St. (at 5th St.). ☎ 415/321-8000. www.calacademy.org.

Admission $7, $4.50 seniors & kids 12–17 & students, $2 kids 4–11, free for kids under 3, free for all the 1st Wed of the month. Daily 10am–5pm.

⑫ ★★ Civic Center. Less than a decade after the 1906 earthquake destroyed City Hall, San Francisco completed an ambitious new administrative and cultural center in grandiose, Beaux Arts style. It contains City Hall, with its 308-foot-(92m-) tall dome, the homes of the San Francisco Symphony, Opera, and Ballet, the main public library, the Asian Art Museum, and other notable buildings. For more details on the Civic Center, refer to the neighborhood tour on page 48. ⏱ 1 hr. Most Civic Center buildings are bordered by Hayes, Franklin & Hyde sts. & Golden Gate Ave. Best time: weekdays during daylight hours.

⑬ Zuni Café. Treat yourselves to dinner at an SF institution, one of the first purveyors of innovative California cuisine (1658 Market St. ☎ 415/552-2522; $$$; see also p 116). For a delicious (and cheaper) alternative, head to **⑭ Vicolo Pizzeria,** an alley-side gem serving memorable cornmeal crust pizzas (150 Ivy Alley ☎ 415/863-2382; $; see also p 115). ●

2 The Best
Special-Interest Tours

San Francisco Waterfront

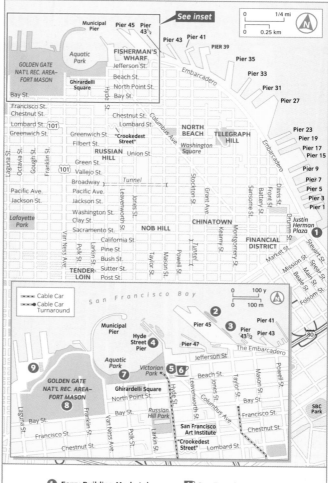

See inset

0	1/4 mi
0	0.25 km

Municipal Pier
Pier 45 Pier 43½
Pier 43 Pier 41
PIER 39
Aquatic Park
FISHERMAN'S WHARF
Jefferson St.
Pier 35
GOLDEN GATE NAT'L REC. AREA—FORT MASON
Beach St.
Pier 33
Ghirardelli Square
North Point St.
Embarcadero
Pier 31
Bay St.
Bay St.
Pier 27
Francisco St.
Chestnut St.
Chestnut St.
Lombard St. 101
Lombard St.
Pier 23
Greenwich St.
NORTH BEACH
Pier 19
Greenwich St.
Greenwich St.
"Crookedest Street"
TELEGRAPH HILL
Pier 17
Filbert St.
Washington Square
Pier 15
Green St.
RUSSIAN HILL Union St.
Pier 9
Vallejo St.
101
Pier 7
Broadway Tunnel
Pier 5
Pacific Ave.
Pacific Ave.
Pier 3
Jackson St.
Jackson St.
Pier 1
Washington St.
Justin Herman Plaza
Lafayette Park
Clay St.
NOB HILL
CHINATOWN
Sacramento St.
FINANCIAL DISTRICT
California St.
Pine St.
Tunnel
Market St.
Bush St.
TENDER-LOIN
Sutter St.
Post St.

- - - Cable Car
- ● - Cable Car Turnaround

San Francisco Bay

0	100 y
0	100 m

Municipal Pier
Pier 45
Pier 41
Hyde Street Pier
Pier 43½ Pier 43
Pier 47
Aquatic Park
The Embarcadero
Victorian Park
Jefferson St.
GOLDEN GATE NAT'L REC. AREA—FORT MASON
Ghirardelli Square
Beach St.
North Point St.
SBC Park
Russian Hill Park
Bay St.
Bay St.
San Francisco Art Institute
Francisco St.
Chestnut St.
"Crookedest Street"
Lombard St.
Chestnut St.

1. Ferry Building Marketplace
2. SS Jeremiah O'Brien
3. USS Pampanito
4. Hyde Street Pier
5. National Maritime Historical Park Visitors Center
6. San Francisco Crepe Cart
7. Maritime Museum
8. Fort Mason
9. Maritime Library

Flanked by the Pacific Ocean to the west and the San Francisco Bay to the north and east, San Francisco possesses a rich seafaring past. It became a trading post in the early 1800s and harbored hundreds of ships after the discovery of gold. During 20th-century global conflicts, the city served as an embarkation point for Pacific-bound servicemen. Take 4 to 5 hours to enjoy this scenic walk through history, and don't forget to bring a sweater. If your schedule allows, take this tour on a Tuesday, Thursday, or Saturday morning, when the thrice-weekly Farmers Market, a San Francisco favorite, takes place at your first stop—the Ferry Building Marketplace.

START: **Ferry Building (at the Embarcadero & Misson St.). Streetcar: F to Ferry Terminal. Bus 2, 7, 14, 21, 66, or 71 to Steuart & Market sts.**

❶ ★★ **Ferry Building Marketplace.** Stroll through this gourmet market inside the **Ferry Building** (p 15, bullet ❷), where tenants sell the best of Northern California's bounty, from bread, pastries, and cheese to chocolate, gourmet coffee, tea, and sushi. Then head outside to watch the ferries depart to Angel Island, Marin County, Oakland, and Alameda. Before the Bay and Golden Gate bridges were constructed, the ferry system included hundreds of boats shuttling both people and goods. If you are lucky enough to be here during the alfresco **Ferry Plaza Farmers Market** *(Tues & Thurs 10am–2pm; Sat 8am–2pm, just outside the main doors of the marketplace; for more details, see p 15, bullet ❸)*, you'll want to add an extra hour to mingle with the locals and check out the stands hawking fine produce, flowers, and readymade snacks by local restaurants. ⏱ *25 min. 1 Ferry Building (at the Embarcadero & Mission St.) Streetcar: F to Ferry Terminal. Bus: 2, 7, 14, 21, 66, or 71 to Steuart & Market sts. After you explore the marketplace, hop on the F streetcar westbound towards Fisherman's Wharf. Exit at Jones and Beach sts., and walk two blocks to Pier 45. Note: Be sure to have your camera out— the streetcar ride takes you along the scenic waterfront.*

Fresh produce and flowers at the Ferry Plaza Farmers Market.

❷ **SS Jeremiah O'Brien.** During World War II, the U.S. ramped up production of warships, revolutionizing building methods by prefabricating several parts at a time in various shipyards. The new technique allowed the U.S. to make ships faster than Germany could sink them. One such "Liberty Ship" was the *O'Brien*, which participated in both the 1944 D-Day invasion and the anniversary celebrations 50 years later. You can tour almost the entire ship—don't miss the flying bridge, the cozy captain's quarters, and the impressive engine room with its *massive* steam pipes. ⏱ *30 min. Pier 45.* ☎ *415/544-0100. www.ssjeremiahobrien.org. Admission $7, $5 seniors, $4 kids 6-14, free military with ID & kids under 6, $20 for family with 2 adults & up to 4 kids under 18. Daily 10am-4pm.*

❸ ★ **USS Pampanito.** On her six Pacific tours in WWII, this submarine sank six Japanese ships and damaged four others, and also helped save 73 British and Australian prisoners of war. The intriguing 20-minute audio tour through the cramped quarters is narrated by former crew members. ⏱ *45 min. Pier 45.* ☎ *415/775-1943. www.maritime. org. Admission (including audio tour) $9, $5 seniors, $3 children 6–12. The $20 family pass for 2 adults & up to 4 kids under 18 includes admission to Hyde St. Pier ships (reviewed below). Sun–Thurs 9am–6pm, Fri–Sat 9am–8pm; summer Thurs–Tues 9am–8pm, Wed 9am–6pm.*

❹ ★★★ **Hyde Street Pier.** This lovely pier houses eight historic, refurbished ships, three of which you can tour. The majestic *Balclutha*, one of the few remaining square-riggers, took her maiden voyage from Cardiff, Wales, in 1887, and over the course of her working life, carried coal, wheat, lumber, and canned salmon from Alaska.

In retirement she appeared in the film *Mutiny on the Bounty.* The captain's quarters, with the picture of his daughter "Inda Francis" (born onboard on a trip from India to San Francisco), are particularly compelling. The 1890 steam ferryboat *Eureka* was the last of 50 paddle-wheel ferries that regularly plied the bay, making its final trip in 1957. The restored 300-foot-long (91m) side-wheeler is loaded with deck cargo, including a sizable collection of antique cars and trucks. The third boat currently on display is the 1907 oceangoing tugboat *Hercules*. ⏱ *25 min. Jefferson & Hyde sts.* ☎ *415/561-6662. www.maritime.org. Admission to walk on pier: free. Admission to board ships: $5, free for children under 16. Daily 9:30am–5pm; summer until 5:30pm.*

❺ **National Maritime Historical Park Visitors Center.** Take a moment to step inside this intriguing visitor center, housed in a refurbished wing of the Cannery, once the site of a major canning facility that packed up California produce bound for export. The visitor center contains wooden models of the Hyde Street pier boats and hosts

Tour the ships at the Hyde Street Pier.

The USS Balclutha and Eureka are two ships permanently docked at the Hyde Street Pier, which is part of the National Maritime Historical Park.

delightful art exhibits with nautical themes. ⏲ *15 min.* ☎ *415/561-6662. www.maritime.org. Free admission. Daily 9:30am–5pm; summer until 7pm. Closed major holidays.*

6 ★ **San Francisco Crepe Cart.** Purchase a ham and cheese or chocolate and banana crepe at this cart located in the tree-shaded Cannery courtyard. With luck, a live folk singer in the adjacent outdoor performance area will provide musical accompaniment. No credit cards. *The Cannery (at Jefferson & Hyde sts.). $.*

7 ★ **Maritime Museum.** This three-story structure shaped like a bright white Art Deco ship holds several model ships spanning many decades and styles—from sailing ships to aircraft carriers. Old photos depict San Francisco a century and a half ago; a particularly memorable one is an 1851 snapshot of hundreds of abandoned boats, deserted by crews dashing off to participate in the gold rush. The second floor has a model radio communications

room and the top floor is made to look like a captain's deck. ⏲ *30 min. 900 Beach St.(at Polk St.).* ☎ *415/ 561-7100. www.maritime.org. Free admission. Daily 10am–5pm. Closed major holidays. Visit anytime, as it's rarely crowded.*

8 ★ **Fort Mason.** Walk east towards the Municipal Pier. At the start of the pier, take the path heading uphill on your left. This collection of piers and buildings belonged to the U.S. military until 1972, and during World War II and the Korean conflict, it served as the point of departure for well over a million American servicemen. ⏲ *30 min. Marina Blvd. (at Buchanan St.)*

9 **Maritime Library.** If you'd like to soak up more maritime history, come here for books, magazines, oral histories, ships' plans, and some 250,000 photos on the subject. Tours can be arranged in advance. Lectures are held monthly. ⏲ *15–30 min. Building E, 3rd floor, Fort Mason Center.* ☎ *415/561- 7038. Free admission. Tues 5–8pm; Wed–Fri 1–5pm; Sat 10am–5pm. Closed all federal holidays.*

Romantic San Francisco

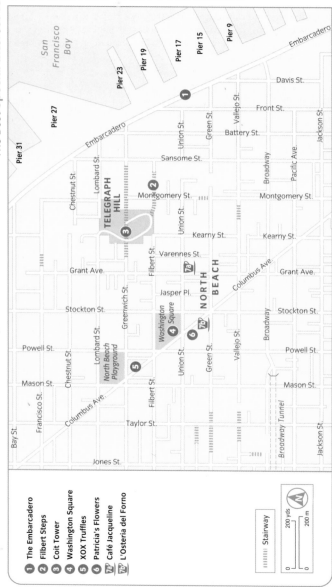

1 The Embarcadero
2 Filbert Steps
3 Coit Tower
4 Washington Square
5 XOX Truffles
6 Patricia's Flowers
🚇 Café Jacqueline
🚇 L'Osteria del Forno

Stairway

200 yds
200 m

With its dazzling vistas and intimate restaurants, San Francisco is made for lovers. This tour takes you from the tranquil waterfront through some of the city's most enchanting hidden neighborhoods to sultry North Beach. Best to begin at 3 or 4pm and end with a romantic dinner. START: **The Embarcadero at Pier 17. Street-car: F to Green St.**

1 ★★ The Embarcadero. Enjoy the lovely views of the Bay Bridge, Treasure Island, and the East Bay. ⏱ *15 min. The Embarcadero at Pier 17. Streetcar: F to Green St.*

2 ★★ Filbert Steps. In this captivating corner of town, the street becomes too steep for cars. As you head uphill, you'll pass lush, flower-bedecked gardens decorating Carpenter Gothic homes (characterized by steeply sloped roofs, pointed arches over windows, and "gingerbread" detailing on the façade) dating from as early as 1870. ⏱ *30 min. Steps start at Filbert & Sansome sts.*

3 ★★ Coit Tower. Catch a glorious sunset over the City by the Bay. If you make it here before 6pm, ascend

The view of downtown from Coit Tower at sunset is magnificent.

to the top of the pillar for a dazzling panorama. For details on Coit Tower, see p 9, bullet **5**. ⏱ *30 min.* ☎ *415/362-0808. Admission to the top $3.75. Daily 10am–6pm.*

4 ★ Washington Square. Stroll through this welcoming park, one of the oldest in the city, which has the feel of an old-world town square. Saints Peter and Paul Church, a local landmark in front of which Joe DiMaggio and Marilyn Monroe famously posed after their marriage in 1957, serves as a lovely backdrop. ⏱ *15 min. Filbert & Stockton sts.*

5 ★ XOX Truffles. After climbing Telegraph Hill, you've earned a stop at this luscious store. Sinful delicacies come in flavors like cognac, and you must try "Clarissa's Favorite." What is it? I'll let you be surprised. ⏱ *15 min. 754 Columbus Ave.* ☎ *415/421-4814. Mon–Sat 9am–6pm. Closed Sun.*

6 ★ Patricia's Flowers. Buy your loved one a rose at this closet-size florist. ⏱ *15 min. 571 Columbus Ave.* ☎ *415/956-4947.*

7A ★★ Café Jacqueline. For an indulgent culmination to your evening, dine at this purveyor of fine soufflés *(1454 Grant Ave., between Green & Union sts.;* ☎ *415/981-5565 $$$; p 101).* A moderately priced alternative is **7B ★★ L'Osteria del Forno,** a cozy Italian favorite *(519 Columbus Ave., between Union & Green sts.;* ☎ *415/982-1124 $$; p 108).*

Downtown **Galleries**

1 49 Geary
2 Meyerovich Gallery
3 John Berggruen
4 Café de la Presse
5 Caldwell Snyder Gallery
6 Hang Gallery

San Francisco has long been on the cutting edge of the American art scene, and the city's downtown galleries provide a rich look at the depth of SF's artistic offerings, including works by masters of the past century, edgy contemporary pieces, and superb photographic prints. Most galleries carry the "San Francisco Bay Area Gallery Guide," which lists current exhibits. ***Note:*** Most galleries open around 10am (noon on weekends) and close around 5:30pm, but on the first Thursday of each month, galleries stay open later and many serve wine and cheese. Best Tuesday through Friday—downtown bustles and all the galleries are open. 🕐 *2 to 4 hours.* START: Bus 16, 17, 49; F Streetcar; BART/Muni: Powell St.

① ★★★ **49 Geary.** This nondescript building houses several of SF's galleries, covering an array of genres. My personal favorites are the **Fraenkel Gallery** (☎ 415/981-2661; closed Sun–Mon) and the **Stephen Wirtz Gallery** (☎ 415/433-6897; closed Sun–Mon). Both houses feature contemporary works and splendid photography exhibits. The **Catharine Clark Gallery** (☎ 415/399-1439; closed Sun–Mon) offers a layaway plan that puts art within most everyone's reach, but her keen eye for talent draws even serious collectors. *49 Geary St. (between Grant Ave. & Kearny St.). Bus 16, 17, 49; F Streetcar, Muni: Powell St.*

② ★ **Meyerovich Gallery.** You'll find paintings, sculpture, and works on paper by masters like Chagall, Matisse, Miró, and Picasso. Meyerovich's Contemporary Gallery holds works by Lichtenstein, Motherwell, Dine, and Hockney. *251 Post St., 4th Floor (between Grant & Stockton sts.). ☎ 415/421-7171. Closed Sun.*

③ ★ **John Berggruen.** This gallery specializes in 20th-century works from artists such as Diebenkorn, Calder, Matisse, Ruscha, and O'Keeffe. *228 Grant Ave. (between Post & Sutter sts.). ☎ 415/781-4629. Closed Sun.*

④ **Café de la Presse.** Sip an espresso at this bustling cafe, decorated with movie posters and racks of newspapers. *352 Grant Ave. (at Bush St.). ☎ 415/398-2680. $.*

⑤ **Caldwell Snyder Gallery.** Works from cutting-edge American, European, and Latin American artists are exhibited in a striking, 9,000-square-foot space. *341 Sutter St. (between Grant Ave. & Stockton St.). ☎ 415/296-7896. Closed Sun.*

⑥ ★★ **Hang Gallery.** Hang features arresting pieces by yet-to-be-discovered artists at excellent prices. Check out the Hang Annex across the street, too. *556 & 557 Sutter St. (between Powell & Mason sts.). ☎ 415/434-4264. Open daily.*

Explore the avant-garde collection at the Hang Gallery.

San Francisco Literati

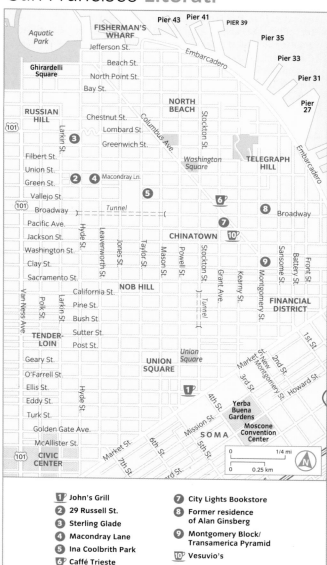

Aquatic Park

FISHERMAN'S WHARF

Pier 43 Pier 41 PIER 39

Pier 35

Pier 33

Pier 31

Pier 27

Ghirardelli Square

Jefferson St.

Beach St.

North Point St.

Bay St.

Embarcadero

RUSSIAN HILL

101

Larkin St.

Chestnut St.

Lombard St.

Greenwich St.

❸

Columbus Ave.

NORTH BEACH

Stockton St.

Washington Square

TELEGRAPH HILL

Embarcadero

Filbert St.

Union St.

Green St.

❷ ❹ Macondray Ln.

Vallejo St.

❺

101 Broadway

Tunnel

❻

❽ Broadway

Pacific Ave.

Jackson St.

Washington St.

Clay St.

Sacramento St.

Hyde St.

Leavenworth St.

Jones St.

Taylor St.

Mason St.

Powell St.

Stockton St.

Grant Ave.

Kearny St.

Montgomery St.

Sansome St.

Battery St.

Front St.

❼

🔟

CHINATOWN

Tunnel

❾

FINANCIAL DISTRICT

California St.

NOB HILL

Van Ness Ave.

Polk St.

Larkin St.

Pine St.

Bush St.

Sutter St.

Post St.

TENDER-LOIN

Geary St.

O'Farrell St.

Ellis St.

Eddy St.

Turk St.

Golden Gate Ave.

McAllister St.

101 **CIVIC CENTER**

Hyde St.

UNION SQUARE

Union Square

❶

Market St.

New Montgomery St.

1st St.

2nd St.

3rd St.

Howard St.

4th St.

Mission St.

5th St.

6th St.

7th St.

3rd St.

SOMA

Yerba Buena Gardens

Moscone Convention Center

0   1/4 mi
0   0.25 km

N

❶ John's Grill

❷ 29 Russell St.

❸ Sterling Glade

❹ Macondray Lane

❺ Ina Coolbrith Park

❻ Caffé Trieste

❼ City Lights Bookstore

❽ Former residence of Alan Ginsberg

❾ Montgomery Block/ Transamerica Pyramid

🔟 Vesuvio's

Mystery writers, poets, authors of nonfiction, social commentators, and many others with a gift of the pen have long made their home in San Francisco. This tour takes you on a historical journey through the city's literary past. ⏱ *2 to 3 hours.* START: **Union Square area, F Streetcar, BART/Muni: Powell St.**

1️⃣ John's Grill. Start your tour at Dashiell Hammet's favored hangout. Although his fictional character Sam Spade ordered chops and a baked potato, don't come for the food, but do come for its great 1940s vibe and to enjoy a drink at the bar. Be sure to check out the *Maltese Falcon* room upstairs. Then jump on the Powell-Hyde cable car around the corner. *63 Ellis St. (between Stockton & Powell sts.).* ☎ *415/986 0069. F Streetcar, BART/Muni: Powell St.*

Neal Cassady (circa 1950). Neal was Kerouac's inspiration for Dean Moriarty, one of the main characters in On the Road.

2️⃣ 29 Russel St. Jack Kerouac lived in the attic of this unassuming cottage with Neal Cassady and Cassady's wife for 6 months in 1952. Kerouac revised *On the Road* here, a stream-of-consciousness novel based on his travels across the country with Cassady, and wrote parts of *Visions of Cody.* The house is now a private residence. ⏱ *10 min. 29 Russel St. (off Hyde St., between Green & Union sts.). Exit the cable car at Green St.*

3️⃣ ★ Sterling Glade. In 1872 poet George Sterling founded San Francisco's Bohemian Club, an influential group of newspapermen,

novelists, and poets that included nature writer John Muir and Sterling's good friend Jack London. Sterling's seminal poem *A Wine of Wizardry* appeared in the 1907 issue of *Cosmopolitan,* with a forward by Ambrose Bierce, who compared Sterling to Milton and Keats. Sadly, Sterling committed suicide in 1926 at the age of 57. Two years later, the city dedicated this hilltop green space in his name. Enjoy lovely views of the Golden Gate Bridge from the northwest corner of the park. ⏱ *15 min. Larkin St. (between Greenwich & Lombard sts.).*

4️⃣ Macondray Lane. Many people believe this steep alley, accessible only to pedestrians, was the model for "Barbary Lane," the Russian Hill residence for the characters in Armistead Maupin's *Tales of the City,* which in 1994 was made into a widely acclaimed public television miniseries. ⏱ *15 min. Off Jones St. (between Union & Green sts.).*

Re-live the 1940s at John's Grill.

Bob Donlin, Neal Cassady, Allen Ginsberg, Robert LaVigne, & Lawrence Ferlinghetti, circa 1956, outside Ferlinghetti's City Lights Bookstore.

5 Ina Coolbrith Park. Josephine Donna Smith, a niece of Mormon founder Joseph Smith, arrived in San Francisco in 1862 as a 21-year-old divorcée and changed her name to Ina Coolbrith. Already a published poet, she joined a circle of writers that included Mark Twain and Ambrose Bierce and became librarian of the Oakland Public Library in 1873, where she introduced a young, poor Jack London to classic literature and inspired him to write. (He would eventually earn fame with such stories as *Call of the Wild* and *White Fang*.) In 1899 she became the only woman named honorary member of the Bohemian Club (see bullet **3**) and according to the plaque at top of this steep park, Coolbrith was named the first Poet Laureate in the country by the state legislature in 1919. Your hike up the many steps to reach the plaque will be rewarded with sweeping North Beach views. ⏱ *15 min. Taylor & Vallejo sts.*

6 ★ Caffé Trieste. The West Coast's first espresso house, still owned by the same family, was a popular hangout of the beatniks, whose photos fill the walls. Best for a cappuccino or a thick pizza slice. *609 Vallejo St. (between Columbus & Grant aves.).* ☎ *415/392-6739.*

Kerouac & the Beat Generation

The 1957 publication of *On the Road* established **Jack Kerouac** as one of the central figures of the Beat Generation, a counterculture movement of writers, poets, and artists with its heart in San Francisco. The Beat movement—which valued freedom of artistic and personal expression—was a reaction to the excessive conformity of postwar America in the 1950s, and included Neal Cassady, William S. Burroughs, Robert LaVigne, Allen Ginsberg, and Lawrence Ferlinghetti. Kerouac unwittingly originated the term **Beat Generation** when he said "We are nothing but a beat generation," but it was the late *San Francisco Chronicle* columnist Herb Caen who coined the term *beatnik* to describe the disheveled literati.

7 ★ City Lights Bookstore.
Founded in 1953 and owned by
Lawrence Ferlinghetti, one of the first
Beat poets to arrive in San Francisco,
City Lights is now a city landmark, a
literary mecca, and one of the last of
the Beat-era hangouts in operation.
An active participant in the Beat
movement, Ferlinghetti established
his shop as a meeting place where
writers and bibliophiles could (and
still do) attend poetry readings and
other events. This vibrant part of the
literary scene and well-stocked book-
shop prides itself on its collection of
art, poetry, and social and political
paperbacks. ⏱ *30 min. 261 Columbus
Ave. (at Broadway).* ☎ *415/362-
8193. www.citylights.com. Daily
10am–midnight.*

**8 Former residence of Alan
Ginsberg.** It was here in 1955
where Ginsberg, a central figure in
the Beat movement, wrote his controversial poem *Howl,* an uncensored
examination of modern life. ⏱ *5 min.
1010 Montgomery St. (at Broadway).*

**9 Montgomery Block/
Transamerica Pyramid.** The landmark Transamerica Pyramid sits on
the site of the former "Montgomery
Block," which in 1853 was, at four
stories, the tallest building in the
American West. Among the many
writers who lived in the block-long

A plaque about Jack Kerouac Street.

building were Mark Twain, Ambrose
Bierce, Jack London, and George Sterling. The lobby was the center of SF
society, and its unusual construction
atop redwood logs allowed it to with-
stand even the 1906 earthquake. The
Montgomery Block building was
demolished in 1959. ⏱ *15 min.
Columbus Ave. & Montgomery St.*

10 ★ Vesuvio's. This excellent
example of pressed-tin architecture
was the preferred watering hole for
the Beats. Order a "Jack Kerouac,"
made with rum, tequila, orange/
cranberry juice, and lime, or a
"Bohemian coffee:" brandy,
amaretto, and a lemon twist.
Opened in 1949, it still maintains its
original bohemian atmosphere. *255
Columbus Ave. (at Jack Kerouac St.).*
☎ *415/362-3370. (See p 122.)*

The mural on the wall outside Vesuvio's, a favorite Beat hangout.

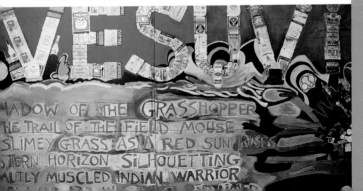

Shop 'til You Drop

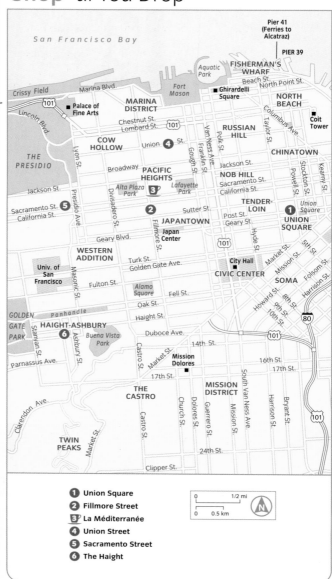

San Francisco Bay

Pier 41
(Ferries to Alcatraz)
PIER 39

Aquatic Park

FISHERMAN'S WHARF

Beach St.
North Point St.

Crissy Field

Marina Blvd.

Fort Mason

■ Ghirardelli Square

NORTH BEACH

101

■ Palace of Fine Arts

Lincoln Blvd

Chestnut St.

MARINA DISTRICT

Lombard St.

101

RUSSIAN HILL

Columbus Ave.

Taylor St.

■ Coit Tower

THE PRESIDIO

COW HOLLOW

Union ❹ St.

Polk St.
Van Ness Ave.
Franklin St.
Gough St.

CHINATOWN

Jackson St.

Stockton St.
Powell St.
Kearny St.

Lyon St.

Broadway

PACIFIC HEIGHTS

Alta Plaza Park ❸

Lafayette Park

NOB HILL

Sacramento St.
California St.

Jackson St.

Presidio Ave.

Divisadero St.

❷

Sutter St.

TENDER-LOIN

❶ Union Square

Sacramento St. ❺
California St.

Fillmore St.

JAPANTOWN

Post St.
Geary St.

Hyde St.

UNION SQUARE

Geary Blvd.

Japan Center

101

Market St.
Mission St.

5th St.

WESTERN ADDITION

Turk St.

Golden Gate Ave.

■ City Hall

CIVIC CENTER

Howard St.

4th St.
8th St.
9th St.
10th St.

Folsom St.

Harrison St.

Univ. of San Francisco

Masonic Ave.

Fulton St.

Alamo Square

Fell St.

SOMA

80

GOLDEN GATE PARK

Panhandle

Oak St.

Haight St.

HAIGHT-ASHBURY

Stanyan St.

Ashbury St.

❻

Buena Vista Park

Duboce Ave.

14th St.

101

Parnassus Ave.

Clarendon Ave.

Castro St.

Market St.

Mission Dolores ■

16th St.
17th St.

South Van Ness Ave.

Harrison St.

Bryant St.

101

THE CASTRO

17th St.

MISSION DISTRICT

TWIN PEAKS

Castro St.

Church St.

Dolores St.

Guerrero St.

Mission St.

24th St.

Market St.

Clipper St.

❶ Union Square
❷ Fillmore Street
❸ La Méditerranée
❹ Union Street
❺ Sacramento Street
❻ The Haight

0 ——— 1/2 mi
0 ——— 0.5 km

N

San Francisco's locally owned boutiques carry cutting-edge fashions, distinctive housewares, rare books, and other unique treasures. I've detailed five shopping zones; I recommend you choose three or four and spend a half or a whole day on this tour; weekday mornings are best if you eschew knocking elbows with crowds of fellow shoppers. Refer to the shopping chapter maps (p 69–70) for more stores in each neighborhood. START: **BART/Muni: Powell St.**

❶ Union Square. Retail's biggest names overlook the square: Macy's, Levi's, and elite brands like Louis Vuitton and Tiffany's. The Gap, Old Navy, and myriad designer boutiques are a stone's throw away. For home products, check out William Sonoma's flagship store and Crate & Barrel. Although chains dominate here, you'll also find a few local originals like Gump's (p 77), famed for its china and glass items. *Between Market, Post, Powell & Grant sts. BART/Muni: Powell St.*

❷ Fillmore Street. Sophisticated urbanites flock to this delightful cafe-lined street, perfect if you feel like puttering through high-priced boutiques. You'll pass Mrs. Dewson's Hats, the wares of which have adorned celebrities, and Nest, with its fetching housewares. Stop by Kiehl's (p 77) to sample a buttery hand cream before visiting Heide Says, a stylishly feminine purveyor of ladies' attire and jewelry. *Fillmore St. (between Sutter & Jackson sts.). Bus: 1, 2, 3, 4, 22.*

Mrs. Dewson and her colorful, whimsical hats.

❸ La Méditerranée. Lunch on hummus, stuffed grape leaves, and pita at this cozy eatery. The chicken Cilicia is superb. *2210 Fillmore St. (between California & Sacramento sts).* ☎ *415/921-2956. $. (p 108).*

❹ Union Street. For more moderately priced clothing boutiques, continue down Fillmore Street to Union Street, which caters to the upper upper-middle-class. *Union St. (between Divisadero & Franklin sts.). Bus: 22, 41, 45.*

❺ Sacramento Street. As an alternative Union Street, you could head to posh Presidio Heights for truly chichi purchases. Shops like Fetish, Sue Fisher King, and Dottie Doolittle stock precious ladies' fashions, home furnishings, and kids' attire. *Sacramento St. (between Lyon & Spruce sts.). Bus: 1 to California St. & Presidio Ave. Walk 1 block to Sacramento St.*

❻ The Haight. If dramatic, non-conservative attire is more your style, there's no better place than the Haight. Very choosy vintage stores abound here; this is where you'll find a hip polyester '60s dress, trendy club gear, or punk-rock T-shirts. My favorite is retro-gear-king Wasteland (p 75). *See also p 36, bullet ❹. Haight St. (between Masonic & Stanyan sts.). Bus: 6, 7, 43.*

Hippie **Haight**

Baker St.

Baker St.

Lyon St.

Lyon St.

2

1

Panhandle

Central Ave.

Central Ave.

Buena Vista Ave. East

Buena Vista Park

Buena Vista Ave. West

4

Masonic Ave.

Masonic Ave.

3

Delmar St.

Ashbury St.

Ashbury St.

6

Fell St.

Oak St.

Page St.

Haight St.

Hayes St.

5

Waller St.

9 8

7

Downey St.

Frederick St.

Clayton St.

Clayton St.

10

Belvedere St.

Panhandle

Cole St.

Cole St.

Carl St.

11

Cole St.

Shrader St.

Shrader St.

12

Haight St.

Beulah St.

Stanyan St.

Stanyan St.

Golden Gate Park

100 y

100 m

0

0

1. Buena Vista Park
2. Janis Joplin's
   Former Residence
3. Magnolia Pub & Brewery
4. Haight Street
5. Intersection of Haight
   and Ashbury streets
6. Former residence
   of the Grateful Dead
7. Anubis Warpus
8. Ashbury Tobacco Center
9. Distractions
10. Free Medical Clinic
11. Former Residence
    of Charles Manson
12. Rainbow Mural

During the 1967 "Summer of Love," thousands of young people flooded Haight-Ashbury (simply the Haight to locals) in search of free love, drugs, and music. As *the* center of hippie culture, this neighborhood captured the world's imagination in the 1960s. Despite the changing times—a Gap store (gasp!) now lies a stone's throw from the corner of Haight and Ashbury—nonconformity still rules here. These days the Victorian townhouse-lined streets where the Dead, Janis Joplin, Jefferson Airplane, and Timothy Leary lived contain a mix of clean-cut residents, hipster 20-somethings, homeless people, and colorful characters (or intentional freaks, depending on your point of view) like tie-dye-wearing former Dead-heads and aging we'll-screw-you flower children. This tour is a must for anyone fascinated by San Francisco's role in the psychedelic '60s. Some stops are private homes or working businesses (not museums); they serve to remind you of the Haight's historical past. 🕐 *3 to 4 hours. Best time: afternoon.*
START: **Buena Vista Park: Bus: 6, 7, 66, 71.**

① ★ **Buena Vista Park.** Climb the pathway and head uphill to get a splendid view of Haight Street, the venerable Victorian buildings surrounding the park, and the city. In 1867 this forest was set aside as the first of SF's city parks. The retaining wall (added in 1930) contains broken marble from an old city cemetery; look around and you'll see some headstone inscriptions. 🕐 *30 min. Bus: 6, 7, 66, 71.*

② ★ **Janis Joplin's former residence.** You won't hear anyone belting out "Me and My Bobby McGee" in this nondescript multiunit complex where Janis lived during the Summer of Love, but it is worth swinging by for pure nostalgia and to admire the neighboring Victorian homes boasting intricate woodwork details. 🕐 *15 min. 122 Lyon St.*

③ ★ **Magnolia Pub & Brewery.** Relax with a pint of Blue Bell Bitter or Prescription Pale Ale (brewed in the basement). Before it was a brewpub, this historic building had an endlessly colorful array of previous incarnations, but in the 1960s it housed the Drogstore Café (a famous hippie gathering spot—NOT named Drugstore, but Drogstore) and former dancer turned curiously shaped dessert-creator Magnolia Thunderpussy and her Ice Cream Parlor (people *still* talk about her inimitable desserts like Montana Banana). Ah, only in the Haight. *1398 Haight St.* ☎ *415/864-7468. magnoliapub.com. $$.*

Vivid colors symbolize Haight Street.

The neighborhood's namesake and most famous intersection.

❹ ★ Haight Street. This block epitomizes the Haight's free-spirited past. Few chain stores or tacky T-shirt shops blot this block. You'll find shops like **Dreams of Katmandu** *(1352 Haight St.; ☎ 415/255-4968)*, where a turquoise facade gives way to a lovely array of Tibetan prayer rugs, tapestries, masks, and Buddha statues. Funky rave shop **Ceiba** *(1463 Haight St.; ☎ 415/437-9598)*, which advertises "Fashion, Music, Art," is just a few steps away, and across the street is **Recycled Records** *(1377 Haight St.; ☎ 415/626-4075)*, which holds an impressive collection of old LPs and 45s. Particularly notable is **Pipe Dreams** *(1376 Haight St. ☎ 415/431-3553)*, aka "The Oldest Smoke Shop in San Francisco." Hundreds of water pipes share shelf space with T-shirts, lighters, and incense. Another intriguing stop is **Bound Together Bookstore** *(1369 Haight St. ☎ 415/431-8355)*, a not-for-profit, volunteer-run bookseller otherwise known as an "Anarchist Collective." Titles here include works by Che Guevarra, Henry David Thoreau, and Noam Chomsky, as well as "The Anarchist Yellow Pages." ⏱ *25 min. Haight St. (between Central & Masonic aves.); most stores open between 11am & 8pm.*

❺ Intersection of Haight and Ashbury streets. The corner of Haight and Ashbury streets is the center of the neighborhood. You've seen the ubiquitous photo of the crisscrossed street signs—here is your chance to take a shot of your own. ⏱ *5 min. Haight at Ashbury.*

❻ Former residence of the Grateful Dead. The Grateful Dead lived here from June 1966 until October 1967, when the police raided the house and arrested everyone inside for marijuana possession. Jerry Garcia was out shopping at the time. Within a few weeks, the band moved to Marin County—but their memory still lives on in the hearts and minds of many Haight hippies and in T-shirts and memorabilia found in local curio shops. Today a private residence, the attractive Victorian shows little trace of its colorful past, with the exception of occasional notes left behind by mourning fans. ⏱ *15 min. 710 Ashbury St.*

❼ Anubis Warpus. Piercings and tattoos are loudly advertised above this shop's glass windows, but those procedures actually take place at the back of the shop. Step inside to admire the collection of punk T-shirts, wacky shoes, and

funky wigs (think purple afro). Shelves of counterculture books and mags (hemp guides and the latest issue of *Fetish Times,* for example) are mainstays here. 🕐 *15 min. 1525 Haight St.* ☎ *415/431-2218. Mon-Fri noon-7pm, Sat-Sun noon-8pm.*

8 Ashbury Tobacco Center. This store, allegedly the inspiration for Jimi Hendrix's song "Red House," sells 1960s paraphernalia, lava lamps, and an assortment of smoking and tobacco accessories. 🕐 *15 min. 1524 Haight St. (at Ashbury St.).* ☎ *415/552-5556. Daily 10am-9:30pm.*

9 Distractions. This head shop will truly leave you agape with its collection of paraphanelia including water pipes, incense, glow sticks, stickers, and disco lights. 🕐 *15 min. 1552 Haight St.* ☎ *415/252-8751. Mon-Fri 11am-7:40pm, Sun 11am-7pm.*

10 Free Medical Clinic. This clinic was set up in 1967 with a mission and philosophy to provide free (and nonjudgmental) medical care. In the beginning, many patients sought help coming down from LSD overdoses. Today the clinic offers everything from help for homeless youths to drug-detox programs. 🕐 *15 min. 558 Clayton St.*

The historic house where the Dead lived in the 60s.

11 Former residence of Charles Manson. The serial murderer lived in this house throughout 1967. It was here that he recruited confused young people into his cult. 🕐 *15 min. 636 Cole St.*

12 Rainbow Mural. Just north of Haight street is a bright, vivid mural depicting the story of evolution painted in 1967 by artist Yana Zegri. She still returns from Florida to touch it up from time to time. 🕐 *15 min. Haight & Cole sts.*

No cost and open-minded health care is offered to the public at this clinic.

Crossing the **Golden Gate Bridge**

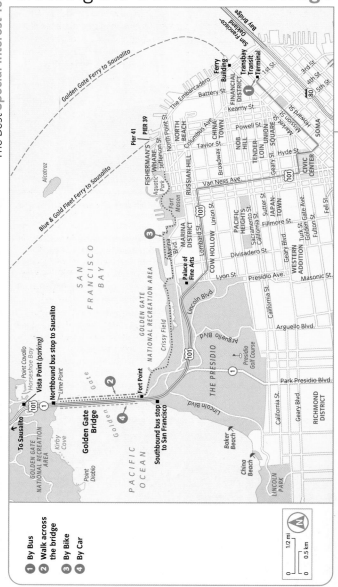

1 By Bus
2 Walk across the bridge
3 By Bike
4 By Car

Golden Gate Ferry to Sausalito

Blue & Gold Fleet Ferry to Sausalito

San Francisco–Oakland Bay Bridge

Ferry Building

Transbay Transit Terminal

1 FINANCIAL DISTRICT

The Embarcadero

Battery St.

Kearny St.

Powell St.

Taylor St.

Columbus Ave.

NORTH BEACH

CHINA-TOWN

NOB HILL

UNION SQUARE

TENDER-LOIN

Broadway

Geary St.

Hyde St.

CIVIC CENTER

Van Ness Ave.

RUSSIAN HILL

MARINA HILL

FISHERMAN'S WHARF

PIER 39

Pier 41

North Point St.

Jefferson St.

Aquatic Park

Fort Mason

3

Marina Blvd.

Lombard St.

MARINA DISTRICT

Union St.

COW HOLLOW

PACIFIC HEIGHTS

Sacramento St.

California St.

Sutter St.

Fillmore St.

JAPAN-TOWN

Geary Blvd.

Turk St.

Golden Gate Ave.

Fulton St.

Fell St.

Divisadero St.

WESTERN ADDITION

Masonic St.

Lyon St.

Palace of Fine Arts

Lincoln Blvd.

Presidio Ave.

California St.

Arguello Blvd.

ALCATRAZ
Alcatraz

SAN FRANCISCO BAY

GOLDEN GATE NATIONAL RECREATION AREA

Crissy Field

THE PRESIDIO

Presidio Golf Course

1

Arguello Blvd.

Lincoln Blvd.

Park Presidio Blvd.

California St.

Geary Blvd.

RICHMOND DISTRICT

Point Cavallo

Horseshoe Bay

Vista Point (parking)

Lime Point

Northbound bus stop to Sausalito

2

Fort Point

GOLDEN GATE NATIONAL RECREATION AREA

Golden Gate Bridge

4

Southbound bus stop to San Francisco

1

To Sausalito

GOLDEN GATE NATIONAL RECREATION AREA

Kirby Cove

Point Diablo

PACIFIC OCEAN

Baker Beach

China Beach

LINCOLN PARK

Golden Gate

80

101

101

Mission St.

Howard St.

Market St.

1st St.

3rd St.

4th St.

5th St.

SOMA

0   1/2 mi
0   0.5 km

The brilliant, red-colored Golden Gate Bridge, often half-veiled by San Francisco's trademark rolling fog, spans tidal currents and ocean waves, connecting the City by the Bay with Marin County to the north. The trek across this awe-inspiring expanse is a fitting part of a visit to the city. This tour should take 2 to 3 hours (depending on how you decide to cross), or all day if you opt to make your visit to the bridge part of an excursion to charming **Sausalito** (p 152). In summer be sure to visit after 10 or 11am (after the morning fog has burned off); all other seasons, visit anytime. *Note:* If you choose to walk or ride across the bridge, this tour may be combined with "The Golden Gate Promenade" tour, p 84.

❶ **By Bus.** To reach the Golden Gate Bridge via public transportation, take a northbound (Marin County-bound) Golden Gate transit bus and return on a southbound (SF-bound) bus. Or consider continuing on a northbound bus to **Sausalito** (p 152). ⏱ *35 min. Golden Gate transit.* ☎ *415/923-2000. golden gatetransit.org. One-way fare: $3.10, $1.55 seniors, $2.80 under 12. All northbound (Marin County–bound) buses stop at the bridge; buses run every 30–60 min. Sausalito buses (2 & 10) run approx. once per hour—call for exact schedules. From SF, northbound buses depart from the Transbay Terminal (Mission & 1st sts.), stopping at Market & 7th sts., the Civic Center & at stops along Van Ness Ave. & Lombard St. Note: If you continue on to Sausalito, you can exit the bus on the south side, walk across the bridge & hop on a Sausalito-bound bus at the bus stop on the north side of the bridge. To return to SF by bus, you must take it from the bus stop on the south side of the bridge (the bus stop on the north side is only for northbound buses).*

❷ **Walk across the bridge.** Crossing the bridge is not always easy (it is usually windy and cold, and the bridge vibrates). But it is worth it for the awe-inspiring vistas. ⏱ *45 min., one-way.*

The view of the city from the Golden Gate Bridge.

You'll never forget the first time you drive over the Golden Gate Bridge.

❸ By Bike. The best way to cross the bridge is on two wheels. Rent bikes at Pier 41 and ride along the scenic SF waterfront of the Golden Gate Promenade (see detailed tour p 84) and along the well-marked bike path up to the Golden Gate Bridge. Return back over the bridge. If you choose to continue on the bridge's northern side along US 101, it's an easy ride downhill to **Sausalito** (p 152), where you can catch a ferry back to Pier 41. ⏱ *2–3 hr, one-way. (⏱ 3–4 hr. including Sausalito & ferry; see p 153, bullet ❶). Bike rentals from Blazing Saddles. Pier 41/Fisherman's Wharf, at Blue & Gold Fleet Ferry Terminal. ☎ 415/202-8888. www.blazingsaddles.com. $7/hr. or $28/24 hr.*

❹ By Car. The fastest way to grasp the immense structure's sheer size is by car. If you drive, cross over the bridge and pull over at the first exit in Marin County (marked VISTA POINT) for breathtaking views of San Francisco. Consider stopping at the parking lot before driving across and walk across the bridge a short distance. After you cross and visit the bridge, consider continuing north with a side trip to **Sausalito** (p 152). ⏱ *5 min. From downtown, drive north on Van Ness Ave. Turn left at Lombard St., which becomes Hwy. 101 N. $5 bridge toll when driving south.* ●

The Golden Gate Bridge

Defying the popular notion that such a bridge could not be built, chief engineer Joseph Baerman Strauss spent $35 million and 4½ years constructing this mammoth project. On May 27, 1937, the Golden Gate Bridge opened to pedestrian traffic (it opened the next day to vehicular traffic). A crowd of over 200,000 proud San Franciscans and others crossed the 1¾-mile- (2.8km-) long bridge on foot. Named for the 400-foot- (120m-) deep Golden Gate Strait that it spans, the bridge's towers rise 746 feet (224m), and the 4,200-foot (1,260m) distance between them remained the longest of any suspension bridge for 27 years. The bridge is also designed to withstand strong winds, able to swing up to 27 feet (8m) in the unlikely event of a 100-mph (161kph) gale. *www.goldengatebridge.org.*

Pacific Heights & Cow Hollow

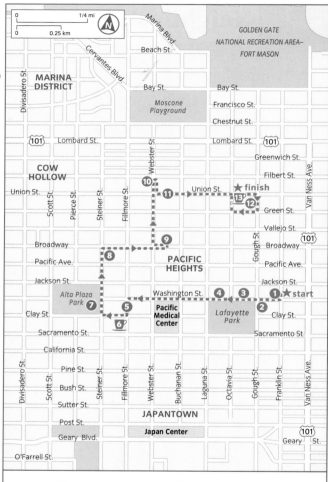

1 Haas-Lilienthal House
2 Gough Street
3 Spreckels Mansion
4 Mary Phelan Mansion
5 Fillmore Street
6 The Coffee Bean and Tea Leaf
7 Alta Plaza Park
8 *Mrs. Doubtfire* house
9 The Hamlin School
10 Vedanta Temple
11 Union Street
12 Octagon House
13 Pane e Vino

Majestic Victorian homes, steep hillsides, charming commercial streets, and sweeping bay vistas permeate this upscale section of San Francisco. The area is so picturesque, Hollywood has filmed several movies in Pacific Heights and Cow Hollow—*Mrs. Doubtfire, Basic Instinct,* and *The Princess Diaries,* to name a few. Note that a few stops in the residential sections are private homes (not museums)—they serve to showcase famous residences and striking examples of Victorian architecture. ⏲ 2 to 3 hours. START: **Franklin St. (at Washington St.). Bus 1, 12, 19, 27, 47, 49, 83. Cable car: California line.**

The Haas-Lilienthal House is a prime example of SF's Victorian architecture.

❶ **Haas-Lilienthal House.** Built in 1886, this flamboyant example of a Queen Anne house (see below) features architectural frills like dormer windows, flying cupolas, ornate trim, and a winsome turret. The Foundation of San Francisco's Architectural Heritage now maintains it as a museum and offers guided tours. ⏲ *1 hr. 2007 Franklin St. (at Washington St.).* ☎ *415/441-3004. www.sfheritage.org/house.html. 1-hr. guided tours $8, $5 seniors & kids under 12. Tours start every 20–30 min. Wed & Sat noon–3pm; Sun 11am–4pm. Bus: 1, 12, 19, 27, 47, 49, 83. Cable car: California line.*

❷ **Gough Street.** The Victorians on this block, all built in 1889, are particularly lovely. Numbers 2004 to 2010 are in the Queen Anne style, while no. 2000 is in the Queen Anne–Eastlake style (marked by elaborate woodwork). *Gough St. (between Washington & Clay sts.).*

❸ **Spreckels Mansion.** Romance novelist Danielle Steel's home is one of the most extravagant in town—built in 1913 for Adolph Spreckels, heir to the sugar empire of German-American industrialist

Queen Anne Architecture

Queen Anne homes dominated Victorian residential architecture from 1880 to 1910. In fact, this style is virtually synonymous with the phrase "Victorian house." Typical characteristics of a Queen Anne home include projecting bay windows, wraparound porches, towers, turrets, balconies, elaborate banisters and spindles, stained glass, decorative trim, and patterned shingles.

Claus Spreckels, who made his fortune refining California sugar beets and Hawaii sugarcane. Houses were razed or physically moved to make room for the mansion, which occupies an entire city block. The original house featured an indoor pool and a circular Pompeian room with a fountain. Despite the home's grand size, it can't fit all of Ms. Steele's 20+ cars, which are parked all over the neighborhood. *2080 Washington St. (between Octavia & Gough sts.).*

④ Mary Phelan Mansion. James Phelan, SF mayor from 1894 to1902 and U.S. senator from 1915 to1921, commissioned this house for his sister Mary, after hers was destroyed in the 1906 earthquake. *2150 Washington St.*

⑤ Fillmore Street. One of the lovelier lanes to stroll along in San Francisco, Fillmore Street is lined with fashionable boutiques and several cafes. *For more on shopping here, see p 33, bullet ②. Fillmore St., between Jackson & Sutter sts.*

⑥ The Coffee Bean and Tea Leaf. Grab a traditional coffee drink or a specialty tea concoction like a Moroccan Mint Latte and chill out at an outdoor table. *2201 Fillmore St.* ☎ 415/447-9733. $.

⑦ Alta Plaza Park. Originally a rock quarry, this park boasts wide views of downtown, grand staircases, a children's playground, and intricate terraced landscaping with stately pine trees and flower gardens. Barbra Streisand drove down the steps in front of Pierce and Clay streets in the 1972 movie *What's Up Doc?*—chips made by this stunt are still visible on the steps (the movie's producers refused to pay for repairs). **Fun tip:** If you stand at the top of the steps and start walking down, you'll feel like you're stepping off a cliff. *Between Steiner, Scott, Clay & Jackson sts.*

⑧ Mrs. Doubtfire house. Remember the film *Mrs. Doubtfire?* Robin Williams played a divorced father who disguised himself as a nanny to spend more time with his kids at this cream-colored Victorian with conical spires. *2640 Steiner St. (between Pacific St. & Broadway Ave.).*

⑨ The Hamlin School. This Italian baroque mansion, built for James Leary Flood, son of millionaire James Flood (one of the original "Bonanza Kings" who struck it rich with the Comstock Lode, an enormous silver strike in Nevada), is now an elite secular K–8 school for girls. Director Garry Marshall shot a portion of *The Princess Diaries* from the

Vividly-colored, intricate trims are typical elements of Queen-Anne homes.

Steiner Street contains rows and rows of elegant Victorian homes.

roof of this structure, using the photogenic hills of SF as a backdrop for his modern-day fairy tale. *2120 Broadway (between Webster & Buchanan sts.).* ☎ *415/674-5426.*

🔟 **Vedanta Temple.** This structure, built from 1905 to 1908, is a temple for the Northern California Vedanta Society, a branch of Hinduism. Its astounding combination of several types of architecture—including Moorish columns, onion domes, and medieval turrets—reflects the Hindu idea that there are numerous paths (or many religions) to reach the same God. *2963 Webster St. (at Filbert St.).*

⓫ **Union Street.** This lengthy lane is the commercial heart of Cow Hollow, so named for the 30 dairy farms that existed here in the 1860s. The street draws locals and visitors for leisure shopping at its swank boutiques. *For more on shopping here, see p 33, bullet* ④.

⓬ **Octagon House.** This unusual, eight-sided, cupola-topped house built in 1861 is maintained by the National Society of Colonial Dames of America. The small museum contains early American furniture and artifacts. Historic documents include signatures of 54 of the 56 signers of the Declaration of Independence. 🕐 *30 min. 2645 Gough St.* ☎ *415/441-7512. Free admission; donation suggested. Limited open hours: 2nd Sun & 2nd & 4th Thurs of the month noon–3pm. Closed Jan & holidays.*

⓭ **Pane e Vino.** Enjoy an espresso and tiramisu, a fine appetizer like carpaccio, or a classic Italian entree at this casual, local favorite. *1715 Union St.* ☎ *415/346-2111. $$.*

All faiths are welcome at the Hindu Vedanta Temple.

The **Marina**

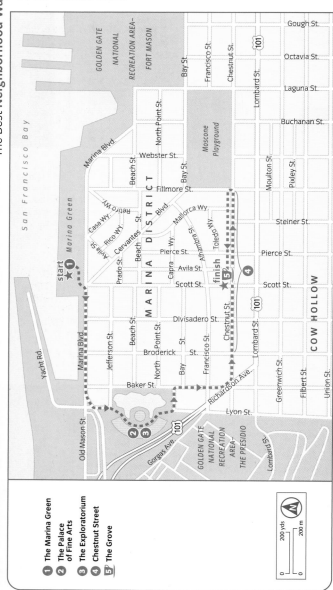

1 The Marina Green
2 The Palace
   of Fine Arts
3 The Exploratorium
4 Chestnut Street
5 The Grove

It is difficult to believe today's swank and wealthy Marina District (nicknamed simply "the Marina") was once home to mud flats. The flats were filled in for the Panama-Pacific Exposition of 1915, held to celebrate the completion of the Panama Canal. This same exposition also left behind the glorious Palace of Fine Arts, a delightful stop on an SF visit. Today the Marina is popular with trendy singles and stroller-pushing parents (grateful for the lack of hills). An address along its patch of green (the Marina Green, your first stop on this tour) is highly coveted for its front-seat views of the bay, the Golden Gate Bridge, Angel Island, and the yacht-filled private marinas that give the neighborhood its name. Take 2 to 3 hours for this tour. START: **Marina Blvd. (between Fillmore & Scott sts.). Bus: 22.**

1 ★★ **The Marina Green.** This stretch of lawn is a popular place to stroll, run, or bike. Check out the musical sculpture called the **Wave Organ** (p 85, bullet **1**). On a typically windy afternoon, you'll see people flying colorful and acrobatic kites. *Marina Blvd. (between Fillmore & Scott sts.). Bus: 22.*

2 ★★★ **The Palace of Fine Arts.** Most of the Panama-Pacific Exposition structures were built of temporary materials. Only this one was left intact and rebuilt in the 1960s. It now houses the Exploratorium (see below). The classical rotunda with curved colonnades, inspired by classic Greek and Roman ruins, is topped with a dramatic orange dome and situated around a lovely pond filled with ducks and geese. *3601 Lyon St. (at Marina Blvd.).*

3 ★★★ **kids** **The Exploratorium.** Described by *Scientific American* as the "the best science museum in the world," (I agree!) this hangarlike hall holds over 650 interactive exhibits that enthrall both kids and adults. *3601 Lyon St., in The Palace of Fine Arts. ☎ 415/397-5673. www.exploratorium.org. Admission $12; $9.50 seniors, students & kids 13–17; $8 kids 4–12; free for kids under 4. Free 1st Wed of the month. Tues–Sun 10am–5pm. Closed Mon except holidays. While the Exploratorium always has a crowd, it's best on weekday afternoons (to avoid school tours) and weekend mornings.*

4 **Chestnut Street.** A stroll along the Marina's upscale retail quarter is a fun way to end your tour. *Chestnut St. (between Fillmore & Broderick sts.).*

5 **The Grove.** Grab an outdoor table and people-watch as you sip a cup of java. *2250 Chestnut St. (at Avila St.). ☎ 415/474-4843. $.*

The Palace of Fine Arts was built for the 1915 Panama-Pacific Exposition.

Civic Center & Hayes Valley

1. San Francisco Main Library
2. Asian Art Museum
3. Civic Center Plaza
4. City Hall
5. Veterans Building
6. War Memorial Opera House
7. Louise M. Davies Symphony Hall
8. Hayes Valley
9. Frjtz
10. Hayes Street
11. Alamo Square Historic District
12. Postcard Row

200 yds

200 m

The Civic Center area, the southwestern section of Market Street, remains somewhat dilapidated, but it contains the notable Civic Center Plaza and a handful of museums and buildings worth a visit for their architectural splendor. After the Civic Center, you'll continue through hip Hayes Valley—where you'll discover the city's highest concentration of Painted Ladies (SF's famous Victorian houses), one cluster of which is reproduced so often on SF post-cards, it has been nicknamed Postcard Row. ⏲ 2 to 4 hours.
START: **100 Larkin St. (at Grove St.). BART/Muni: Civic Center.**

① ★ San Francisco Main Library. San Francisco's 376,000-square-foot (35,000 sq. m) main library opened in 1996; its facade (Sierra White granite) came from the same quarry that provided the stone for other Civic Center buildings, built 8 decades earlier. Step inside to appreciate the five-story atrium and the bridges across light wells that connect floors. The four-story stair-case travels up along a panel featuring 160 author names inscribed on small protruding glass shades. Fiber-optic light beams project the names onto the panel. Patrons continue to endow additional names; the panel can accommodate up to 200 more shades. ⏲ 30 min. 100 Larkin St. (at Grove St.). ☎ 415/557-4400. Mon 10am–6pm; Tues 9am–8pm; Fri, Sat, Tues 12–6pm.

② ★★★ Asian Art Museum. After 35 years in Golden Gate Park, this museum moved in 2003 to its current quarters. Gae Aulenti, the Milanese architect renowned for her adaptive use of historic structures into museum space (she transformed a Paris train station into the Musée d'Orsay), renovated the former Main Library, creating 37,500 square feet (3,500 sq. m) of exhibition space. The museum has one of the Western world's largest collections of Asian art, covering 6,000 years and encompassing cultures across Asia. Its collection includes world-class sculptures, paintings, bronzes, ceramics, and jade. ⏲ 1-2 hours. 200 Larkin St. (at Fulton St.). ☎ 415/581-3500. www.asianart.org. Admission $10, $7 seniors, $6 youths 13–17, free for children under 12. $5 after

With more than 15,000 objects of art, you won't get bored at the Asian Art Museum.

Beaux Arts Architecture

From about 1885 to 1920, Beaux Arts architecture flourished in America's wealthier cities. Architects trained at Paris's *Ecole des Beaux-Arts* designed grandiose structures combining classic Greek and Roman forms with French and Italian Renaissance styles. The penchant for massive stone buildings festooned with columns, garlands, and other ornamental flourishes was best suited to government buildings, railroads stations, public libraries, museums, and other lofty edifices. The architects were part of the "City Beautiful" movement that sought to improve the American urban environment through neoclassical architecture. The creation of more inviting city centers was expected to inspire civic pride, elevate residents morally and culturally, and put American cities on par with their European counterparts. Following the devastating 1906 earthquake, the rebuilding of SF's entire city center in the Beaux Arts style marked a deliberate effort to lift the city's spirits and proclaim its resilience.

5pm every Thurs; free 1st Tues of every month. Tues–Sun 10am–5pm (Thurs until 9pm).

3 Civic Center Plaza. From the middle of the plaza, take a moment to appreciate the neoclassically styled buildings (inspired by the turn-of-the-20th-century "City Beautiful" idea—see above) that surround you. Today the entire Civic Center is designated a National Historic Landmark District. *Between Polk, McAllister & Grove sts. & Van Ness Ave.*

4 City Hall. The impressive 308-foot (92m) dome on this 1915 building is taller than the one on the U.S. Capitol and is one of the largest domes in the world. City Hall, another prime example of Beaux Arts architecture, is adorned by real gold leaf on portions of the

The gold adorning City Hall's dome is a fine example of the Beaux Arts-detail displayed in the Civic Center buildings.

dome and much of the exterior. The interior rotunda is made of oak and limestone, and has a monumental marble staircase. *400 Van Ness Ave. (between McAllister & Grove sts.).* ☎ 415/554-4000. Mon–Fri 8am–5pm.

5 Veterans Building. This 1932 structure was designed by Arthur Brown, the architect of City Hall and the War Memorial Opera House, as a tribute to World War I veterans. Today the theater hosts cultural events and classical-music recitals. *401 Van Ness Ave. (between McAllister & Grove sts.).* ☎ 415/621-6600. Mon–Fri 8am–5pm.

6 War Memorial Opera House. The home of the San Francisco Opera was built in remembrance of fallen World War I soldiers. It was also the site of the signing of the U.S.-Japan peace treaty in 1951, marking the formal end of World

It is crystal clear why the perfectly picturesque "Painted Ladies" adorn so many SF postcards.

War II. *301 Van Ness Ave. (at Grove St.).* ☎ *415/621-6600.*

7 Louise M. Davies Symphony Hall. This curved, modern structure, named for one of its benefactors, was completed in 1980. The design did not inspire great enthusiasm, and a $10-million renovation was required in 1992 to improve the acoustics. *201 Van Ness Ave. (at Grove St.).* ☎ *415/552-8000.*

8 Hayes Valley. This vibrant, hip neighborhood was once best known for its homeless population, but the 1989 earthquake destroyed two noisy, unattractive freeway on-ramps here that kept businesses and pedestrians away. Now, the area is a haven for new designers and galleries, and restaurants and bars.

9 Frjtz. This funky spot dubs itself a "DJ Art teahouse." Try their tasty Belgian fries served in a paper cone or their sweet and savory crepes. *579 Hayes St. (at Laguna St.).* ☎ *415/864-7654. www.frjtzfries. com. $.*

10 Hayes Street. The area's main shopping drag features eclectic and unique shops carrying everything from antiques and clothes by local designers to fine Italian shoes (see the shopping chapter, p 67, for details on stores in this area). Or stop by some of the galleries, including **Octavia's Haze Gallery** (498 Hayes St.; ☎ 415/255-6818), with hand-blown art glass from Italy, Seattle, and the Bay Area; and **Polanco** (393 Hayes St.; ☎ 415/252-5753), which highlights Mexican art. *Hayes St. (between Franklin & Buchanan sts.).*

11 Alamo Square Historic District. San Francisco's most remarkable Victorian homes perished in the 1906 post-earthquake fires, which swept through downtown. To prevent the fires from spreading westward, firemen dynamited the mansions along Van Ness Avenue. Although the fire did cross Van Ness in some places, many homes west of the thoroughfare were spared. A small area around Alamo Square has such a great concentration of these homes that it has been designated a historic area. *Historic District between Divisadero, Webster & Fell sts. & Golden Gate Ave.*

12 Postcard Row. SF's ornate Victorians are fondly referred to as "Painted Ladies." Of these, the most famous lie on the south end of Alamo Square, with a backdrop of the San Francisco skyline providing a striking contrast. Take a look at (and your own shot of) the oft-photographed view from atop Alamo Park. *Hayes St. (between Steiner & Scott sts.).*

Russian Hill & North Beach

1 Polk Street
2 Boulange de Polk
3 Lombard Street
4 Telegraph Hill & Coit Tower
5 Washington Square Park
6 Saints Peter & Paul Church
7 Firemen Statue
8 North Beach Museum
9 Molinari Delicatessen
10 Biordi Arts Imports
11 City Lights Bookstore
12 Bill Weber Mural
13 Tosca

Street grade greater than 18%
Stairway

0 — 200 yds
0 — 200 m

Stroll through the vibrant urban landscape of North Beach (otherwise known as San Francisco's Italian Quarter) and Russian Hill, and follow the steep curves of Lombard Street, with its lush gardens and breathtaking views. Take your time enjoying these neighborhoods like a local: indulging in simple luxuries like sitting and people-watching at sidewalk cafes. Take 2 to 3 hours in a morning or an afternoon for this tour. START: **Bus 19; Cable car: Powell-Hyde lines.**

1 Polk Street. This is the main drag on Russian Hill, so named for the Russian seamen who sailed south from Alaska to hunt sea otters for their skins. Those who died on the expeditions are reputedly buried on the top of this hill at Vallejo Street but no trace of the graves exists today. Polk Street's young, urban, and European feel helps define the hill today, though it's less trendy than **Pacific Heights** (p 42) or the **Marina** (p 46). *Polk St. (between California & Chestnut sts.). Bus: 19. Cable car: Powell-Hyde lines.*

The interior of Coit Tower contains murals painted by local artists—the scenes reflect the mood of CA in the early 1930's.

2 Boulange de Polk. This excellent cafe serves croissants as good as any in Paris, plus a fine café au lait. *2310 Polk St. ☎ 415/345-1107. $.*

3 Lombard Street. Although locals don't get why tourists will wait in 3-block-long car lines (on summer weekends) to drive here, the windy curves and stately homes of Lombard Street do have their charm. Take my advice: Walk this street, don't drive it. Vibrant hydrangeas are in bloom each spring, and year-round you'll take in a brilliant view of Coit Tower and the Bay Bridge. *Lombard St. (between Hyde & Leavenworth sts.).*

4 Telegraph Hill & Coit Tower. Named for a semaphore that was installed here in 1850 to alert residents of ships' arrivals, the hill was home to various immigrant groups, from Chileans and Peruvians to Irish, and later to Italians. When the fire of 1906 came to Telegraph Hill, its Italian residents saved many homes by dousing the flames with 500 barrels of red-wine-soaked blankets and burlap bags. The crown of the hill is the landmark **Coit Tower** (for details see p 9, bullet **5**). *If your feet tire, catch the 39 bus at Union and Union St. & Columbus Ave., which heads up to Coit Tower.*

Explore Lombard Street on foot, and you'll have more time to enjoy all its details, like this ornate house number.

• 1033-37 LOMBARD •
CROOKEDEST ST.

Washington Square Park, flanked by St. Peter & Paul Church, is a quiet expanse of green in North Beach.

⑤ Washington Square Park. This land was designated a public park in 1847, making it one of the oldest parks in the city. Feeling like an old-world town plaza, it draws residents of all stripes who come to sun themselves on the lawn, read a book on a park bench, or watch their children play in the playground on the northwest corner. *Columbus & Filbert sts.*

⑥ Saints Peter & Paul Church. This is the religious center of the neighborhood's Italian community. Since the Italians who came to North Beach in the 1870s were primarily fishermen, it became known as "the Church of the Fishermen," and yearly processions to bless the fishing fleet still start out here. Inside, check out the elaborate altar carved by Italian craftsmen, the ornate columns, and the stained-glass windows. Today masses are given in English, Italian, and Chinese. *666 Filbert St. (between Powell & Stockton sts.).* ☎ *415/421-0809. Mass in English Sundays at 7:30am, 8:45am, & 1pm. Mass in Chinese Sundays at 10:15am. Mass in Italian Sundays at 11:45am.*

⑦ Firemen Statue. This bronze statue of three firemen and a damsel in distress was created in 1933 at the bequest of local character Lillie Hitchcock Coit, who was saved from a tragic fire as a young girl and became devoted to firemen. Upon her death in 1929, she endowed one-third of her estate to the SF Board of Supervisors "for the purpose of adding beauty to the city." The city used money to build Coit Tower (p 9, bullet ⑤), which contrary to popular belief is not meant to resemble a fire hose—it is simply a fluted column. *Columbus Ave. (between Union & Filbert sts.).*

⑧ North Beach Museum. This tiny museum has photos of old North Beach, including shots of its early Irish, Chinese, and Italian settlers. *Inside US Bank, 2nd floor. 1435 Stockton St. (at Columbus Ave.).* ☎ *415/391-6210 (US Bank telephone; no telephone for the museum). Free admission. Mon–Fri 9am–5pm; Sat 9am–1pm.*

9 ★ **Molinari Delicatessen.**
This shop has been supplying the
city with imported and house-made
Italian foods since 1896. Beware:
The mouthwatering Italian sand-
wiches are enormous! *373 Columbus
Ave.* ☎ *415/421-2337. www.
molinarideli.com. $.*

10 ★ **Biordi Art Imports.** Biordi
has been importing fine pottery from
central Italy since 1946. The elegant
ceramic plate ware is gorgeous. *412
Columbus Ave. (btwn Green & Vallejo
sts.)* ☎ *415/392-8096. See p 74 for a
full review.*

11 ★ **City Lights Bookstore.**
This legendary bookstore is one
of the last Beat-era hangouts in
operation, owned by famed beatnik
Lawrence Ferlinghetti. *261 Columbus
Ave.* ☎ *415/362-8193. www.city
lights.com. Daily 10am–midnight.
See p 31, bullet* 7.

12 **Bill Weber Mural.** This atten-
tion-grabbing mural, restored in
2004, covers two sides of a residential building. It depicts the history of
North Beach and Chinatown with
icons like jazz musicians, Italian
fishermen, the Imperial Dragon, and
Herb Caen, whose *San Francisco
Chronicle* columns, always at the

The window of City Lights bookstore.

epicenter of local politics and
society were a facet of SF life for
nearly 6 decades. *Broadway &
Columbus sts.*

13 ★ **Tosca.** One of the city's oldest cafes, dating from 1919, has
for years attracted politicians and
socialites. Order a "house cappuccino," really a hot chocolate with
brandy. *242 Columbus Ave.* ☎ *415/
986-9651. $.*

An abundance of Italian specialties at Molinari's Deli.

Japantown

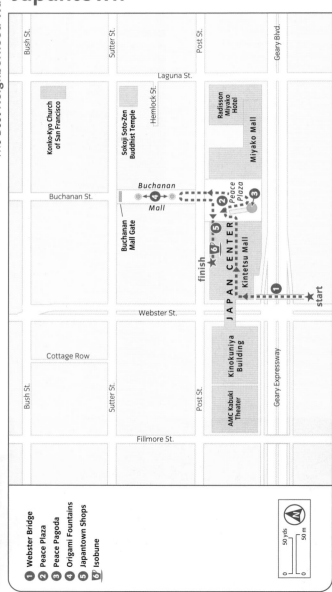

Bush St.

Sutter St.

Post St.

Geary Blvd.

Laguna St.

Hemlock St.

Konko-Kyo Church
of San Francisco

Sokoji Soto-Zen
Buddhist Temple

Radisson
Miyako Hotel

Miyako Mall

Buchanan

Buchanan St.

Mall

Peace
Plaza

Buchanan
Mall Gate

JAPAN CENTER

Kintetsu Mall

finish

start

Webster St.

Cottage Row

Kinokuniya
Building

Bush St.

Sutter St.

Post St.

Geary Expressway

AMC Kabuki
Theater

Fillmore St.

❶ Webster Bridge
❷ Peace Plaza
❸ Peace Pagoda
❹ Origami Fountains
❺ Japantown Shops
❻ Isobune

N

50 yds

50 m

0

0

Japantown once housed over 100,000 Japanese-American residents. When they were forcibly interned in camps during World War II, other settlers moved in, among them African Americans recruited to work in the shipyards. Today less than 15,000 Japanese-Americans remain in San Francisco. Although few of them live here, Japantown remains their cultural center. This tour should take 2 hours. START: **Webster St. & Geary Blvd. Bus: 2, 3, 4, 22, 38.**

1 Webster Bridge. Built in the style of Japanese pedestrian bridges, this arched walkway spans several lanes of traffic over the city's widest thoroughfare, Geary Boulevard. Its height provides a good overview of Japantown, which today covers just six square blocks, down from over 40 blocks in the 1930s. *Webster St. & Geary Blvd. Bus: 2, 3, 4, 22, 38.*

2 Peace Plaza. The Japan Center, a collection of Japanese shops and restaurants, was opened in 1968. It seemed very modern at the time, but looks less impressive today. The serenely empty space

The five-tiered peace pagoda was built as an offer of friendship from Japan to the United States.

between the two buildings is the Peace Plaza. Take a moment to examine the unusually austere fountain, where water cascades horizontally across a hard-edged cement surface. *Between Fillmore, Laguna & Posts sts. & Geary Blvd.*

3 Peace Pagoda. This concrete structure was designed by Japanese architect Yoshiro Taniguchi as a gesture of goodwill from the people of Japan. *Peace Plaza.*

4 Origami Fountains. Noted Japanese-American sculptor Ruth

Asawa designed these bronze sculptures in the style of the traditional Japanese art of paper folding. The airy, delicate sculptures, reminiscent of paper fans, contrast with the heavy stone benches that encircle them. The benches are a good place to relax and observe the water rippling through the "folds" in the sculptures to the ground below. *Nihonmachi Pedestrian Mall, Buchanan St. (between Post & Bush sts.).*

5 Japantown Shops. Explore the array of Japanese shops selling bonsai, kimonos, and ceramics. For excellent bargains on Japanese tableware, head to the basement of **Soko Hardware** (p 78). *In the Japan Center.*

6 Isobune. Pluck California rolls or *maguro* tuna sushi off little boats that cruise by on an aquatic conveyor belt in front of you. Just be sure to come at lunch or dinnertime; in off-hours you'll see limp fish that has been around the loop one too many times. *1737 Post St. (in the Japan Center).* ☎ 415/563-1030. $$.

Chinatown

1 The Dragon's Gate

2 Grant Avenue

3 St Mary's Square

4 Old St. Mary's Cathedral

5 Waverly Place

6 Tin How Temple

7 Golden Gate Fortune Cookie Co.

8 Stockton Street

9 Chinese Historical Society

10 Bank of Canton

11 Portsmouth Square

12 R&G Lounge

The first Chinese arrived in California in the 1800s to work as servants. During the gold rush, thousands left war and famine in their own country to seek their fortunes in the California "Gold Mountain." By 1851, 25,000 Chinese were working in California, most of them living in SF's Chinatown. But California didn't live up to expectations. First employed in the gold mines and later on the railroads, Chinese laborers were essentially indentured servants who faced constant prejudice. The 1906 earthquake and fire destroyed much of Chinatown, and Chinese refugees swamped relief camps outside the city center. An effort by city officials to permanently relocate them failed, and Chinatown continued to grow and thrive, in part because Chinese people were not allowed to buy homes elsewhere until 1950. Today it remains a complete community where residents shop, socialize, attend school, exercise, worship, and play. ⏱ *3–4 hours.* START: **Bush & Grant sts. Bus: 2, 3, 4, 15, 30, 45 to BART/Muni: Montgomery St.**

① The Dragon's Gate. Chinatown's best-known entryway mirrors traditional gateway arches found in many Chinese villages. The stone lions on either side of the arch are meant to protect against evil spirits. The dragons and fishes on the pagoda atop the arch signify prosperity. *Bush & Grant sts. Bus: 2, 3, 4, 15, 30, 45. BART/Muni: Montgomery St.*

② Grant Avenue. This bustling street lined with shops whose wares—from herbal medicine to jewelry—overflow onto sidewalk tables is the main thoroughfare.

Look up at the vibrant colors of the banners strung over the street like an urban canopy. The predominant red is for good luck, gold is for prosperity, and green for longevity. *Grant Ave. (between Bush & Jackson sts.).*

③ St. Mary's Square. Italian-born sculptor Beniamino Bufano created the imposing stainless-steel statue of Sun Yat-Sen, the first president of the Republic of China. Sun Yat-Sen traveled the world to raise money and support for the overthrow of the Qing Dynasty in mainland China. It is believed that he

Dried Seahorses are just one of many animal, herbal, and mineral products used in Traditional Chinese medicine.

wrote a new constitution for his country while living in San Francisco in 1911. *East of Grant Ave. (between Pine & California sts.).*

④ Old St. Mary's Cathedral. The first cathedral in California was built in 1854 by Chinese laborers using Chinese granite. The interior was destroyed by fire following the 1906 earthquake and rebuilt 3 years later. Today the church has an active congregation and many outreach programs. *660 California St. (at Grant Ave.).* ☎ 415/228-3800. www.oldsaintmarys.org. *Mass Mon–Fri 8:30am & 12:05pm, Sat 12:05pm, Sun 8:30am & 11am.*

⑤ Waverly Place. This alley between Sacramento and Washington streets is also known as the "Street of Painted Balconies," where everything from verandas to fire escapes are rendered in vivid shades of red, yellow, and green. Here you'll also find many fascinating shops, including the **Clarion Music Center** *(816 Sacramento St., at Waverly Place;* ☎ 415/391-1317*)*, selling musical instruments from all over the world, and **Bonsai Villa** *(825 Clay St., at Waverly Place;* ☎ 415/ 837-1688*)*, filled with (what else!) miniature trees in tiny pots. Several clinics offer traditional Chinese remedies including acupuncture. *East of*

Grant Ave. (between Sacramento & Washington sts.).

⑥ Tin How Temple. Climb three flights of stairs to one of the oldest Chinese temples in America. Established in 1852, it has an elaborate altar holding a statue of Tin How, or Tien Hou, "Queen of the Heavens and Goddess of the Seven Seas." You're likely to see people here meditating or praying. Admission is free, but consider giving a donation or buying incense. *125 Waverly Place (between Clay & Washington sts.).*

⑦ Golden Gate Fortune Cookies Co. Grab a bag of freshly made fortune cookies in this tiny, low-tech factory. Enjoy them like the locals do: unfolded and fortuneless. Take another moment to enjoy the murals of typical Chinatown life in the alley. *56 Ross Alley (between Washington & Jackson sts.).* ☎ 415/ 781-3956. $.

⑧ Stockton Street. While Grant Street may appeal to tourists, this is where Chinatown locals do their shopping. In grocery stores, pigs hang from hooks and crates overflow with exotic vegetables and fruits. Live frogs, turtles, eels, and other sea creatures are also available. Also on

Fortune cookies at the Golden Gate Fortune Cookie Co. are folded by hand.

Bustling Stockton Street teems with both familiar and foreign-to-western-eyes fresh produce.

this street are traditional herb shops selling dried plants and animal parts, for use in prescriptions written by traditional Chinese healers. Still other stores sell ceremonial "money" and paper goods to be burnt as offerings to ancestors. Even DVD players and washing machines made out of paper are sold for burning purposes, as no one knows for sure what's needed in the afterlife. *Stockton St. (between Sacramento St. & Broadway).*

9 Chinese Historical Society. Founded in 1963 to record and disseminate information about the history and contributions of America's Chinese immigrants, the society displays documents, photographs, and artifacts such as clothing from the earliest immigrants, traditional herbs, and the original Chinatown telephone book. *965 Clay St. (between Stockton & Powell sts.).* ☎ *415/391-1188. Tues–Fri 11am–4pm; Sat–Sun noon–4pm. Admission $3, $2 college students & seniors, $1 kids 6–17.*

10 Bank of Canton. Dating from 1909, this colorful pagoda-like structure is the oldest Asian-style edifice in Chinatown. Until 1945 it housed the China Telephone Exchange,

which was famous for its operators who were fluent in numerous Chinese dialects and English, and who knew (by heart!) the phone number of virtually every Chinatown resident. *743 Washington St. (between Grant Ave. & Kearny St.).*

11 Portsmouth Square. Captain John B. Montgomery of the USS *Portsmouth* raised a flag here in 1846 to declare San Francisco part of the United States. A year later, California's first public school was opened on the plaza, and just a year after that Sam Brannan announced the discovery of gold in the state. Today the square is an important communal center for Chinatown residents, who practice tai chi, gamble over cards, or bring children to frolic here. *Next to Kearny St., between Washington & Clay sts.*

12 R&G Lounge. Is your stomach growling for an authentic Cantonese meal but you're overwhelmed by so many choices on each block? Why not try this local favorite? *(See p 112 for full review). 631 Kearny St. (at Commercial St.).* ☎ *415/982-7877. $$.*

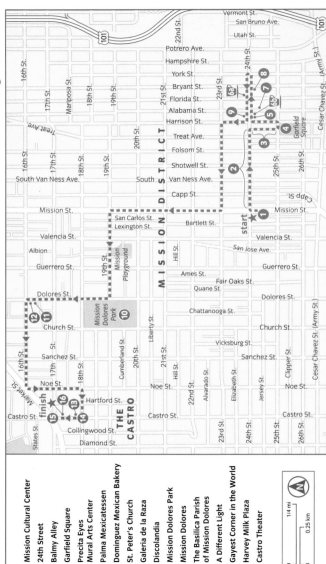

The **Mission** & the **Castro**

Vermont St.
San Bruno Ave.
Utah St.

101

Potrero Ave.
Hampshire St.
York St.
Bryant St.
Florida St.
Alabama St.
Harrison St.
Treat Ave.
Folsom St.
Shotwell St.
South Van Ness Ave.
Capp St.

Mission St.
Valencia St.
Albion
Guerrero St.
Dolores St.
Church St.

16th St.
17th St.
18th St.
19th St.

Treat Ave.

16th St.
17th St.
18th St.
19th St.

Mariposa St.

22nd St.

21st St.

23rd St.

24th St.

Cesar Chavez St. (Army St.)

101

Garfield Square

San Carlos St.
Lexington St.

Bartlett St.

Hill St.

Mission Playground

19th St.

25th St.
26th St.

Capp St.

San Jose Ave.

start

Mission St.
Valencia St.
Guerrero St.
Dolores St.
Church St.

Ames St.
Fair Oaks St.
Quane St.

Chattanooga St.

Liberty St.

Vicksburg St.

Sanchez St.

Clipper St.

Noe St.

Cumberland St.

21st St.

22nd St.

Hill St.

Alvarado St.

Elizabeth St.

Jersey St.

23rd St.
24th St.
25th St.
26th St.

Cesar Chavez St. (Army St.)

Mission Dolores Park

Mission Dolores Park

16th St.
17th St.
18th St.

Sanchez St.
Noe St.

Hartford St.

THE CASTRO

Castro St.
Collingwood St.
Diamond St.

States St.

Market St.

finish

N

1/4 mi
0.25 km

0

1 Mission Cultural Center
2 24th Street
3 Balmy Alley
4 Garfield Square
5 Precita Eyes
5a/5b Mural Arts Center
6a Palma Mexicatessen
6b Dominguez Mexican Bakery
7 St. Peter's Church
8 Galeria de la Raza
9 Discolandia
10 Mission Dolores Park
11 Mission Dolores
12 The Basilica Parish of Mission Dolores
13 A Different Light
14 Gayest Corner in the World
15 Harvey Milk Plaza
16 Castro Theater

As one of the last somewhat-affordable-for-San-Francisco places to live in town, the dynamic Mission draws many Latin-American immigrants and young, alternative types who call this neighborhood home. In addition to charming Latino markets and colorful Victorian-era homes, there are hundreds of vivid murals brightening up the sides of buildings and storefronts with religious, historic, political, or playful motifs. Next door is the Castro, a vibrant, politically active (and largely gay) neighborhood with a strong sense of community. Take 3 to 4 hours to explore these diverse neighborhoods far off the beaten tourist path. START: **Bart: 24th St.**

1 Mission Cultural Center. This nonprofit organization promotes Latino cultural arts and offers dance, painting, and folk-art classes. Note the mural above the entrance, which depicts Aztec gods, dancing skeletons, and seemingly destitute farmers in a desert. ⏱ *30 min. 2868 Mission St. (at 25th St.).* ☎ *415/643-5001. www.missionculturalcenter. org. Gallery hours: 10am-5pm Tues-Sat. $2 admission. BART: 24th St.*

2 24th Street. This leafy street lined with Mexican bakeries and other distinctly Latino stores is the neighborhood's commercial heart. Among the many colorful murals you'll see here is one on the corner of South Van Ness Avenue entitled *Carnaval*, depicting the city's Latin residents celebrating the Carnaval SF festival that occurs yearly the last weekend in May. *24th St. (from Mission to York sts.).*

3 ★★ Balmy Alley. This year-round outdoor gallery is a high point of a visit to the Mission. The murals first appeared some 3 decades ago, but in 1984 a group called PLACA began painting them everywhere—fences, garage doors, and the backs of the homes that flank this tiny alley. Some murals are political, some philosophical, some silly—but all are great fun to contemplate. *Balmy Alley (between 24th & 25th sts.).*

4 Garfield Square. Visitors are drawn here for the many murals, such as *The Primal Sea* on 26th Street or the 1973 Diego Rivera mural

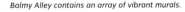

Balmy Alley contains an array of vibrant murals.

with Mayan and Aztec themes, on Harrison Street. Be sure also to check out the brightly decorated homes, including those across the street from the Rivera mural. *Between 25th, 26th, & Harrison sts. & Treat Ave.*

5 **Precita Eyes Mural Arts Center.** This group is responsible for many of the local murals, including *The Primal Sea.* Precita Eyes sponsors mural contests and teaches art classes. Inquire inside this cheerful center about new murals in the area. *2981 24th St. (between Harrison & Alabama sts.).* ☎ *415/285-2287. www.precitaeyes.org.*

Pick up a Mexican snack or meal (tortillas are handmade on-site!) at this local, take-out only favorite: **6A** **La Palma Mexicatessen** *(2884 24th St. at Bryant St.;* ☎ *415/647-1500; $);* or try a pan dulce (sweet bread) from **6B** **Dominguez Mexican Bakery** *(2951 24th St. at Alabama St.;* ☎ *415/821-1717; $).*

7 **St. Peter's Church.** The impassioned mural adorning this church depicts Aztec gods, Spanish conquistadors, and ravaged native peoples. *24th St. (at Florida St.).*

8 **Galeria de la Raza.** Dedicated to fostering public appreciation of Chicano/Latino art and culture, this small gallery holds captivating exhibitions and performances. Its gift shop, filled with Latin-American imports, is also worth visiting. *2857 24th St. (at Bryant St.).* ☎ *415/826-8009. www. galeriadelaraza.org.*

9 **Discolandia.** Step inside this popular Latin-American CD shop and don't be surprised if you find yourself doing a little shake to a salsa beat. *2964 24th St. (at Alabama St.).*

10 **Mission Dolores Park.** Take a stroll and admire the sublime city views. Established in 1905, it served as a refugee camp for over 1,600 families made homeless by the 1906 earthquake and subsequent fire. *Dolores St. (between 18th & 20th sts.).*

11 ★★ **Mission Dolores.** Officially known as Mission of San Francisco de Assisi, this was the 6th of 21 California missions on the California coast. The mission itself was established in 1776 by Father Junipero Serra, but the structure was built 15 years later, using a combination of indigenous and Spanish building techniques. It is

The handmade tortillas at La Palma Mexicatessen are a local favorite.

Contemplate the stained-glass depiction of St. Francis of Assisi inside SF's oldest standing structure, Mission Dolores.

SF's oldest building, having survived several earthquakes. Note the vegetable-dye-painted ceiling with its Native-American tribal pattern, and the graveyard, dating from 1830. While some of the wooden tombstones are no longer legible, reading the names of early pioneers is stirring. (*Fun fact:* Hitchcock filmed scenes for *Vertigo* here.) *3321 16th St. (Dolores St.)* ☎ *415/621-8203. Admission $3, $2 kids. 40-min. audio tour $5. May–Oct daily 9am–4:30pm; Nov–Apr daily 9am–4pm. www.missiondolores.org.*

⓬ **The Basilica Parish of Mission Dolores.** This church, completed in 1918, replaced a former church destroyed in the 1906 earthquake. The coat of arms with the papal insignia on the altar symbolizes the church's special status as a "basilica," so designated in 1952. The stained-glass windows depict the city's patron saint, St. Francis of Assisi, and California's 21 missions. *3321 16th St. (at Dolores St.).* ☎ *415/621-8203. Daily 8am–noon & 1–4pm.*

⓭ **A Different Light.** The city's best gay and lesbian bookstore hosts many readings and other events. Drop in for books on the history of the Castro. Another store worth checking out is Cliff's Variety (p 77). *489 Castro St. (at 18th St.).* ☎ *415/431-0891. www.adlbooks. com. Daily 10am–11pm.*

⓮ **Gayest Corner in the World.** This proud moniker for the intersection of 18th and Castro streets highlights the Castro's difficult history and proud resilience. No plaque proclaims this to be the gayest intersection on earth, but most Castro residents will affirm that it is and may point to the profusion of rainbow flags as proof. During the 1970s the gay community moved into this working-class neighborhood, fixing up homes and establishing openly gay businesses. With the election of Harvey Milk, acceptance by the wider community seemed assured. The Milk assassination and the AIDS epidemic a decade later fueled the community's

This plaque depicts the late Harvey Milk, a heroic local politician who fought to improve gay rights in the 1970s.

political activism. *Corner of 18th & Castro sts.*

⓯ **Harvey Milk Plaza.** Named after the first openly gay politician elected to public office in the U.S., this plaza is the starting point for the city's many gay marches and rallies. Milk, who was on the city board of supervisors, and liberal Mayor George Moscone, were both assassinated at City Hall in 1978 by conservative ex-supervisor Dan White. White's so-called "Twinkie defense" resulted in a mere 7-year prison sentence. Shocked by the verdict, both the gay and heterosexual communities stormed **City Hall** (see p 50, bullet ❹) during the "White Night Riot" on May 21, 1979. In 1997, on the 20th anniversary of Milk's election victory, then-mayor Willie Brown raised a rainbow flag on the plaza's flagpole. Several plaques exist here: one at the base lists the names of past and present openly gay and lesbian state and local officials. *Castro St. (at Market St.).*

⓰ **Castro Theatre.** Consider ending your tour with a flick at this 1922 Art Deco structure created by celebrated Bay Area designer Timothy Pfleuger. This is a true movie palace, with its own "Mighty Wurlitzer Organ" played on special occasions. The theater screens movie classics. *429 Castro St. (between 17th & 18th sts.).* ☎ *415/621-6120. www.castrotheatresf.com. Tickets $8.50, $5.50 children.* ●

UCSF AIDS HEALTH PROJECT
THE SILENT ROAR: MGM

The landmark Castro Theatre is one of the best-preserved 1920s-style movie houses in the United States.

Best Bets

Best **Take-Home Gifts**
★★ Canton Bazaar, *616 Grant Ave.*
(p 76)

Best **Shoe Store**
★★ Gimme Shoes, *50 Grant Ave.;*
416 Hayes St.; 2358 Fillmore St.
(p 74)

Best **Wine Shop**
★★ Wine Club San Francisco,
953 Harrison. (p 81)

Best **Scotch & Champagne**
Store
★★ D&M, *2200 Fillmore St. (p 80)*

Best **Galleries**
★★ 49 Geary St., *49 Geary St.*
(p 71)

Best **Glassware**
★★ Gump's, *135 Post St. (p 77)*

Best **Toy Store**
★ Ambassador Toys, *Two Embar-*
cadero Center (p 81)

Best **Used Books**
★ Green Apple Books and Music,
506 Clement St. (p 72)

Most Outrageous Clothes &
Accessories
★ Piedmont, *1452 Haight St. (p 75)*

Best **Museum Shop**
★★ SFMOMA MuseumStore,
151 3rd St. (p 77)

Best **Vintage-Clothing Store**
★ Crossroads Trading, *1519 Haight*
St.; 2231 Market St.; 1901 Fillmore
St. (p 75)

Best **Designer Discounts**
★★ Jeremy's, *2 S. Park St. (p 73)*

Best **Place for Unusual**
Instruments
★★ Lark in the Morning,
The Cannery, 2801 Leavenworth St.
(p 79)

Best **Cheese Shop**
★★ Cowgirl Creamery's Artisan
Cheese Shop, *Ferry Building*
Marketplace (p 80)

D & M on Fillmore is the finest purveyor of scotch & champagne in SF.

Shopping: East of Van Ness Ave.

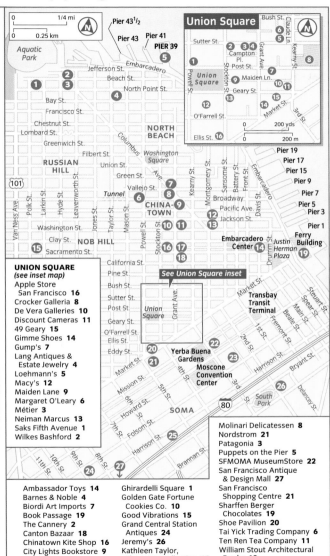

UNION SQUARE
(see inset map)
Apple Store
  San Francisco **16**
Crocker Galleria **8**
De Vera Galleries **10**
Discount Cameras **11**
49 Geary **15**
Gimme Shoes **14**
Gump's **7**
Lang Antiques &
  Estate Jewelry **4**
Loehmann's **5**
Macy's **12**
Maiden Lane **9**
Margaret O'Leary **6**
Métier **3**
Neiman Marcus **13**
Saks Fifth Avenue **1**
Wilkes Bashford **2**

Ambassador Toys **14**
Barnes & Noble **4**
Biordi Art Imports **7**
Book Passage **19**
The Cannery **2**
Canton Bazaar **18**
Chinatown Kite Shop **16**
City Lights Bookstore **9**
Cowgirl Creamery's
  Artisan Cheese Shop **19**
Crown Point Press **23**

Ghirardelli Square **1**
Golden Gate Fortune
  Cookies Co. **10**
Good Vibrations **15**
Grand Central Station
  Antiques **24**
Jeremy's **26**
Kathleen Taylor,
  The Lotus Collection **13**
Lark In The Morning
  Musique Shoppe **2**

Molinari Delicatessen **8**
Nordstrom **21**
Patagonia **3**
Puppets on the Pier **5**
SFMOMA MuseumStore **22**
San Francisco Antique
  & Design Mall **27**
San Francisco
  Shopping Centre **21**
Sharffen Berger
  Chocolates **19**
Shoe Pavilion **20**
Tai Yick Trading Company **6**
Ten Ren Tea Company **11**
William Stout Architectural
  Books **12**
Wine Club San Francisco **25**
The Wok Shop **17**

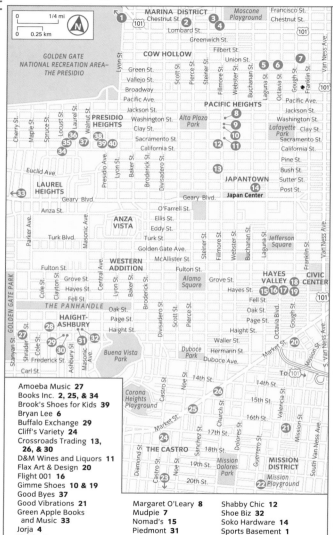

Amoeba Music **27**
Books Inc. **2, 25, & 34**
Brook's Shoes for Kids **39**
Bryan Lee **6**
Buffalo Exchange **29**
Cliff's Variety **24**
Crossroads Trading **13, 26, & 30**
D&M Wines and Liquors **11**
Flax Art & Design **20**
Flight 001 **16**
Gimme Shoes **10 & 19**
Good Byes **37**
Good Vibrations **21**
Green Apple Books and Music **33**
Jorja **4**
Kiehl's **9**
MAC Modern Appealing Clothing **18**
Maison de Belles Choses **40**
Manifesto **17**

Margaret O'Leary **8**
Mudpie **7**
Nomad's **15**
Piedmont **31**
Pumpkin, Hip Clothes for Cool Kids **38**
Rabat **3 & 23**
Ruby's Artist Cooperative **22**

Shabby Chic **12**
Shoe Biz **32**
Soko Hardware **14**
Sports Basement **1**
Steel Gallery **36**
Union Street Goldsmith **5**
Wasteland **28**
Woodchuck Antiques **35**

Shopping from A to Z

Antiques

Grand Central Station Antiques
SOMA A vast collection of inexpensive antique European and American furniture. *333 9th St. (between Folsom & Harrison sts.)* ☎ *415/252-8155. www.gcsantiques.com. DISC, MC, V. Bus: 12, 19. Map p 69.*

Kathleen Taylor, the Lotus Collection FINANCIAL DISTRICT The place for decorative antique textiles including tapestries, wall hangings, pillows, and table covers. *445 Jackson St. (between Sansome & Montgomery sts.)* ☎ *415/398-8115. www.ktaylor-lotus.com. AE, MC, V. Closed Sun. Bus: 12, 15. Map p 69.*

★★ Lang Antiques & Estate Jewelry UNION SQUARE An impressive collection of vintage engagement rings, antique time-pieces, lockets, and brooches. *323 Sutter St. (between Stockton St. & Grant Ave.)* ☎ *415/982-2213. www.langantiques.com. AE, DC, DISC, MC, V. Closed Sun. Bus: 2, 3, 4, 30, 45. Map p 69.*

★ San Francisco Antique & Design Mall POTRERO HILL Over 200 antique specialists show their stuff at this huge warehouse space. *701 Bayshore Blvd.* ☎ *415/656-3530. www.sfantique.com. AE, DISC, MC, V. Bus: 9. Map p 69.*

★ Woodchuck Antiques PRESIDIO HEIGHTS Fashionable SF homeowners head here for 19th- and early-20th-century lamps, chandeliers, and bronzes. *3597 Sacramento St. (at Locust St.)* ☎ *415/922-6416. www.sanfranciscoantiquedealers.com/woodchuck. AE, MC, V. Closed Sun. Bus: 1, 4. Map p 70.*

Kathleen Taylor is THE place for antique textiles, like this Late Ming Dynasty brocade.

Art

★ Crown Point Press SOMA Excellent etchings from U.S. and international artists, usually priced from $1,000 to $5,000. *20 Hawthorne St. (off Howard St., between 2nd & 3rd sts.)* ☎ *415/974-6273. www.crownpoint.com. MC, V. Closed Sun–Mon. Bus: 15, 30, 45. Map p 69.*

★★ 49 Geary Street UNION SQUARE You'll find several top galleries here and on Sutter and Post streets. See also p 26. *49 Geary St.(between Grant Ave. & Kearny St.) Streetcar: F. Most galleries closed Sun–Mon. Bus: 16, 17, 50. BART/ Muni: Powell St. Map p 69.*

Steel Gallery PRESIDIO HEIGHTS Danielle Steel's gallery specializes in contemporary paintings and sculptures from new and emerging artists. *3524 Sacramento St. (between Laurel & Locust sts.)* ☎ *415/885-1655. www.steelgalleryinc.com. MC, V. Closed Sun–Mon. Bus: 1, 4. Map p 70.*

Books

Barnes & Noble FISHERMAN'S WHARF An enormous superstore of this popular chain. *2550 Taylor St., (between Bay & N. Point sts.)* ☎ *415/292-6792. AE, DISC, MC, V. Cable Car: Powell/Hyde line. Map p 69.*

The Best Shopping

★ **Book Passage** FINANCIAL DISTRICT   This independent bookseller stocks books on cooking, sustainable agricultural, ecology, local history, and regional travel. *Ferry Building Marketplace, The Embarcadero (at Market St.)* ☎ 415/863-8688. *www.bookpassage.com. AE, DISC, MC, V. Streetcar: F. Map p 69.*

★ **Books Inc.** PRESIDIO HEIGHTS, COW HOLLOW, AND CASTRO   The oldest independent bookseller in town has spot-on customer service. *3515 California St. (at Locust St.)* ☎ 415/221-3666. *Bus: 1, 4. 2251 Chestnut St. (at Avila St.)* ☎ 415/931-3633. *Bus: 22, 30. 2275 Market St. (at Noe St.)* ☎ 415/864-6777. *Streetcar: F. www.booksinc.net. AE, DISC, MC, V. Map p 70.*

★ **City Lights Bookstore** NORTH BEACH   Founded by Lawrence Ferlinghetti in 1953, this landmark shop still stocks avant-garde and alternative literature. *261 Columbus Ave. (at Broadway St.)* ☎ 415/362-8193. *www.citylights.com. AE, DISC, MC, V. Bus: 15, 30, 41. Map p 69.*

★ **Green Apple Books and Music** RICHMOND   SF's best used-book store has more than 60,000 new and 100,000 used books, including rare graphic comics, an enticing cookbook selection, and art books. *506 Clement St. (at 6th Ave.)* ☎ 415/387-2272. *www.greenapple books.com. DISC, MC, V. Bus: 2, 38. Map p 70.*

★ **William Stout Architectural Books** FINANCIAL DISTRICT   You could lose yourself amid the glossy books devoted to architecture and design. *804 Montgomery St. (at Jackson St.)* ☎ 415/391-6757. *www.stoutbooks.com. MC, V. Closed Sun. Bus: 12, 15, 30, 41. Map p 69.*

Department Stores

Macy's UNION SQUARE   It can be tough to actually find what you're looking for at this thickly stocked behemoth, but sales are impressive. The men's store is across the street. *170 O'Farrell St. (between Powell & Stockton sts.)* ☎ 415/397-3333. *www.macys.com. AE, MC, V. Streetcar: F. Bus: 30, 38, 45. Map p 69.*

Neiman Marcus UNION SQUARE   Most items here are mercilessly expensive, but the third floor occasionally has good sales on items by lines/designers like Theory and Marc Jacobs. *150 Stockton St. (at Geary St.)* ☎ 415/362-3900. *www.neiman marcus.com. AE, MC, V. Bus: 30, 38, 45. Streetcar: F. Map p 69.*

★ **Nordstrom** UNION SQUARE   An excellent shoe department, knowledgeable service, and clothing for the whole family are some

City Lights contains an impressive selection of art, poetry, & political paperbacks.

of the bonuses of this well-run department store. *865 Market St. (at 5th St.)* ☎ *415/243-8500. www. nordstrom.com. AE, DC, DISC, MC, V. Bus: 27, 30, 38, 45. Streetcar: F. Map p 69.*

Saks Fifth Avenue UNION SQUARE   You'll find only top designers here, at top prices. The men's store is down the street. *384 Post St. (at Powell St.)* ☎ *415/ 986-4300. Men's store: 220 Post St.* ☎ *415/986-4300. www.saksfifth avenue.com. AE, DC, DISC, MC, V. Bus: 2, 3, 4, 38. Cable car: Powell lines. Map p 69.*

Electronics
★ Apple Store San Francisco UNION SQUARE   This is one beautiful store brought to you by the makers of very hip electronics. *1 Stockton St. (at Market St.)* ☎ *415/392-0202. www.apple.com. AE, DC, DISC, MC, V. Bus: 30, 38, 45. Streetcar: F. Map p 69.*

Discount Cameras UNION SQUARE   An authorized dealer for all major brands of photographic, digital, and video equipment. Most repairs done in 3 to 5 days. *33 Kearny St. (between Geary & Post sts.)* ☎ *415/392-1103. www.discount camera.com. AE, DC, DISC, MC, V. Bus: 38. Streetcar: F. Map p 69.*

Fashion
Children's
★ Maison de Belles Choses PRESIDIO HEIGHTS   The *très chere* kiddie clothes here are imported from France to save you the trouble of flying there yourself. *3263 Sacramento St. (at Presidio Ave.)* ☎ *415/ 345-1797. AE, DISC, MC, V. Bus: 1, 3, 4. Map p 70.*

Mudpie COW HOLLOW   This refined store stocks elegant baby and kids' clothes, accessories, and

children's furniture, but prices are extreme. Check the basement for sale items. *1694 Union St. (at Gough St.)* ☎ *415/771-9262. AE, MC, V. Bus: 41, 45. Map p 70.*

★★ Pumpkin, Hip Clothes for Cool Kids PRESIDIO HEIGHTS   Groovy, well-priced clothes for boys and girls up to age 12 who want to set themselves apart from the Gap-pack. *3366 Sacramento St. (between Walnut St. & Presidio Ave.)* ☎ *415/ 567-6780. www.pumpkinbabes.com. AE, DISC, MC, V. Bus: 1, 3, 4. Map p 70.*

Discount
★★ Jeremy's SOMA   You'll find an astonishing array of top designer fashions, from shoes to suits, at rock-bottom prices. *2 S. Park St. (between Bryant & Brannan sts.)* ☎ *415/882-4929. www.jeremys. com. AE, MC, V. Bus: 10, 15. Map p 69.*

Loehmann's UNION SQUARE   The national discount designer chain has a convenient location in downtown SF. *222 Sutter St. (between Grant Ave. & Kearny St.)* ☎ *415/982-3215. www.loehmanns. com. DISC, MC, V. Bus: 2, 3, 4, 15, 30, 45. Map p 69.*

Men's
Bryan Lee COW HOLLOW   A swank shop that will prepare gents for a night on the town or a day at the office. *1814 Union St. (at Octavia St.)* ☎ *415/923-9918. AE, DC, DISC, MC, V. Bus: 22, 41, 45. Map p 70.*

Nomads HAYES VALLEY   Distressed and vintage trousers, shirts, and leather jackets from European and American designers. *556 Hayes St. (between Laguna & Octavia sts.)* ☎ *415/864-5692. www.nomads-sf. com. AE, DC, DISC, MC, V. Bus: 21. Map p 70.*

★★★ **Wilkes Bashford** UNION SQUARE   SF's best-known men's clothing store. SF resident and comedian Robin Williams is among the high-profile customers who shop here for the finest European fashions. *375 Sutter St. (at Stockton St.)* ☎ *415/986-4380. www.wilkes bashford.com. AE, DC, DISC, MC, V. Bus: 2, 3, 4, 30, 45. Map p 69.*

Shoes

Brook's Shoes for Kids PRE-SIDIO HEIGHTS   Stylish European and American brands sold by a knowledgeable and friendly staff. *3307 Sacramento St. (at Presidio Ave.)* ☎ *415/440-7599. www.brooks shoesforkids.com. AE, DISC, MC, V. Bus: 1, 3, 4. Map p 70.*

★★ **Gimme Shoes** UNION SQUARE, HAYES VALLEY, AND PACIFIC HEIGHTS   This über-fashionable, sparse store has the coolest designer shoes in town. *50 Grant Ave. (between Geary & O'Farrell sts.)* ☎ *415/434-9242. Cable car: Powell-Mason or Powell-Hyde. 416 Hayes St. (at Gough St.)* ☎ *415/ 864-0691. Bus: 21. 2358 Fillmore St. (between Washington & Clay sts.)* ☎ *415/441-3040. Bus: 1, 22.*

www.gimmeshoes.com. AE, DISC, MC, V. Map p 69 & 70.

Shoe Biz HAIGHT   Teens and 20-somethings will appreciate the funky shoes—like tennis shoes, skate shoes, and bright red leather boots—at moderate prices. *1446 Haight St. (between Ashbury St. & Masonic Ave.)* ☎ *415/864-0990. Bus: 6, 7, 66, 71. 3810 24th St. (between Church & Blanche sts.)* ☎ *415/821-2528. Streetcar: J. BART to 24th St. then bus 48. www.shoe bizsf.com. AE, DISC, MC, V. Map p 70.*

Shoe Pavilion UNION SQUARE   This West Coast chain sells discontinued or overstocked designer and brand-name shoes at big discounts. *838 Market St. (between Stockton & Powell sts.)* ☎ *415/834-1436. www.shoepavilion.com. AE, DISC, MC, V. Cable car: Powell-Hyde or Powell-Mason. Streetcar: F. Map p 69.*

Unisex

★ **MAC Modern Appealing Clothing** HAYES VALLEY   Hip, affordable clothes—including tailored suits and fashionable separates—from designers like Paul Smith and

Did you wear out your shoes hiking up a Nob hill? You'll find a new pair at Gimme Shoes.

The famous red-heeled legs looming over the entrance to Piedmont.

Laurie B. *387 Grove St. (at Gough St.)* ☎ *415/863-3011. AE, MC, V. Bus: 21. Map p 70.*

★ **Manifesto** HAYES VALLEY Two local designers show off their groovy, retro designs with everything from sweaters and dresses to hats and ties. *514 Octavia St. (at Hayes St.)* ☎ *415/431-4778. www. piedmontsf.com. AE, MC, V. Closed Mon. Bus: 21. Map p 70.*

Vintage Clothing

Buffalo Exchange HAIGHT This Haight shop is crammed with old and new attire from the 1960s, 1970s, and 1980s. It's a good place to espy the latest street fashions. *1555 Haight St. (between Clayton & Ashbury sts.)* ☎ *415/431-7733. www.buffaloexchange.com. MC, V. Bus: 6, 7, 66, 71. Map p 70.*

★ **Crossroads Trading** HAIGHT, CASTRO, AND PACIFIC HEIGHTS Unlike other thrift stores, Crossroads gets some of its merchandise from wholesalers, so you'll also find new items in various sizes. *1519 Haight St. (at Ashbury St.)* ☎ *415/355-0555. Bus: 6, 7, 66, 71. 2231 Market St. (between Noe & Sanchez sts.)* ☎ *415/ 626-8989. Streetcar: F. 1901 Fillmore St. (at Bush St.)* ☎ *415/775-8885. Bus: 1, 2, 3, 4, 22. www.crossroads trading.com. MC, V. Map p 70.*

Good Byes PRESIDIO HEIGHTS This consignment shop offers excellent deals on high-quality attire and shoes for men and women. *3464 Sacramento St. & 3483 Sacramento St. (between Laurel & Walnut sts.)* ☎ *415/346-6388. www.goodbyessf. com. DISC, MC, V. Bus: 1, 3, 4. Map p 70.*

★ **Piedmont** HAIGHT Absolutely outrageous women's garments and accessories—sold mostly to men. If in your heart of hearts you've ever coveted any of the gaudy get-ups you've seen on drag queens, this is the place to find them. . . . The giant fishnet legs over the entrance are *so* totally The Haight. *1452 Haight St. (at Ashbury)* ☎ *415/864-8075. www. manifestoclothing.com. AE, MC, V. Closed Mon. Bus: 21. Map p 70.*

★ **Wasteland** HAIGHT The staff is choosy about what they'll take in, so clothing and accessories here are hip and retro at the same time. *1660 Haight St. (at Belvedere St.)* ☎ *415/ 863-3150. AE, MC, V. Bus: 6, 7, 66, 71. Map p 70.*

Women's

★★ **Jorja** COW HOLLOW For that special event, Jorja stocks $200 to $800 gowns and accessories that look like they cost three times the price. *2015 Chestnut St.*

(at Fillmore St.) ☎ 415/674-1131. AE, MC, V. Bus: 22, 30. Map p 70.

★★★ **Maiden Lane** UNION SQUARE   Top designers like Marc Jacobs have boutiques on this pedestrian alley. Louis Vuitton, Kate Spade, and others are nearby. Major upscale designers without their own SF store can be found at Saks Fifth Avenue or Neiman Marcus. (see "Department Stores"). *Maiden Ln., off Stockton St. Bus: 30, 38, 45. Map p 69.*

★★ **Margaret O'Leary** PACIFIC HEIGHTS AND FINANCIAL DISTRICT   Irish-born O'Leary began knitting elegant sweaters in SF in 1987. Now she has several swanky boutiques, which also carry accessories from other designers. *2400 Fillmore St. (at Washington St.).* ☎ *415/771-9982. Bus: 1, 12, 22. 1 Claude Ln. (off Sutter St., between Grant Ave. & Kearny St.)* ☎ *415/391-1010. (Claude Ln. location closed Sun–Mon). Bus: 2, 3, 4, 15, 30, 45. www. margaretoleary.com. AE, DISC, MC, V. Map p 69 & 70.*

★★ **Métier** UNION SQUARE   For classic, and pricey, attire from European ready-to-wear lines and designers, plus exquisite jewelry from LA designer Cathy Waterman, head to Métier. *355 Sutter St. (between Stockton St. & Grant Ave.)* ☎ *415/989-5395. www.metiersf.com. AE, MC, V. Closed Sun. Bus: 2, 3, 4, 30, 45. Map p 69.*

★★ **Rabat** MARINA AND NOE VALLEY   The minimalist surroundings perfectly match the stylish designer clothing and accessories. The shoes are to-die-for. *2080 Chestnut St. (at Mallorca Way)* ☎ *415/929-8868. Bus: 22, 30. 4001 24th St. (at Noe St.)* ☎ *415/282-7861. Streetcar: J. BART to 24th St. then bus 48. AE, DISC, MC, V. Map p 70.*

Gifts & Souvenirs

★ **Biordi Art Imports** NORTH BEACH   Beautiful examples of hand-painted Majolica dishes and serving pieces nearly too pretty to use. *412 Columbus Ave. (at Vallejo St.)* ☎ *415/392-8096. www.biordi. com. AE, DC, DISC, MC, V. Closed Sun. Bus: 15, 30, 41. Cable car: Powell-Mason. Map p 69.*

★★ **Canton Bazaar** CHINATOWN   This multilevel store carries Chinese porcelain, jade, antiques, and hand-carved furniture. *616 Grant Ave.*

Intricately painted dinnerware fill the shelves at Biordi Art Imports.

Family-owned Flax Art & Design has been fostering creativity in SF for over 60 years.

(between California & Sacramento sts.) ☎ 415/362-5750. AE, DISC, MC, V. Bus: 1, 15, 30, 45. Map p 69.

★★ **Cliff's Variety** CASTRO This only-in-SF shop is loaded with amusing, useful, necessary, or just plain fun items, among them art supplies. *479 Castro St. (at 18th St.)* ☎ 415/431-5365. AE, DC, DISC, MC, V. Streetcar: F. Map p 70.

★★ **Flax Art & Design** MISSION FLAX carries just about every art and design supply you can think of, plus crafts, children's art supplies, frames, and calendars. *1699 Market St. (at Valencia St.)* ☎ 415/552-2355. www.flaxart.com. AE, DISC, MC, V. Streetcar: F. Map p 70.

Good Vibrations MISSION AND NOB HILL This straightforward, layperson's sex-toy, book, and video emporium is geared mostly towards women, but not exclusively. *603 Valencia St. (at 17th St.)* ☎ 415/522-5460. Bus: 22, 26. Bart to 16th St. *1620 Polk St. (at Sacramento St.).* ☎ 415/345-0400. Bus: 1, 19. Cable car: California line. www.goodvibes.com. AE, DISC, MC, V. Map p 70.

★★ **Kiehl's** PACIFIC HEIGHTS This is one of the few retail locations of the 150-plus-year-old cosmetics firm. *2360 Fillmore St. (at Washington St.)* ☎ 415/359-9260. www.kiehls.com. AE, DC, MC, V. Bus: 1, 22. Map p 70.

★★ **SFMOMA MuseumStore** SOMA With an array of artistic books, jewelry, and intelligent toys, it's one of the more clever gift shops around. *151 3rd St. (between Mission & Howard sts.)* ☎ 415/357-4035. www.sfmoma.com. AE, DISC, MC, V. Bus: 9, 15, 30, 45. Map p 69.

Tai Yick Trading Company CHINATOWN This is a real find for tiny china tea sets, miniature Chinese bowls, and all kinds of porcelain and pottery. *1400 Powell St. (at Broadway St.)* ☎ 415/986-0961. www.tai yick.com. AE, DC, DISC, MC, V. Bus: 12, 15, 30, 45. Cable car: Powell-Mason. Map p 69.

Housewares & Furnishings
★★ **Gump's** UNION SQUARE Founded in 1861, this SF institution offers tasteful home accessories

Gump's is a SF institution, selling fine frills for the home.

including fine crystal, elegant tableware, and other artful items, along with superlative service. *135 Post St. (between Grant Ave. & Kearny St.)* ☎ *415/982-1616. www.gumps.com. AE, DISC, MC, V. Bus: 2, 3, 4, 15, 30, 45. Map p 69.*

★ **Shabby Chic** PACIFIC HEIGHTS Rachel Ashwell's airy English designs are now well known through her TV series and design books. Check out one of her first stores for slipcover furniture, poplin and linen bedding, and home accessories. *2185 Fillmore St. (between California & Sacramento sts.)* ☎ *415/771-3881. www.shabby chic.com. AE, DISC, MC, V. Bus: 1, 3, 22. Map p 70.*

★ **Soko Hardware** JAPANTOWN A great selection of ceramic plates, tea sets, sake cups, and more at bargain prices. *1698 Post St. (at Buchanan St.)* ☎ *415/931-5510. MC, V. Bus: 2, 3, 4, 38. Map p 70.*

The Wok Shop CHINATOWN This shop has every conceivable implement for Chinese cooking, including woks, brushes, and oyster knives. It also sells plenty of kitchen

utensils. *718 Grant Ave. (at Sacramento St.)* ☎ *415/989-3797 or 888/ 780-7171. www.wokshop.com. AE, DC, DISC, MC, V. Bus: 1, 30, 45. Cable Car: California line. Map p 69.*

Jewelry

★ **De Vera Galleries** UNION SQUARE Designer Frederico de Vera's unique rough-stone jewelry collection, art glass, and vintage knickknacks are too beautiful to pass up and too expensive to be a painless purchase. *29 Maiden Ln. (between Grant Ave. & Kearny St.)* ☎ *415/788-0828. www.devera objects.com. AE, MC, V. Closed Sun–Mon. Bus: 30, 38, 45. Streetcar: F. Map p 69.*

★★ **Ruby's Artist Cooperative** MISSION As the name suggests, Ruby's provides a venue for local jewelry makers to show their delightful, one-of-a-kind creations. *3602 20th St. (at Valencia St.)* ☎ *415/550-8052. www.rubygallery. com. MC, V. Bus: 12, 27. Streetcar: J. BART to 16th or 24th St. Map p 70.*

★ **Union Street Goldsmith** COW HOLLOW A showcase for Bay Area goldsmiths, this exquisite shop sells a contemporary collection of fine custom-designed jewelry in platinum and gold. *1909 Union St. (at Laguna St.)* ☎ *415/776-8048. www.unionstreetgoldsmith.com. AE, DC, DISC, MC, V. Bus: 22, 41, 45. Map p 70.*

Music & Musical Instruments

★★ **Amoeba Music** HAIGHT *The* music store for young San Franciscans, with a huge collection of LPs, plus CDs and cassettes. *1855 Haight St. (between Shrader & Stanyan sts.)* ☎ *415/831-1200. www.amoebamusic.com. DISC, MC, V. Bus: 6, 7, 66, 71. Map p 70.*

Would you prefer a mandolin, a xylophone, or perhaps a flute? You'll find them all—and more—at Lark in the Morning.

★★ Lark in the Morning Musique Shoppe
FISHERMAN'S WHARF   An incredible selection of musical instruments, books, recordings, videos, and musical artwork from over 50 cultures. *The Cannery, 2801 Leavenworth St. (at Beach St.)* ☎ *415/922-4277. www.larkinthe morning.com. AE, DC, DISC, MC, V. Bus: 10, 30. Cable car: Powell-Hyde. Map p 69.*

Amoeba Music carries CDs plus a massive selection of classic LPs (remember those?).

Shopping Centers & Complexes
The Cannery FISHERMAN'S WHARF   Several tourist-oriented shops are in this charmingly restored former fruit-canning facility. *2801 Leavenworth St. (at Jefferson St.)* ☎ *415/771-3112. www.delmonte square.com. Bus: 10, 30. Streetcar: F. Map p 69.*

Crocker Galleria FINANCIAL DISTRICT   This glass-domed pavilion features several high-end shops selling expensive and classic designer creations. *50 Post St. (between Kearny & Montgomery sts.)* ☎ *415/393-1505. www.shopatgalleria.com. Bus: 2, 3, 4, 15, 30, 45. Map p 69.*

★ Ghirardelli Square FISHERMAN'S WHARF   Along with the quaint gift shops at this former chocolate factory comes a priceless view. This is a perfect spot to shop for SF's famous chocolate: Ghirardelli's flagship store, the Ghirardelli Soda Fountain & Chocolate Shop (see p 106) is located within the square. *900 North Point St. (at Larkin St.)* ☎ *415/775-5500. www.ghirardellisq. com. Bus: 10, 30. Streetcar: F. Map p 69.*

San Francisco Shopping Centre SOMA Anchored by Nordstrom, this attractive mall has some more interesting chains like Kenneth Cole and some less interesting ones. *865 Market St. (at 5th St.)* ☎ *415/495-5656. www. westfield.com/sanfrancisco. Bus: 27, 30, 38, 45. Streetcar: F. Map p 69.*

Specialty Foods, Wines & Liquors
For **Ghirardelli chocolate,** *see "Ghirardelli Square" above.*

★★ Cowgirl Creamery's Artisan Cheese Shop FINANCIAL DISTRICT Top-notch domestic and international cheeses, in addition to award-winning selections from Cowgirl Creamery's own Point Reyes facility, plus cheese tools, boards, and books about cheese. *Ferry Building Marketplace, 1 Ferry Building on The Embarcadero at Mission St.* ☎ *415/362-9354. www. cowgirlcreamery.com. MC, V. Streetcar: F. Map p 69.*

★★ D&M Wines and Liquors PACIFIC HEIGHTS This unassuming shop boasts amazing champagnes and French brandies, plus one of the world's best single-malt scotch selections. *2200 Fillmore St. (at Sacramento St.)* ☎ *415/346-1325. www.dandm.com. AE, MC, V. Bus: 1. Map p 70.*

★ Golden Gate Fortune Cookies Co. CHINATOWN Buy fortune cookies hot off the press at this tiny, alley-side Chinatown shop. Bring your own messages and watch them being folded into the cookies. *56 Ross Alley (between Washington & Jackson sts.).* ☎ *415/781-3956. No credit cards. Bus: 30, 45. Cable car: Powell-Mason. Map p 69.*

★ Molinari Delicatessen NORTH BEACH Since 1896, Molinari has been supplying SF with imported meats, cheeses, wines, and canned goods at very moderate prices. *373 Columbus Ave. (at Vallejo St.)* ☎ *415/421-2337. www.molinari deli.com. MC, V. Closed Sun. Bus: 12, 15, 30, 41. Map p 69.*

★★ Sharffen Berger Chocolates FINANCIAL DISTRICT In 1996 a former winemaker and his business partner decided to make the finest chocolates possible. Judge their success for yourself. *Ferry Building Marketplace, 1 Ferry Building, on The Embarcadero at Mission St..* ☎ *415/981-9150. www. scharffenberger.com. AE, DISC, MC, V. Streetcar: F. Map p 69.*

The SF Shopping Center downtown is an endlessly entertaining mall to explore on a damp, foggy afternoon.

Specialty tea from Ten Ren Tea Co. is a fun, inexpensive, and light gift to tote home.

★ Ten Ren Tea Company

CHINA-TOWN   In addition to a selection of 50 varieties of tea, you'll be offered a steaming cup of tea when you walk in. *949 Grant Ave. (between Washington & Jackson sts.)* ☎ *415/362-0656. www.tenren. com. AE, DC, MC, V. Bus: 1, 15, 30, 45. Cable car: California line. Map p 70.*

Wine Club San Francisco

SOMA   The largest wine merchant in the West offers bargain-basement prices. *953 Harrison St. (between 5th & 6th sts.)* ☎ *415/512-9086. www.thewineclub.com. AE, MC, V. Bus: 12, 19, 27. Map p 69.*

Sporting Goods: Clothing & Equipment

Patagonia FISHERMAN'S WHARF An excellent source for high-quality fleece and outerwear. *770 North Point St. (between Hyde & Leavenworth sts.)* ☎ *415/771-2050. www. patagonia.com. AE, DC, DISC, MC, V. Bus: 10, 30. Cable car: Powell-Hyde. Map p 69.*

★★ Sports Basement

PRESIDIO & MISSION BAY   Although signs on the walls still read FROZEN FOODS and BAKERY at this former military PX, it now stocks SF's best-priced selection of sporting goods. *610 Mason St. (in the Presidio)* ☎ *415/437-0100. Bus: 28, 29, 76. 1301 6th St. (between Owens & 16th sts.)* ☎ *415/437-0100. Bus: 15. www.sportsbasement.com. AE, DC, DISC, MC, V. Map p 70.*

Toys

★ Ambassador Toys

FINANCIAL DISTRICT   Classic European dolls, wonderful wooden toys, clever games, and books are among the great playthings at this delightful store. *2 Embarcadero Center (at Sacramento St., between Front & Davis sts.)* ☎ *415/345-8697.*

Your child will be mesmerized by the traditional toys on sale at Ambassador Toys.

www.ambassadortoys.com. AE, DISC, MC, V. Bus: 1. Cable car: California line. Map p 69.

Chinatown Kite Shop CHINATOWN From world-class stunt fliers to more modest models, an awesome array of kites is on display here. *717 Grant Ave. (at Sacramento St.)* ☎ *415/989-5182. www.chinatownkite.com. AE, DC, DISC, MC, V. Bus: 1, 15, 30, 45. Cable car: California line. Map p 69.*

Puppets on the Pier FISHERMAN'S WHARF Kittens, bunnies, dragons, and even cockroaches are just some of the amazing puppets here. *Pier 39, on The Embarcadero at Grant Ave., Fisherman's Wharf.* ☎ *415/781-4435. www.puppetdream.com. AE, DISC, MC, V. Bus: 10, 15. Streetcar: F. Map p 69.*

Travel Goods
Flight 001 HAYES VALLEY Jetsetters will find hip travel accessories like sleek luggage, "security friendly" manicure sets, and other midair must-haves. *525 Hayes St. (between Laguna & Octavia sts.)* ☎ *415/487-1001. www.flight001.com. AE, DISC, MC, V. Bus: 21. Map p 70.* ●

5 Great Outdoors

The **Golden Gate** Promenade

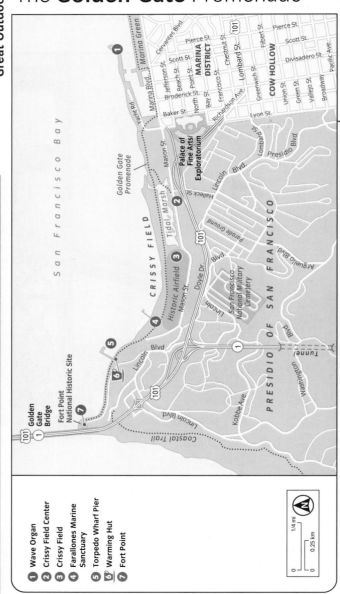

1 Wave Organ
2 Crissy Field Center
3 Crissy Field
4 Farallones Marine Sanctuary
5 Torpedo Wharf Pier
6 Warming Hut
7 Fort Point

1/4 mi

0 0.25 km

T he **Golden Gate Promenade** is a 3½-mile (5.5 km) paved trail hug-
ging the San Francisco Bay. Not only is it the city's most scenic biking, jogging, and walking path, it is also surprisingly flat! The promenade
lies within the pristine Golden Gate National Recreation Area (one of the
largest urban parks in the world), which is maintained by the National
Park Service. Come at any time of the day, but note that in summer the
mornings may be foggy, while the late afternoon is usually windy. ***Note:***
This tour can be done on foot or by bike (see p 166 for bike rental info),
and may be combined with the "Crossing the Golden Gate Bridge" tour
(p 38). 🕐 2 to 3 hours. START: **Bus 30 to Broderick & Beach sts.**

❶ ★ kids **Wave Organ.** This is an
amazing (and musical) piece of envi-
ronmental art. Tubes emerge from
the water below through a concrete
and rock structure, capturing the
ebb and flow of the ocean currents
in strange humming sounds. *Marina
Breakwater. Baker St. & Marina
Blvd. Bus: 30 to Broderick & Beach
sts.* ☎ *415/561-0360. Free.*

❷ **Crissy Field Center.** Stop
here to pick up maps and information about Crissy Field. This commu-
nity-run facility also leads walks
through the area. 🕐 *15 min. 603
Mason St. (at Halleck St.).* ☎ *415/
561-7690. www.crissyfield.org/
center. Wed–Sun 9am–5pm.*

❸ ★★★ kids **Crissy Field.** This
100-acre (40-hectare) site contained
what was a military airstrip until 1936.
It lay abandoned until 1996, when
individuals and civic organizations
worked to put in over 100,000 native
plants and restored its natural
ecosystem. Today it contains a tidal
marsh, beaches, and marvelous wind-
ing paths. *Old Mason & Baker sts.*

❹ kids **Farallones Marine Sanctuary.** This small house offers information and imaginative exhibits on
the local marine wildlife. 🕐 *15 min.*
☎ *415/561-6625. www.farallones.
org. Wed–Sun 10am–5pm.*

❺ **Torpedo Wharf Pier.** Walk to
the end of this pier for brilliant views
of the Golden Gate and Alcatraz.

*Fort Point sits under the Golden Gate
Bridge.*

❻ **Warming Hut.** Order organic
gourmet sandwiches and explore
the ecologically correct gift shop
while you wait. Consider eating at
the outdoor picnic tables. *Daily
9am-5pm. Presidio Building 983.*
☎ *415/561-3040. $.*

❼ **Fort Point.** Hastily completed
by the U.S. Army Corps of Engineers
at the onset of the Civil War, this formidable brick fortress at the foot of
the Golden Gate Bridge was used as
a base of operations to build the
bridge and was manned by soldiers
during World War II. 🕐 *15 min.
Fri–Sun 10am–5pm. To continue with
the "Crossing the Golden Gate
Bridge" tour (p 38), follow the signs
to the walking and biking trails lead-
ing to the Golden Gate Bridge.*

Land's End

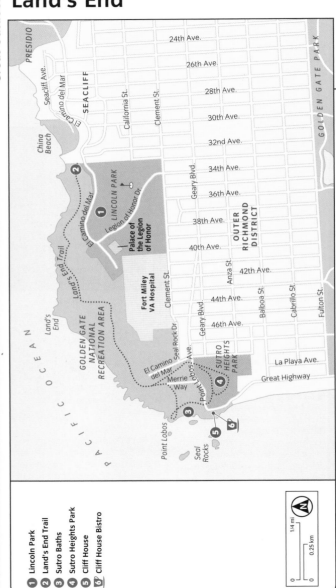

1. Lincoln Park
2. Land's End Trail
3. Sutro Baths
4. Sutro Heights Park
5. Cliff House
6. Cliff House Bistro

This **poetically rocky point** known as Land's End, juts out into the wide expanse of the Pacific. This dramatic and striking section of the coast boasts rugged views of the violent surf, and the feeling that you are standing at the edge of the world. You'll marvel that these wild cliffs are contained within urban San Francisco. It's generally chilly and windy here—dress warmly. ⏱ *1–2 hours.* START: **Bus: 1, 38 to Clement St. & 33rd Ave.**

1 Lincoln Park. This 275-acre boasts Monterey cypresses and contains the **California Palace of the Legion of Honor** (p 12, bullet **5**). *Clement St. & 33rd Ave. Bus: 1, 38.*

2 Land's End Trail. Spectacular views of the Pacific's waves crashing against the cliffs, twisted cypress trees, and unusual rock formations accompany you on this 1½-mile (2.4km) trek. *Eagle's Point.* ☎ *415/ 561-4395 to verify hours.*

3 Sutro Baths. San Francisco millionaire Adolph Sutro opened these baths in 1897. Seven pools of various temperatures held 1.7 million gallons of water and could accommodate up to 10,000 people at a time. The baths burned in 1966, but the concrete ruins of these mega-pools remain.

4 Sutro Heights Park. This small park on a bluff overlooking Ocean Beach was once the home of Adolph Sutro, a Prussian émigré who created the Sutro Tunnel to reach the Comstock silver lode, and also served as mayor of San Francisco. *La Playa Ave. & Geary Blvd.*

5 Cliff House. This neoclassical structure, acquired by the National Park Service in 1977, contains viewing decks looking out to Seal Rocks, home to a colony of sea lions and marine birds, and two restaurants— upscale and pricey Sutro's, and the Cliff House Bistro (see below); both boast breathtaking ocean views. *1090 Point Lobos (Geary St., west of 48th Ave.).* ☎ *415/386-3330. www. cliffhouse.com. Daily 9am–9:30pm.*

6 Cliff House Bistro. This casual, old-fashioned sandwich-and-salad spot in the Cliff House provides a warm respite from the wind. The view is worth the inflated prices. *Inside the Cliff House. $$.*

Rocky pillars jut majestically out of the water at Ocean Beach.

Golden Gate Park

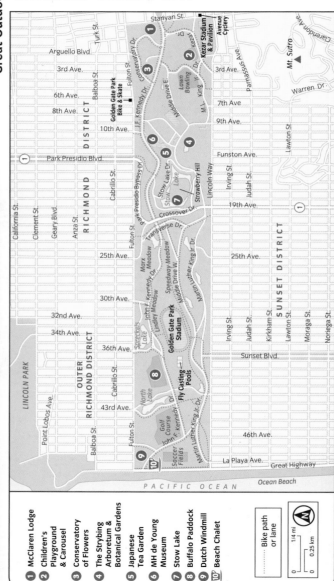

1 McClaren Lodge

2 Children's
Playground
& Carousel

3 Conservatory
of Flowers

4 The Strybing
Arboretum &
Botanical Gardens

5 Japanese
Tea Garden

6 MH de Young
Museum

7 Stow Lake

8 Buffalo Paddock

9 Dutch Windmill

10 Beach Chalet

.... Bike path
or lane

0   1/4 mi
0   0.25 km

Golden Gate Park is the jewel of San Francisco—this narrow strip of green stretches inland from the Pacific Ocean, creating a magical 1017-acre rectangle containing a myriad of treasure—museums, bison paddocks, windmills, flower gardens, and walking, jogging, and biking trails to name a few (see p 166 and bullet ⑦ on the next page for bike rental info). I've listed my favorite stops and activities, but take a day to explore this outdoor wonder at leisure. ***Note:*** If your schedule allows, visit on a Sunday, when one of the main throughways (JFK Dr.) is closed to car traffic. START: **Fell & Stanyan Sts. Bus 5, 21.**

① **McLaren Lodge and Park Headquarters.** This entry to the park honors John McLaren, park superintendent from 1890 to 1943, who transformed the barren land into a lush urban retreat and developed a new strain of grass to hold the sandy soil, built windmills to pump water for irrigation, and spent 40 years constructing a natural wall to prevent erosion from the ocean. Stop by for detailed information on the park. ***Note:*** If you want to explore the park by bike, see bullet ⑦ for rental info. ⏱ *30 min. Fell & Stanyan sts.* ☎ *415/831-2700. www. parks.sfgov.org. Bus: 5, 21.*

② kids **Children's Playground & Carousel.** Built in 1887 as the first public children's playground in the U.S., it now features huge slides, a fabulous climbing structure, and a decorative 1912 carousel from Buffalo, N.Y. ⏱ *30 min. Kezar Dr. (at 1st Ave.). 50¢ per ride.*

③ ★ **Conservatory of Flowers.** In 1995 a massive windstorm damaged 40% of the glass tiles in this 1878 public conservatory. It reopened in 2003 after a $25-million restoration, which also rescued from the wreckage a century-old tropical philodendron. The striking glass structure and path-filled gardens showcase rare orchids, carnivorous flora, and plants from five continents. ⏱ *1 hour. Off John F. Kennedy Dr., near Stanyan St. entrance.* ☎ *415/666-7001. www.conservatory*

Built in 1967, the Conservatory of Flowers is the oldest public conservatory in the western hemisphere.

offlowers.org. $5; $3 kids 12–17, seniors 65 & over & students; $1.50 kids 5–11. Open Tues–Sun 9am–4:30pm.

④ **The Strybing Arboretum & Botanical Gardens.** Over 6,000 species of plants, flowering trees, and theme gardens grace this splendid oasis. Docents give free tours daily at 1:30pm. ⏱ *1 hour. 9th Ave. (at Lincoln Way).* ☎ *415/661-1316. www.strybing.org. Free admission. Mon–Fri 8am–4:30pm; Sat–Sun 10am–5pm.*

The Japanese Tea Garden created by Makoto Hagiwara, a wealthy Japanese landscape designer.

5 ★★ kids **Japanese Tea Garden.** This pristine garden features koi ponds, Japanese maples, and bonsai. Highlights include a 1790 bronze Buddha, a Shinto wooden pagoda, a Zen Garden, and an outdoor teahouse. Kids love scaling the Drum Bridge. ⏱ *1 hour. Music Concourse (at Tea Garden Drive, off Concourse Drive near Martin Luther King Jr Drive).* ☎ *415/752-4227. Admission $3.50, $1.25 seniors & kids 6–12, kids under 6 free. Entrance free from 8:30–9am. Daily 8:30am–5pm; summer until 6pm.*

6 **MH de Young Museum.** In October 2005 the de Young reopened in Golden Gate Park. The museum features a superb collection of art from Africa, Oceania, and the Americas. Its controversial new home, designed by architects Herzog & de Meuron, includes a gleaming copper facade and 84,000 square feet of gallery space. ⏱ *1 hour. 75 Tea Garden Dr.* ☎ *415/750-3600. www.thinker.org/deyoung. Call for hours and admission prices.*

7 kids **Stow Lake.** Tool around this sublime man-made lake in a boat. This is also where you can come to rent a bike. *Stow Lake Boat House, 50 Stow Lake Dr.* ☎ *415/752-0347. Rowboats $13/hr., pedal boats $17/hr. 4 passengers/boat max. Wheel Fun Rentals.* ☎ *415/668-6699. Mountain bikes $8/hr., $20/4 hrs., $25/day; cruiser bikes $6/hr., $15/ 4 hrs., $20/all day.*

8 **Buffalo Paddock.** Drop by and visit these enormous mammals, descendents of the original creatures brought here in 1891, when the park also had elk, bears, and goats. *On John F. Kennedy Dr.*

9 **Dutch Windmill.** This was one of two windmills that pumped water to a reservoir on Strawberry Hill in the middle of the park. *Great Hwy. & Fulton St.*

10 **Beach Chalet.** The food here is secondary to the stunning ocean view. If you aren't hungry, hang at the bar area to grab hot cocoa or perhaps a house-made beer (brewed on site!). I recommend their sampler rack—six mini-mugs of their brews served in a tiny Lazy Susan. *1000 Great Hwy. (between Fulton & Lincoln Way).* ☎ *415/386-8439. www.beach chalet.com. $$.* ●

The Best Dining

Dining Best Bets

Best **Celebrity-Chef Meal**
★★★ Michael Mina $$$$ Westin St. Francis Hotel, 335 Powell St. (p 109)

Best **Chinese Restaurant**
★ R & G Lounge $$ 631 Kearny St. (p 112)

Best **Diner**
★ Taylor's Refresher $ 1 Market St. (p 114)

Best **Burger**
★ Burger Joint $ 700 Haight St. and 807 Valencia St. (p 100)

Best **Seafood**
★★★ Aqua $$$ 252 California St. (p 99)

Best **Bakery**
★ Tartine $ 600 Guerrero St. (p 114)

Best **Dim Sum**
★★ Ton Kiang $ 5821 Geary Blvd. (p 115)

Best **Wood-Fired Pizza**
★★ A16 $$ 2355 Chestnut St. (p 99)

Best **French Restaurant**
★★★ Fleur de Lys $$$$ 777 Sutter St. (p 104)

The Cliff House may be pricey, but it is more than worth it for its view of the Pacific Ocean.

Most **Worth the Wait**
★★★ The Slanted Door $$$ 1 Market St. (p 113)

Most **Romantic**
★★ Café Jacqueline $$$ 1454 Grant Ave. (p 101)

Best **Belly Dancer/Moroccan Food**
★★ Aziza $$ 5800 Geary Blvd. (p 99)

Best **Outdoor Dining Area**
★ Park Chalet $$ 1000 Great Hwy. (p 111)

Best **Neighborhood Italian**
★★ Antica Trattoria $$ 2400 Polk St. (p 98)

Best **Thai**
★ Khan Toke $$ 5937 Geary Blvd. (p 107)

Best **Sidewalk Cafe**
★ Boulange de Polk $ 2310 Polk St. (p 53)

Best **Brunch**
★ Ella's $ 500 Presidio Ave. (p 104)

Best **Vegetarian**
★★ Greens $$$ Building A, Fort Mason Center (p 106)

Best **Ice Cream**
★ Mitchell's Ice Cream $ 688 San Jose Ave. (p 110)

Best **Burrito**
★ Taqueria Pancho Villa $ 3071 16th St. (p 114)

Best **View**
Cliff House $$$ 1090 Point Lobos (p 102)

Best **Pre-Theater Meal**
★★ Cortez $$$ 550 Geary St. (p 103)

Best **Four-Star Meal at Two-Star Prices**
★ Clementine $$ 126 Clement St. (p 102)

The Mission & Environs **Dining**

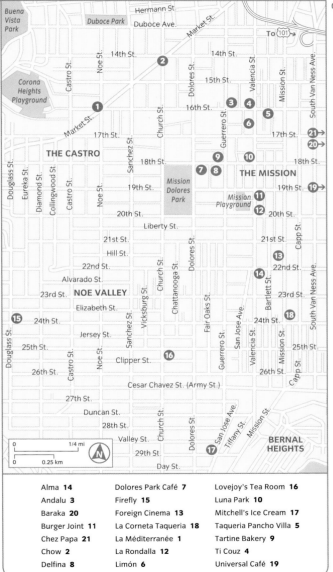

Alma **14**

Andalu **3**

Baraka **20**

Burger Joint **11**

Chez Papa **21**

Chow **2**

Delfina **8**

Dolores Park Café **7**

Firefly **15**

Foreign Cinema **13**

La Corneta Taqueria **18**

La Méditerranée **1**

La Rondalla **12**

Limón **6**

Lovejoy's Tea Room **16**

Luna Park **10**

Mitchell's Ice Cream **17**

Taqueria Pancho Villa **5**

Tartine Bakery **9**

Ti Couz **4**

Universal Café **19**

San Francisco **Dining**

A16 **1**
Ana Mandara **29**
Antica Trattoria **36**
Betelnut **7**
Blue Mermaid
  Chowder House **33**
Boulevard **51**
Burger Joint **19**
Café Kati **14**
Café Marimba **2**

Cha Cha Cha's **17**
Citizen Cake **24**
The Citrus Club **16**
Dragon Well **3**
East Coast West
  Delicatessen **42**
Ella's **12**
Eos Restaurant
  & Wine Bar **18**
Fog City Diner **40**

Franciscan **35**
Fresca **10**
Fringale **45**
Gary Danko **30**
Ghirardelli Soda Fountain
  & Chocolate Shop **32**
Greens **6**
Harris' **41**
Hawthorne Lane **46**
Hayes Street Grill **27**

Berkeley

Indian Oven **22**
IN-N-OUT Burger **34**
Isa **4**
Isobune **15**
Jardiniere **25**
Juban Yakiniku House **15**
La Méditerranée **11**
Long Life Noodle Company
  & Jook Joint **52**
McCormick & Kuleto's **31**

Memphis Minnie's **21**
Okoze **38**
One Market **48**
Ozumo **53**
Pane e Vino **8**
Quince **9**
Restaurant LuLu **44**
RNM **20**
The Slanted Door **50**
Sociale **13**

Suppenkuche **23**
Swan Oyster Depot **43**
Swensen's **37**
Taylor's Refresher **49**
Town's End **47**
Vicolo Pizzeria **26**
Yank Sing **54**
ZA Pizza **39**
Zao Noodle Bar **5, 10**
Zuni Café **28**

BERKELEY *(See inset)*
Chez Panisse **1**

Union Square & Environs **Dining**

Pacific Ave.

Jackson St.

Mason St.

Powell St.

Stockton St.

CHINATOWN

Washington St.

Taylor St.

Grant Ave.

Clay St.

Jones St.

NOB HILL ❶

Sacramento St.

Grace Cathedral

Huntington Park

California St.

Pine St.

Stockton Tunnel

Bush St.

❶❷

Sutter St.

Grant Ave.

❸ ❹ Cosmo Pl.

Campton Pl.

Post St. ❾

UNION SQUARE ⓫

Union Square

Maiden

Jones St.

Shannon St.

Taylor St.

❺❻
❽
❼

Geary St.

Mason St.

Powell St.

Stockton St.

O'Farrell St.

Ellis St.

C. Magnin St.

Ellis St.

Market St.

4th St.

❿

⓭

⓬

Aqua **24**

B44 **17**

Bocadillos **22**

Brindisi Cucina di Mari **18**

Café Claude **15**

Cortez **6**

Dottie's True Blue Café **7**

Fifth Floor **13**

Fleur de Lys **3**

Garden Court Restaurant **14**

Grand Café **8**

Great Eastern Restaurant **20**

Kokkari Estiatorio **23**

Le Colonial **4**

Michael Mina **11**
Millennium **5**
Naan-N-Curry **21**
Nob Hill Café **1**
Postrio **9**
Puccini & Pinetti **10**
R & G Lounge **19**

Sam's Grill **16**
Sanraku **2**
Tadich Grill **25**
The Terrace **12**
Town Hall **27**
Yank Sing **26**

North Beach **Dining**

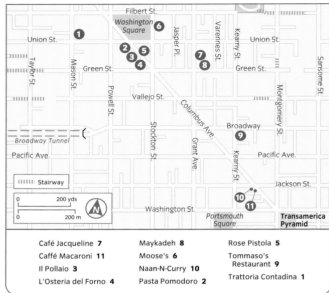

Café Jacqueline **7**

Caffé Macaroni **11**

Il Pollaio **3**

L'Osteria del Forno **4**

Maykadeh **8**

Moose's **6**

Naan-N-Curry **10**

Pasta Pomodoro **2**

Rose Pistola **5**

Tommaso's
Restaurant **9**

Trattoria Contadina **1**

San Francisco Dining **A to Z**

★ **Alma** THE MISSION *LATIN*
"Nuevo Latino" creations like butternut squash and queso fresco empanadas or orange-chipotle BBQ duck are served in warm, inviting digs. *1101 Valencia St.(at 22nd St.)* ☎ *415/401-8959. Entrees $16–$22. MC. V. Dinner Tues–Sat. Bus: 14, 49. BART: 24th St. Map p 93.*

★ **Ana Mandara** FISHERMAN'S WHARF *VIETNAMESE* Palm trees, colonial architecture, and Indochinese cuisine transport you to Vietnam. Have the mango soup with durian sorbet for dessert. *891 Beach St. (at Polk St.)* ☎ *415/771-6800. Entrees $18–$32. AE, DC, DISC, MC, V. Lunch Mon–Fri, dinner daily. Bus: 10, 30. Cable car: Powell-Hyde. Map p 94.*

★ **Andalu** THE MISSION *CALIFORNIA* Eclectic dishes, from ahi tartar tacos to Coca-Cola braised short ribs, are meant to be shared in this buzzing Mission site. *3198 16th St. (at Guerrero St.)* ☎ *415/ 621-2211. Small plates $5–$13. AE, DISC, MC, V. Dinner Tues–Sat. Bus: 14, 22, 49. BART: 16th St. Map p 93.*

★★ **Antica Trattoria** RUSSIAN HILL *ITALIAN* SF's best neighborhood trattoria, serving stately pastas, fishes, and meats with high-quality, seasonal ingredients. *2400 Polk St. (at Union St.)* ☎ *415/928-5797. Entrees $9.50–$20. DC, MC, V. Dinner Thurs–Sun. Bus: 19, 41, 45. Map p 94.*

Richmond & Sunset **Dining**

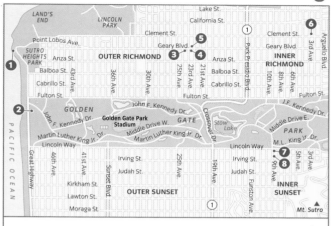

Aziza **5**
The Canvas Café/Gallery **7**
Clementine **6**
Cliff House **1**

Khan Toke **3**
Park Chalet **2**
Park Chow **8**
Ton Kiang **4**

0   1/2 mi

0   0.5 km

★★★ **Aqua** FINANCIAL DISTRICT *SEAFOOD/CALIFORNIA* Resplendent seafood stunningly presented against a chic, opulent backdrop. *252 California St. (between Battery & Front sts.)* ☎ *415/956-9662. Entrees $30–$40. AE, DC, DISC, MC, V. Lunch Mon–Fri, dinner nightly. BART/Muni: Montgomery St. Cable car: California line. Map p 96.*

Aqua Restaurant's King Salmon "En Papilotte" with lemon potato croquettes, cipollini onions, warm dill & caviar cream.

★★ **A16** MARINA *ITALIAN* A chic crowd comes for superb wood-fired pizza and delectable dishes like house-made fennel sausage. Its exciting wine list features 40 wines served by the glass and carafe. Named for the highway to Naples, Italy. *2355 Chestnut St. (between Scott & Divisadero sts.)* ☎ *415/771-2216. Entrees $8–$20. AE, DC, MC, V. Lunch Wed–Fri, dinner daily. Bus: 22, 30. Map p 94.*

★★ **Aziza** RICHMOND *MOROCCAN* This is my favorite spot for Moroccan food. Delicious North African cuisine is served on decorative plates under colorful arches, with friendly service and weekend belly dancers. *5800 Geary Blvd. (at 22nd Ave.)* ☎ *415/752-2222. Entrees $10–$20. MC, V. Dinner Wed–Mon. Bus: 38. Map p 99.*

★ **Baraka** POTRERO HILL *MOROC-CAN* Delectable Moroccan tapas in a festive, cozy atmosphere that makes sharing all the more fun. *288 Connecticut St. (at 18th St.)* ☎ *415/ 255-0387. Entrees $17–$26. AE, MC, V. Dinner daily. Bus: 22. Map p 93.*

★ **Betelnut** MARINA *ASIAN* Ten years on, this Pan-Asian eatery remains packed. Try Cecilia's minced chicken in lettuce cups and the Shanghai steamed dumplings. *2030 Union St. (at Buchanan St.)* ☎ *415/ 929-8855. Entrees $14–$20. DC, DISC, MC, V. Lunch & dinner daily. Bus: 41, 45. Map p 94.*

B44 FINANCIAL DISTRICT *CATALAN* A Catalan-style bistro serving nine kinds of paella in a European-style pedestrian alley with outdoor tables. *44 Belden Place. (between Bush & Pine sts.)* ☎ *415/986-6287. Entrees $16–$22. AE, DC, MC, V. Lunch Mon–Fri, dinner daily. Bus: 15. BART/Muni: Montgomery St. Map p 96.*

kids **Blue Mermaid Chowder House** FISHERMAN'S WHARF *AMERICAN* The simple menu of tasty chowders, salads, and a few heartier dishes ranks above other wharf choices. *495 Jefferson St. (at Hyde St.)* ☎ *415/771-2222. Entrees $7–$22. AE, DC, DISC, MC, V. Break-fast, lunch & dinner daily. Bus: 10, 30. Cable car: Powell-Hyde. Map p 94.*

★ **Bocadillos** FINANCIAL DISTRICT *SPANISH/TAPAS* Forget pricey tapas spin-offs. Bocadillos' well-priced authentic vittles are all the rage. Good luck getting a seat at the communal table. *710 Montgomery St. (at Washington St.)* ☎ *415/982-2622. Entrees $3–$12. AE, DC, MC, V. Breakfast & lunch Mon–Fri, dinner Mon–Sat. Bus: 12, 15. Map p 96.*

★★★ **Boulevard** SOMA *AMERICAN* The grand decor and sumptuous cuisine have been attracting SF's most stylish diners for over a decade. *1 Mission St. (at Steuart St.)* ☎ *415/*

Enjoy a meal at the intricately decorated Boulevard.

543-6084. Entrees $24–$32. AE, DC, DISC, MC, V. Lunch Mon–Fri, dinner daily. Bus: 12. BART/Muni: Embar-cadero. Map p 94.

Brindisi Cucina di Mare FINAN-CIAL DISTRICT *ITALIAN/SEAFOOD* From stuffed calamari to pasta, all moderately priced entrees are hearty and flavorful. *88 Belden Place. (at Pine St.)* ☎ *415/593-8000. Entrees $12–$22. AE, DISC, MC, V. Lunch & dinner Mon–Sat. Bus: 15. BART/Muni: Montgomery St. Map p 96.*

★ kids **Burger Joint** HAIGHT *HAMBURGERS* Burgers made with naturally raised beef and awesome milkshakes are enjoyed in a vinyl-rich 1950s setting. *700 Haight St. (at Pierce St.)* ☎ *415/864-3833. Entrees $5–$7. MC, V. Lunch & dinner daily. Bus: 6, 7, 66, 71. Map p 94. 807 Valencia St. (between 19th & 20th sts.).* ☎ *415/824-3494. Bus: 14, 49. BART: 16th St. Map p 93.*

★ **Café Claude** FINANCIAL DIS-TRICT *FRENCH* Parisian bistro cheer in an enchanting alley-side nook. *7 Claude Ln. (off Sutter St., between Grant Ave. & Kearny St.)* ☎ *415/ 392-3515. Entrees $10–$18. AE, DC, DISC, MC, V. Lunch Mon–Sat, dinner Tues–Sat. Bus: 2, 3, 4, 15, 30, 45. Cable car: Powell lines. Map p 96.*

★★ Café Jacqueline NORTH BEACH *SOUFFLES* Consistently voted SF's most romantic restaurant. Too bad, because even "just friends" should try the artful, all-soufflé menu. *1454 Grant Ave. (between Green & Union sts.)* ☎ *415/981-5565. Soufflés for 2 $30–$50. AE, DC, DISC, MC, V. Dinner Wed–Sun. Bus: 15, 30, 41. Cable car: Powell-Mason. Map p 98.*

★★ Café Kati PACIFIC HEIGHTS *ASIAN FUSION* East meets West in an intimate neighborhood favorite. Thai red curry seafood or Caesar salad with Cajun cornmeal catfish are among the scrumptious options. *1963 Sutter St. (between Fillmore & Webster sts.)* ☎ *415/775-7313. Entrees $21–$27. AE, MC, V. Dinner Tues–Sun. Bus: 2, 3, 4, 22, 38. Map p 94.*

★ kids Café Marimba MARINA *MEXICAN* Fresh Oaxacan cuisine like red-snapper tacos served in a colorful setting. Homemade tortillas and guacamole shine. *2317 Chestnut St. (at Divisadero St.)* ☎ *415/776-1506. Entrees $8–$14. AE, MC, V. Lunch & dinner daily. Bus: 22, 30. Map p 94.*

★ Caffé Macaroni NORTH BEACH *ITALIAN* Hearty Neapolitan dishes like gnocchi with Gorgonzola make this hole in the wall a true find. Thank goodness there are two outdoor tables. *59 Columbus Ave. (at Jackson St.)* ☎ *415/956-9737. Entrees $9.50–$15. No credit cards. Dinner Mon–Sat. Bus: 15, 41. Map p 98.*

The Canvas Cafe/Gallery SUNSET *AMERICAN/COFFEEHOUSE* This loftlike space next to Golden Gate Park triples as an art gallery, lounge, and cafe. Come for the sandwich, soup, salad, and pizza fare, or try an entree like the tamale pie or homemade macaroni and cheese. *1200 9th Ave. (at Lincoln Way)* ☎ *415/504-0060. Entrees $6.35–$8.70. AE, MC, V. Breakfast, lunch & dinner daily. Live music Thurs–Sun evenings until 2am (drinks only after 10pm). Bus: 6, 66, 71. Muni: 9th & Irving. Map p 99.*

★ Cha Cha Cha's HAIGHT *CARIBBEAN* Tapas like Cajun shrimp and spicy Caribbean entrees are jazzed up with tropical decor and festive Latin rhythms. *1801 Haight St. (at Shrader St.)* ☎ *415/386-7670. Entrees $13–$16. MC, V. Lunch & dinner daily. Bus: 7, 66, 71. Map p 94.*

Chez Panisse BERKELEY *CALIFORNIA* The famous Alice Water's restaurant still deliver's a changing menu with fresh ingredients—the definition of California Cuisine (see box p 103). *1517 Shattuck Ave. (between Cedar & Vine sts.)* ☎ *510/548-5525. Entrees $50-$75 (prix-fixe). AE, DC, DISC, MC, V. Dinner Mon. to Sat. BART: Downtown Berkeley. Map p 94.*

Alice Waters, the queen of California Cuisine, in her kitchen at the famed Chez Panisse.

★ **Chez Papa** POTRERO HILL
FRENCH   Tasty goodies like grilled figs with goat cheese, prosciutto, and watercress or roasted filet mignon with a truffle foie gras sauce combine with cramped quarters for a très French dining experience at this busy Potrero Hill bistro. *1401 18th St. (at Missouri St.)* ☎ *415/255-0387. Entrees $16–$30. AE, DC, MC, V. Lunch Mon–Sat, dinner nightly. Bus: 22. Map p 93.*

★ **Chow** CASTRO *AMERICAN*
Local, organic ingredients are behind the comforting victuals like chicken potpie, wood-fired pizzas, and roasted meats. Relaxed decor and moderate prices, too. *215 Church St. (at Market St.)* ☎ *415/552-2469. Entrees $6–$11. MC, V. Lunch & dinner daily. Bus: 22. Muni: Castro. Map p 93.*

★ **Citizen Cake** HAYES VALLEY
CALIFORNIA   What started as a bakery is now a pre-show destination for the symphony, opera, and ballet crowd. Leave room for dessert. *399 Grove St. (at Gough St.)* ☎ *415/ 861-2228. Entrees $16–$30. MC, V. Breakfast Tues–Fri, lunch Tues–Fri & Sun, dinner Tues–Sat, brunch Sat– Sun. Bus: 21. Map p 94.*

The Citrus Club HAIGHT *ASIAN*
Locals queue up for Vietnamese-inspired noodle dishes in a casual setting. *1790 Haight St. (at Shrader St.)* ☎ *415/387-6366. Entrees $5–$8. MC, V. Lunch & dinner daily. Bus: 7, 66, 71. Map p 94.*

★ **Clementine** RICHMOND
FRENCH   This upscale gem offers both classic French cuisine and bistro standards with impeccable service. Desserts tend to be on the traditional side (think crème brûlée). The generous portions and moderate prices—especially with the prix-fixe option—make this a true find. *126 Clement St. (at 2nd Ave.)* ☎ *415/387-0408. Entrees $15–$19. MC, V. Dinner Tues–Sat. Bus: 2, 38. Map p 99.*

Cliff House SUNSET *AMERICAN*
Breathtaking ocean views and charming early-20th-century decor make up for the uninspired food. *1090 Point Lobos Ave. (just west of 48th Ave. Geary Blvd. turns into Point Lobos Ave. after 43rd Ave.)* ☎ *415/386-3330. Entrees $13–$28. AE, DC, DISC, MC, V. Breakfast, lunch & dinner daily. Bus: 18, 38. Map p 99.*

California Cuisine is based on using seasonal, local products like bright ripe yellow and red cherry and pear tomatoes.

California Cuisine

What is California cuisine? The birth of California cuisine can be traced to chef Alice Waters, owner of Berkeley's Chez Panisse (p 101), which has been hailed as the best restaurant in the country. Waters revolutionized American cuisine by championing the use of fresh, seasonal, and local ingredients. Her own culinary revelation came during a year spent in France, where she lived next to a market street that teemed with fresh, high-quality produce.

The fact that Waters's grand vision came while she was overseas highlights California cuisine's multicultural, transnational character. It draws from the entire world, and as such, it is always evolving. While Waters was inspired by the produce of France, other California chefs have drawn on the cooking of Italy or the Middle East. Today, Asian and South American flavors turn up in many Californian dishes. *But the key thread that unites all California cuisine is this: a strong preference for uncomplicated dishes with superior ingredients that change with the seasons.*

The Bay Area's location and immigrant history were central to the development of this epicurean style. Today you still find several family farms (many organic) and ranches (specializing in naturally raised meats and poultry) surrounding San Francisco. Add the Pacific's bounty of fresh seafood, and the city's treasure trove of ethnic influences, and you've got what makes San Francisco a perfect city to sample California cuisine.

★★ **Cortez** UNION SQUARE *MEDITERRANEAN/TAPAS* This hopping member of the small-plates scene serves exceptional, if pricey, morsels—including tasty soups in shot glasses. *550 Geary St. (at Taylor St.)* ☎ *415/292-6360. Small plates $6–$17. AE, MC, V. Dinner daily. Bus: 2, 3, 4, 38. Map p 96.*

★★ **Delfina** THE MISSION *ITALIAN* Locals love this first-rate Tuscan fare with a cool, vibrant ambience. *3621 18th St. (between Dolores & Guerrero sts.)* ☎ *415/552-4055. Entrees $12–$18. MC, V. Dinner daily. Bus: 14, 33, 49. Muni: Castro. BART: 16th St. Map p 93.*

★ kids **Dolores Park Cafe** MISSION *AMERICAN/BREAKFAST* Enjoy healthy sandwiches or a simple latte on the sunny deck across from Dolores Park. *501 Dolores St. (at 18th St.)* ☎ *415/621-2936. Sandwiches/salads $5–$6.25. AE, MC, V. Breakfast, lunch & dinner daily. Fri music nights until 9:30pm. Bus: 33. Muni: Castro. BART: 16th St. Map p 93.*

★ **Dottie's True Blue Cafe** UNION SQUARE *AMERICAN/BREAKFAST* Ample portions of cornmeal pancakes, eggs, and gourmet sausages. Lunch features salads and burgers. Kitschy decor. *522 Jones St. (between Geary & O'Farrell sts.)* ☎ *415/885-2767. Entrees $5–$10. DISC, MC, V. Breakfast & lunch Wed–Mon. Bus: 2, 3, 4, 27, 38. Cable car: Powell lines. Map p 96.*

★ **kids Dragon Well** MARINA *CHINESE* Chinese with a California bend: super fresh ingredients and less oil. Terrific. *2142 Chestnut St. (between Pierce & Steiner sts.)* ☎ *415/474-6888. Entrees $7–$11. MC, V. Lunch & dinner daily. Bus: 22, 30. Map p 94.*

kids East Coast West Delicatessen RUSSIAN HILL *DELICATESSEN* One of SF's few true Jewish delis sells matzo ball soup, chicken liver sandwiches, and blintzes. Highchairs and boosters are available for children. *1725 Polk St. (at Washington St.)* ☎ *415/563-3542. Entrees $3.50–$13. AE, MC, V. Breakfast, lunch & dinner daily. Bus: 12, 19, 27, 47, 49. Map p 94.*

★ **Ella's** PRESIDIO HEIGHTS *AMERICAN/BREAKFAST* SF's best brunch, with a wait to prove it. Fresh breads, awesome pancakes, and appetizing omelets. Dinner features neoclassical American cuisine. *500 Presidio Ave. (at California St.)* ☎ *415/441-5669. Entrees $7.50–$13. MC, V. Breakfast & lunch daily, dinner Mon–Fri. Bus: 1, 2, 4. Map p 94.*

★ **Eos Restaurant & Wine Bar** COLE VALLEY *ASIAN FUSION* Sleek interior, unconventional small plates, and great wines—a truly fine combination. *901 Cole St. (at Carl St.)* ☎ *415/566-3063. $9–$16. AE, DC, DISC, MC, V. Dinner daily. Bus: 6, 43. Muni: Carl & Cole. Map p 94.*

★★ **Fifth Floor** SOMA *FRENCH* Winner of countless restaurant awards, come here to experience an original and well-executed French meal in a swank space. Sommelier Belinda Chang is one of the country's best. *12 4th St. (in the Hotel Palomar, at Market St.)* ☎ *415/348-1555. Entrees $33–$65. AE, DC, DISC, MC, V. Dinner Mon–Sat. Bus: 30, 45. Map p 96.*

★★ **Firefly** NOE VALLEY *AMERICAN* A charming neighborhood nook offering sumptuous, upscale comfort food made with organic, local ingredients. *4288 24th St. (at Douglass St.)* ☎ *415/821-7652. Entrees $15–$19. AE, MC, V. Dinner daily. BART: 24th St. & transfer to bus 48. Map p 93.*

★★★ **Fleur de Lys** UNION SQUARE *FRENCH* Regal decor, unparalleled service, and superlative French cuisine from a celebrated SF chef. This epitome of luxurious dining is the city's most traditional and classic French affair. *777 Sutter St. (between Jones & Taylor sts.)* ☎ *415/673-7779. Prix-fixe menu from $68. AE, DC, DISC, MC, V. Dinner Mon–Sat. Bus: 2, 3, 4, 27. Map p 96.*

Modern French cuisine and zebra-striped carpeting lends a chi chi vibe to Fifth Floor.

Catch a flick with dinner at Foreign Cinema's alfresco tables.

Fog City Diner TELEGRAPH HILL
AMERICAN Immortalized in a Visa
TV ad, the chrome exterior belies a
sleek interior. Come for the bayside
scenery and order simply. *1300
Battery St. (at The Embarcadero)*
☎ *415/982-2000. Entrees $11–$19.
DC, DISC, MC, V. Lunch Mon–Fri, din-
ner daily, brunch Sat–Sun. Bus: 10.
Streetcar: F. Map p 94.*

★★ Foreign Cinema THE MISSION
CALIFORNIA/MEDITERRANEAN
Dine inside in the chic digs or outside
under the stars (among abundant
heat lamps). Oscar-quality films are
projected onto the outdoor courtyard
wall. A lengthy oyster list, fresh
salads, and hearty entrees like a
grilled rib-eye satisfy all tastes. *2534
Mission St. (between 21st & 22nd sts.)*
☎ *415/648-7600. Entrees $22–$30.
AE, MC, V. Dinner Tues–Sun, brunch
Sat–Sun. Bus: 14, 49. BART: 24th St.
Map p 93.*

Franciscan FISHERMAN'S WHARF
CALIFORNIA One of the better
wharf options—with a terrific view
and agreeable food. *Pier 43½. (at
The Embarcadero)* ☎ *415/362-7733.
Entrees $13–$26. AE, DC, DISC, MC, V.
Lunch & dinner daily. Bus: 10, 30.
Streetcar: F. Map p 94.*

★★ Fresca PACIFIC HEIGHTS
PERUVIAN Exemplary ceviche and
inspired Peruvian fare like braised
pork in adobo sauce keep Fresca
jam-packed. *2114 Fillmore St. (at
California St.)* ☎ *415/447-2668.
Entrees $13–$24. AE, MC, V. Lunch
Mon–Fri, dinner daily. Bus: 1, 22.
Map p 94.*

★★ Fringale SOMA *FRENCH*
Even after founding chef Gerald
Hirigoyen left to open hot spots
Piperade and Bocadillos (p 100),
Fringale still serves excellent French
Basque fare. *570 4th St. (between
Brannan & Bryant sts.)* ☎ *415/543-
0573. Entrees $14–$23. AE, MC, V.
Lunch Tues–Fri, dinner Mon–Sat.
Bus: 15, 30, 45. Map p 94.*

★ Garden Court Restaurant
SOMA *AFTERNOON TEA* Elegant
service in a lovely historic setting.
*Palace Hotel, 2 New Montgomery St.
(at Market St.)* ☎ *415/512-1111.
Tea service $30–$40. Entrees $14–
$24. AE, DC, MC, V. Breakfast daily,
lunch Mon–Sat, brunch Sun, tea
Sat 2–4pm. BART/Muni: Montgomery
St. Map p 96.*

★★★ **Gary Danko** FISHERMAN'S WHARF *CALIFORNIA* SF's best restaurant boasts a sleek interior, flawless service, outstanding wines, and a superlative menu that changes daily. Reserve 4 weeks ahead, or try your luck at the bar. *800 North Point St. (at Hyde St.)* ☎ *415/749-2060. Prix-fixe menu from $58. AE, DC, DISC, MC, V. Dinner daily. Bus: 10, 30. Cable car: Powell-Hyde. Map p 94.*

kids **Ghirardelli Soda Fountain & Chocolate Shop** FISHERMAN'S WHARF *ICE CREAM* The ever-present line attests to consistently great chocolate. *Ghirardelli Sq., 900 North Point St. (at Larkin St.)* ☎ *415/ 771-4903. Desserts $5–$9. AE, DISC, MC, V. Mon–Thurs 10am–10:30pm; Fri–Sat 10am–midnight; Sun 10am–11pm. Bus: 10, 30. Cable car: Powell-Hyde. Map p 94.*

★ **Grand Café** UNION SQUARE *CALIFORNIA/FRENCH* A majestic Beaux Arts interior and inspired dishes attract the theater crowd for dinner or drinks. *501 Geary St. (at Taylor St.)* ☎ *415/292-0101. Entrees $11–$17 lunch, $19–$28 dinner; Petit Café $9.50–$16. AE, DC, DISC, MC, V. Breakfast & lunch Mon–Sat, dinner*

Gary Danko won the prestigious James Beard Foundation's "Best New Restaurant" award in 2000; today, it still lives up to its acclaim.

daily, brunch Sun. Bus: 2, 3, 4, 27, 38. Cable car: Powell lines. Map p 96.

Great Eastern Restaurant CHINATOWN *CHINESE* Order your ultrafresh seafood from the fish tanks and you'll eat well. Don't be steered to more familiar Chinese dishes. *649 Jackson St. (between Grant Ave. & Kearny St.)* ☎ *415/986-2500. Entrees $8–$30. AE, MC, V. Lunch & dinner daily. Bus: 12, 15, 30, 45. Map p 96.*

★★ **Greens** MARINA *VEGETARIAN* The fabulous flavors and stunning views will impress even dedicated carnivores. *Building A, Fort Mason Center (by Buchanan & Marina sts.).* ☎ *415/771-6222. Entrees $15–$19; Sat prix-fixe $46. AE, DISC, MC, V. Lunch Tues–Sat, dinner Mon–Sat, brunch Sun. Bus: 28, 30. Map p 94.*

Harris' RUSSIAN HILL *STEAK* Every town has a proper steakhouse, and this is San Francisco's. Meat lovers swoon. *2100 Van Ness Ave. (at Pacific Ave.) 415/673-1888. Entrees $24–$42. AE, DC, DISC, MC, V. Dinner daily. Bus: 12, 19, 27, 47, 49. Map p 94.*

★★ **Hawthorne Lane** SOMA *CALIFORNIA* This elegant establishment thrills diners with imaginative dishes like spicy rock shrimp and acorn squash soup with lobster won tons. *22 Hawthorne Ln. (off Howard St., between 2nd & 3rd sts.)* ☎ *415/ 777-9779. Entrees $24–$34. DC, DISC, MC, V. Lunch Mon–Fri, dinner daily. Bus: 10, 15, 30, 45. Map p 94.*

★ **Hayes Street Grill** HAYES VALLEY *CALIFORNIA/SEAFOOD* Very fresh fish or naturally raised meats simply prepared with the finest ingredients. *320 Hayes St. (between Franklin & Gough sts.)* ☎ *415/863-5545. Entrees $18–$23. AE, DC, DISC, MC, V. Lunch Mon–Fri, dinner daily. Bus: 21. Map p 94.*

★ **Il Pollaio** NORTH BEACH *CHICKEN* Fragrant roast chicken or other meat, salads, and a few sides are all you'll

The main dining room Grand Café is set in an elegant turn of the-20th-century ballroom.

find at this simple, tasty eatery. *555 Columbus Ave. (between Union & Green sts.)* ☎ *415/362-7727. Entrees $6.95–$17. DISC, MC, V. Lunch & dinner Mon–Sat. Cable car: Powell-Mason. Bus: 15, 30, 41. Map p 98.*

★ **Indian Oven** HAIGHT *INDIAN* There's always a line for the formidable curries, tandoori specials, and naan breads. *233 Fillmore St. (between Haight & Waller sts.)* ☎ *415/626-1628. Entrees $8–$19. AE, DC, DISC, MC, V. Dinner daily. Bus: 6, 7, 22, 66, 71. Map p 94.*

kids **IN-N-OUT Burger** FISHERMAN'S WHARF *HAMBURGERS* This popular California chain serves its burgers on toasted buns with extrathin fries. *333 Jefferson St. (between Leavenworth & Jones sts.)* ☎ *800/786-1000. www.in-n-out.com. Entrees $1.65–$2.80. No credit cards. Lunch & dinner daily. Bus: 10, 30. Streetcar: F. Map p 94.*

★★ **Isa** MARINA *CALIFORNIA/FRENCH* Inventive "French tapas" like truffled risotto and heavenly potato-wrapped sea bass. Check out the delightful, heated patio—perfect for SF's brisk but sunny days. *3324 Steiner St. (between Lombard & Chestnut sts.)* ☎ *415/567-9588. Entrees $9–$17. MC, V. Dinner Mon–Sat. Bus: 22, 30. Map p 94.*

Isobune JAPANTOWN *JAPANESE/SUSHI* Pluck sushi off boats on an aquatic conveyer belt. Come when it's busy; at off hours the *maguro* is limply waiting to be fished. *1737 Post St. (in the Japan Center)* ☎ *415/563-1030. 2 pieces of sushi, $1.80–$3.75. MC, V. Lunch & dinner daily. Bus: 38. Map p 94.*

★ **Jardiniere** HAYES VALLEY *FRENCH* Symphony and opera patrons complete a night on the town with dinner at this affluent Civic Center staple. *300 Grove St. (at Franklin St.)* ☎ *415/861-5555. Entrees $22–$38. AE, DC, DISC, MC, V. Dinner daily. Bus: 21. Map p 94.*

Juban Yakiniku House JAPANTOWN *JAPANESE* Grill your own thin slices of beef, chicken, and shrimp right at the table. *1581 Webster St. (in the Japan Center)* ☎ *415/776-5822. Entrees $7.50–$20. AE, MC, V. Lunch & dinner Wed–Mon. Bus: 38. Map p 94.*

★ **Khan Toke** RICHMOND *THAI* Take off your shoes, sit at a low table, and enjoy an authentic Thai meal brought by a traditionally clad server in a space reminiscent of a Bangkok palace. Order the fried bananas for dessert. *5937 Geary Blvd. (between 23rd and 24th aves.)* ☎ *415/668-6654. Entrees $8–$13. AE, DC, MC, V. Dinner daily. Bus: 38. Map p 99.*

★★ **Kokkari Estiatorio** FINANCIAL DISTRICT *GREEK* Wonderful seasonal dishes and Greek classics prepared with an expert California touch—all in a warm, upscale setting. *200 Jackson St. (at Front St.)* ☎ *415/981-0983. Entrees $19–$34. AE, DC, DISC, MC, V. Lunch Mon–Fri, dinner Mon–Sat. Bus: 10. Map p 96.*

★ kids **La Corneta Taqueria** THE MISSION *MEXICAN* Of the myriad Mission taquerias, this is one of the best. Stand in line to choose the fillings for your mammoth burrito. *2731 Mission St. (between 23rd & 24th sts.)* ☎ *415/643-7001. Entrees $3–$12. MC, V. Lunch & dinner daily. Bus: 14, 49. BART: 24th St. Map p 93.*

La Méditerranée PACIFIC HEIGHTS AND NOE VALLEY *MEDITERRANEAN* A casual, narrow storefront serving up satisfying hummus, stuffed grape leaves, and the like. The chicken cilicia in phyllo dough is super. *2210 Fillmore St. (at Sacramento St.)* ☎ *415/921-2956. 288 Noe St. (at Market St.) www.cafelamed.com. Entrees $7.25–$14. AE, MC, V. Lunch & dinner Mon–Sat. Bus: 1, 22. Map p 93.*

La Rondalla THE MISSION *MEXICAN* It's a fiesta every night here with year-round Christmas lights, mariachi music, and a long menu of Mexican dishes. Potent margaritas keep the party going. *901-903 Valencia St. (at 20th St.)* ☎ *415/647-7474. Entrees $8–$12. No credit cards. Dinner daily. Bus: 14, 49. BART: 24th St. Map p 93.*

Le Colonial UNION SQUARE *VIETNAMESE* Swanky colonial-style decor. I suggest grabbing appetizers and drinks upstairs in the sultry lounge. *20 Cosmo Place (off Post St., between Jones & Taylor sts.).* ☎ *415/931-3600. Entrees $8–$33. AE, MC, V. Dinner daily. Bus: 2, 3, 4, 27, 38. Map p 96.*

Artichokes are just one of many vegetables grown locally.

★★ **Limòn** THE MISSION *PERUVIAN* Peruvian is all the rage, and the stunning ceviche dishes at Limon show you why. The "Picante de Mariscos" is divine. *524 Valencia St. (between 16th & 17th sts.)* ☎ *415/252-0918. Entrees $10–$18. AE, MC, V. Lunch & dinner daily. Bus: 14, 22, 33, 49. BART: 16th St. Map p 93.*

kids **Long Life Noodle Company & Jook Joint** SOMA *ASIAN* Good, cheap noodles served every which way. *139 Steuart St. (between Mission & Howard sts.)* ☎ *415/281-3818. (Additional location in the Sony Metreon food court). Entrees $5.50–$9. MC, V. Lunch & dinner Mon–Fri. Bus: 15, 30, 32, 45. Streetcar: F. Map p 94.*

★★ **L'Osteria del Forno** NORTH BEACH *ITALIAN* There are always as many people lined up outside as seated inside the cozy dining room that serves some of North Beach's best Italian. *519 Columbus Ave. (between Union & Green sts.)* ☎ *415/982-1124. Entrees $11–$13. No credit cards. Lunch & dinner Wed–Mon. Bus: 15, 30, 41. Cable car: Powell-Mason. Map p 98.*

Lovejoy's Tea Room CASTRO *AFTERNOON TEA* Crustless sandwiches, scones, and a bountiful tea selection. Lovejoy's doubles as an antiques shop, so go ahead and buy the tea set you're sipping from. *1351 Church St. (at Clipper St.)* ☎ *415/648-5895. Tea service $12–$19. MC, V. Tea Wed–Sun 11am–5:30pm. Muni: Castro. Map p 93.*

★ **Luna Park** THE MISSION *CALIFORNIA FRENCH* Healthy portions of satisfying food keep hip, young diners coming back to this noisy hot spot. *694 Valencia St. (at 18th St.)* ☎ *415/553-8584. Entrees $9.50–$16. AE, MC, V. Lunch Mon–Fri, dinner daily, brunch Sat–Sun. Bus: 14, 49. BART: 16th St. Map p 93.*

★ **Maykadeh** NORTH BEACH *PERSIAN* Local Iranians seek Maykadeh for refined Persian fare, like eggplant with mint garlic sauce and lamb filet marinated in lime, yogurt, and saffron. *470 Green St. (between Grant Ave. & Kearny St.)* ☎ *415/362-8286. Entrees $13–$24. MC, V. Lunch & dinner daily. Bus: 15, 30, 41, 45. Cable car: Powell-Mason. Map p 98.*

★ **McCormick & Kuleto's** FISHERMAN'S WHARF *SEAFOOD* The stellar view, elegant decor, and well-prepared fish compensate for the massive space and overly

long menu. *900 North Point St. (in Ghirardelli Square, at Hyde St.)* ☎ *415/929-1730. Entrees $11–$31. AE, DC, DISC, MC, V. Lunch & dinner daily. Bus: 10, 30. Cable car: Powell-Hyde. Map p 94.*

★ **Memphis Minnie's** HAIGHT *BARBECUE* SF's best BBQ serves up slow-cooked brisket and succulent pulled pork with three kinds of sauce and a roll of paper towels at every table. *576 Haight St. (at Steiner St.)* ☎ *415/864-8461. Entrees $6.25–$13. AE, MC, V. Lunch & dinner Tues–Sun. Bus: 6, 7, 22, 66, 71. Map p 94.*

★★★ **Michael Mina** UNION SQUARE *CALIFORNIA* A bustling dining room with 20-foot (6 m)-high ceilings, expert waiters clad in sleek charcoal grey, world class sommeliers, and a multitude of startlingly vibrant and luscious flavors make this a not-to-be-missed dining experience. Just beware that portions are overly generous, and you absolutely must save room for the astonishingly delicious desserts. *335 Powell St. (in the Westin St. Francis Hotel, at Geary St.).* ☎ *415/397-9222. Prix-fixe $88-$120. AE, DC, DISC, MC, V. Dinner daily. Cable car: Powell line. Map p 96.*

The grand entrance to Michael Mina's superb cuisine.

Millennium UNION SQUARE *VEGAN* No animal products are used to make everything from vegetarian sausages to truffled vegetable gratin. This place proves that a meatless menu does *not* mean you have to sacrifice taste. *580 Geary St. (at Jones St.) ☎ 415/345-3900. Entrees $18–$21. AE, DC, DISC, MC, V. Dinner daily. Bus: 2, 3, 4, 27, 38. Map p 96.*

★ kids Mitchell's Ice Cream THE MISSION *ICE CREAM* Take a number and wait to order creamy, exotic ice creams like sweet corn, avocado, Mexican chocolate, and everyone's favorite, baby coconut. *688 San Jose Ave. (at 29th St., just south of where Guerrero St. turns into San Jose Ave.) ☎ 415/648-2300. $2.10–$5.30. No credit cards. Lunch & dinner daily. Bus: 14, 49. Muni: Church & 30th St. Map p 93.*

★★★ Moose's NORTH BEACH *AMERICAN* Local politicos and well-heeled clientele seek this North Beach institution for an innovative take on classic American cuisine that relies on the finest local and organic ingredients. Think Atlantic cod with Dungeness crab couscous or roasted venison chop with yam gratin and bitter chocolate port wine sauce. *1652 Stockton St. (between Filbert & Union sts.) ☎ 415/989-7800. Entrees $11–$36. AE, DC, DISC, MC, V. Lunch Thurs–Sat, dinner daily, brunch Sun. Bus: 15, 30, 41, 45. Cable car: Powell-Mason. Map p 98.*

Naan-N-Curry NORTH BEACH *INDIAN/PAKISTANI* Good, cheap Indian/Pakistani food: tandoori-oven meats, savory curries, and warm naan breads. *533 Jackson St. (at Columbus Ave.) ☎ 415/693-0499. Entrees $5–$10. MC, V. Lunch & dinner daily. Bus: 15, 41. Map p 96.*

★ Nob Hill Café NOB HILL *ITALIAN* For down-home ambience (and prices) amidst the posh Nob Hill alternatives, squeeze into this neighborhood nook. *1152 Taylor St. (between Sacramento & Clay sts.) ☎ 415/776-6500. Entrees $8–$15. DC, DISC, MC, V. Breakfast, lunch & dinner daily. Bus: 1. Cable car: California line. Map p 96.*

★★ Okoze RUSSIAN HILL *JAPANESE* The owner shops at the fish market

Open since 1953, Mitchell's Ice Cream's original owner Larry Mitchell imports fresh fruit from the Philippines to make his famous tropical flavors.

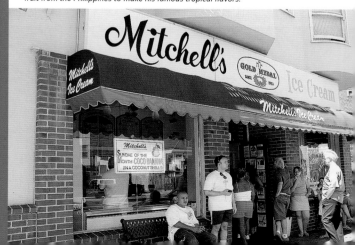

Craving a plate of traditional spaghetti and meatballs? Try Pasta Pomodoro.

5 mornings a week for the freshest sushi in town. *1207 Union St. (at Hyde St.)* ☎ *415/567-3397. 2 pieces sushi $4–$12. AE, DC, DISC, MC, V. Dinner daily. Cable car: Powell-Hyde. Bus: 41, 45. Map p 94.*

★★ **One Market** FINANCIAL DISTRICT *CALIFORNIA* It's all big here: the space, windows, view, prices, flavor, and the tasty farm-fresh menu. Around happy hour a corporate crowd convenes at the bar. *1 Market St. (at Steuart St.)* ☎ *415/777-5577. Entrees $20–$33. AE, DC, DISC, MC, V. Lunch Mon–Fri, dinner Mon–Sat. BART/Muni: Embarcadero. Map p 94.*

Ozumo SOMA *JAPANESE* Ultrahip diners come to this sleek space for fresh sushi, creative entrees, and excellent sake. *161 Steuart St. (between Mission & Howard sts.)* ☎ *415/882-1333. Entrees $25–$30. AE, DC, DISC, MC, V. Dinner daily. Bus: 12. BART/Muni: Embarcadero. Map p 94.*

★ **Pane e Vino** COW HOLLOW *ITALIAN* Exceptionally prepared, unfussy Tuscan dishes that keep locals coming back for more. *1715 Union St. (at Gough St.)* ☎ *415/346-2111. Entrees $10–$25. AC, MC, V. Lunch Mon–Thurs, dinner daily. Bus: 41, 45. Map p 94.*

★ kids **Park Chalet** SUNSET *CALIFORNIA* A glass ceiling and glass walls that open onto a garden patio make this the nicest outdoor space in town, even if you're inside. Food is decent if not fabulous, but this is a great standby at the western end of Golden Gate Park. This place is an extension of the Beach Chalet (p 90). *1000 Great Hwy. (at Fulton St.)* ☎ *415/386-8439. Entrees $10–$24. AE, DC, DISC, MC, V. Breakfast, lunch & dinner daily. Bus: 5, 18, 31, 38. Muni: Ocean Beach. Map p 99.*

★ kids **Park Chow** SUNSET *AMERICAN* Like Chow (p 102) in the Castro, Park Chow balances eclectic American fare from Cobb salads to pasta to sandwich specials, a lively atmosphere, and amazing value. *1240 9th Ave. (between Lincoln Way & Irving St.)* ☎ *415/665-9912. Entrees $6–$11. MC, V. Lunch & dinner daily, Brunch Sat & Sun. Bus: 6, 66, 71. Muni: 9th & Irving. Map p 99.*

kids **Pasta Pomodoro** NORTH BEACH *ITALIAN* This chain, with locations around the city, serves good, basic Italian food at very reasonable prices. Highchairs and boosters are available. *655 Union St. (at Columbus Ave.)* ☎ *415/399-0300. www.pastapomodoro.com. Entrees $6.75–$8.95. MC, V. Lunch & dinner daily. Bus: 15, 30, 41. Cable car: Powell-Mason. Map p 98.*

★ **Postrio** UNION SQUARE *CALIFORNIA* Celebrity chef Wolfgang Puck's creation remains a delightful, and lovely, place to dine. *545 Post St. (in the Prescott Hotel, between Taylor & Mason sts.)* ☎ *415/776-7825. Entrees $16–$27. AE, DC, DISC, MC, V. Lunch & dinner daily. Bus 2, 3, 4. Map p 96.*

★ kids **Puccini and Pinetti** UNION SQUARE *ITALIAN* Kids design their own pizzas, while parents order classics like eggplant parmigiana. *129 Ellis St. (at Cyril Magnin St., between Mason & Powell sts.)* ☎ *415/392-5500. Entrees $12–$16 lunch, $14–$20 dinner. AE, DC, DISC, MC, V. Lunch Mon–Sat, dinner daily. BART/Muni: Powell St. Cable car: Powell lines. Map p 96.*

★★ **Quince** PACIFIC HEIGHTS *ITALIAN* Refined, seasonally changing dishes in a discreet, elegant setting keep the reservations booked. *1701 Octavia St. (at Bush St.)* ☎ *415/775-8500. Entrees $16–$27. AE, MC, V. Dinner daily. Bus: 2, 3, 4. Map p 94.*

★ kids **R & G Lounge** CHINATOWN *CHINESE* SF's best Chinatown restaurant, but it helps to know what to order. The salt-and-pepper crab is the signature dish. If they have live prawns in the tank, try them split in half with minced garlic. I also recommend the filet mignon beef with snow peas and XO sauce, and Fu King fried rice (a risotto-ish starch). Try to sit upstairs. *631 Kearny St. (at Commercial St.)* ☎ *415/982-7877. Entrees $10–$50. AE, DC, DISC, MC, V. Lunch & dinner daily. Bus: 15, 30. Map p 96.*

★ **Restaurant LuLu** SOMA *CALIFORNIA/FRENCH* Savor excellent roasted meats and seasonal items like prawn risotto with summer squash in a busy, multilevel space. *816 Folsom St. (between 4th & 5th sts.)* ☎ *415/495-5775. Entrees $15–$30. AE, DC, MC, V. Lunch & dinner daily. Bus: 30, 45. Map p 94.*

★ **RNM** HAIGHT *AMERICAN* A hip jewel amid modest Haight surroundings serving small and large plates of American fare with a European twist. *598 Haight St. (at Steiner St.)* ☎ *415/551-7900. Entrees $12–$24. MC, V. Dinner Tues–Sat. Bus: 6, 7, 22, 66, 71. Map p 94.*

★ **Rose Pistola** NORTH BEACH *ITALIAN* Come for the always-tasty antipasti and the bustling scene. The

A transformed 1910 warehouse houses the bustling & modern Restaurant Lulu.

The Slanted Door's spring rolls, stuffed with shrimp, pork, and mint, are served with a Vietnamese peanut sauce.

entrees are not as consistent. *532 Columbus Ave. (between Green & Union sts.)* ☎ *415/399-0499. Entrees $19–$36. AE, MC, V. Lunch Sun–Thurs, dinner daily. Bus: 15, 30, 41. Cable car: Powell-Mason. Map p 98.*

Sam's Grill FINANCIAL DISTRICT *ITALIAN/SEAFOOD* Grab a comfy booth and order charbroiled fish, roasted chicken, or simple pasta dishes at one of SF's oldest restaurants. *374 Bush St. (at Belden Place, between Kearny & Montgomery sts.)* ☎ *415/421-0594. Entrees $10–$27. AE, DC, DISC, MC, V. Lunch & dinner Mon–Fri. Bus: 15. BART/Muni: Montgomery St. Map p 96.*

★ **Sanraku** UNION SQUARE *JAPAN-ESE* Some of the freshest sushi in town. Decor is minimal, but the price is right. Highchairs and boosters are available. *704 Sutter St. (at Taylor St.)* ☎ *415/771-0803. (Additional location in the Sony Metreon food court). Entrees $8.50–$25. AE, DC, DISC, MC, V. Lunch & dinner daily. Bus: 2, 3, 4, 27. Map p 96.*

★★★ **The Slanted Door** FINANCIAL DISTRICT *VIETNAMESE* Despite two moves to bigger spaces, there's a perpetual crowd for Charles Phan's delectable cooking. This is SF's most popular restaurant; call ahead. *Ferry Bldg., 1 Ferry Plaza (at The Embarcadero & Market St.)* ☎ *415/861-8032. Entrees $10–$26 dinner. AE, MC, V. Lunch & dinner daily. BART/Muni: Embarcadero. Map p 94.*

★ **Sociale** PRESIDIO HEIGHTS *ITALIAN* Locals head to this court-yard nook behind a tony shopping street for superb Tuscan fare. Out-door tables on warm days are a plus. *3665 Sacramento St. (between Locust & Spruce sts.)* ☎ *415/921-3200. Entrees $12–$24. MC, V. Lunch & dinner Mon–Sat. Bus: 1, 4. Map p 94.*

★ **Suppenkuche** HAYES VALLEY *GERMAN* An excellent beer selection and well-prepared Bavarian classics make this an unlikely hot spot among trendy young locals. *601 Hayes St. (at Laguna St.)* ☎ *415/252-9289. Entrees $8.50–$17. AE, DISC, MC, V. Dinner daily, brunch Sun 10am–2:30pm. Bus: 21. Map p 94.*

★ **Swan Oyster Depot** RUSSIAN HILL *SEAFOOD* The lunch line for a cup of chowder and oysters on the

Grab a plate of clam cocktails at the Swan Oyster bar, little more than a narrow fish market with 20-odd stools.

half shell at this 1912 cubby hole fortunately moves quickly. *1517 Polk St. (between California & Sacramento sts.)* ☎ *415/673-1101. Seafood cocktails $8–$15. Oysters $7.50/half dozen. No credit cards. Mon-Sat 8am-5:30pm. Bus: 1, 19. Map p 94.*

kids Swensen's Creamery RUSSIAN HILL *ICE CREAM* This is the original Swensen's, since 1948. No exotic flavors, but three kinds of vanilla. *1999 Hyde St. (at Union St.)* ☎ *415/775-6818. Cones $2.45–$3.95. AE, MC, V. Sun & Tues–Thurs noon–10pm, Fri–Sat noon–11pm. Bus: 41, 45. Cable car: Powell-Hyde. Map p 94.*

Tadich Grill FINANCIAL DISTRICT *AMERICAN/SEAFOOD* Suits and tourists alike appreciate the clubby feel of SF's oldest restaurant, serving traditional seafood. Prepare to stand in line. *240 California St. (between Battery & Front sts.)* ☎ *415/391-2373. Entrees $15–$34. MC, V. Lunch & dinner Mon–Sat. BART/Muni: Montgomery St. Cable car: California line. Map p 96.*

★ **kids Taqueria Pancho Villa** THE MISSION *MEXICAN* This humble standby is one of the best

taquerias in the city. *3071 16th St. (between Mission & Valencia sts.)* ☎ *415/864-8840. Entrees $1.35–$16. AE, MC, V. Lunch & dinner daily. Bus: 14, 22, 49. BART: 16th St. Map p 93.*

★ **Tartine Bakery** THE MISSION *BAKERY* Crowds linger after 4pm to snap up hot-from-the-oven bread before it sells out. Sandwiches are also tasty. *600 Guerrero St. (at 18th St.)* ☎ *415/487-2600. Sandwiches $6–$10. AE, MC, V. Mon 8am–2pm; Tues–Wed 7:30am–7pm; Thurs–Fri 7:30am–8pm; Sat 8am–8pm; Sun 9am–8pm. Bus: 14, 33, 49. BART: 16th St. Map p 93.*

★ **kids Taylor's Refresher** FINANCIAL DISTRICT *HAMBURGERS* SF branch of a 1949 Sonoma classic diner. Gourmet burgers with naturally raised beef and farmers market fixin's—delicious. *1 Ferry Bldg., 1 Ferry Plaza (at The Embarcadero & Market St.)* ☎ *866/328-3663. Entrees $3–$13. AE, DC, DISC, MC, V. Lunch & dinner daily. BART/Muni: Embarcadero. Map p 96.*

★ **The Terrace** NOB HILL *BRUNCH* An extensive buffet including a caviar station, world-class jazz performers, and a lovely garden courtyard—simply the most opulent brunch in the city. *Ritz-Carlton Hotel, 600 Stockton St. (at California St.)* ☎ *415/773-6198. Brunch $65 adults, $32 kids 5–12. AE, DC, DISC, MC, V. Brunch Sun 10:30am–2pm. Cable car: All lines. Map p 96.*

★ **Ti Couz** MISSION *CREPES* Square buckwheat crepes with fillings like sausage, smoked salmon, or goat cheese. Sunny outdoor tables, too. *3108 16th St. (at Valencia St.)* ☎ *415/252-7373. Crepes $2–$10. MC, V. Lunch & dinner daily. Bus: 14, 22, 49. BART: 16th St. Map p 93.*

Tommaso's Restaurant NORTH BEACH *ITALIAN/PIZZA* Pass XXX-rated storefronts to sit at a communal table and have excellent wood-fired pizzas and other Italian classics. *1042 Kearny St. (between Broadway St. & Pacific Ave.)* ☎ *415/398-9696. Entrees $10–$19. AE, DC, MC, V. Dinner Tues–Sun. Bus: 12, 15. Map p 98.*

★★ **kids Ton Kiang** RICHMOND *CHINESE* Number one for dim sum. Sip tea and choose from trays laden with stuffed crab claws, pork buns, and snow-pea shoots. Save room for the custard pancakes. *5821 Geary Blvd. (between 22nd & 23rd aves.)* ☎ *415/387-8273. Dim sum $2–$5.50 each. AE, DC, DISC, MC, V. Lunch & dinner daily. Bus: 38. Map p 99.*

★★★ **Town Hall** SOMA *AMERICAN* This celebrated newcomer specializes in New American cuisine, with a tilt toward New Orleans. *342 Howard St. (at Fremont St.)* ☎ *415/908-3900. Entrees $19–$26. AE, DC, MC, V. Lunch Mon–Fri, dinner daily. Bus: 10, 14, 15. Map p 96.*

★ **Town's End** SOMA *AMERICAN/ BRUNCH* Baskets of homemade breads accompany meals at this low-key joint, with a lovely outdoor space. *2 Townsend St. (at The Embarcadero)* ☎ *415/512-0749. Entrees $6.50–$11 brunch, $9–$17 dinner. AE, DC, MC, V. Breakfast & lunch Tues–Fri, dinner Tues–Sat, brunch Sat–Sun 8am– 2:30pm. Bus: 10. Muni: Brannan & Embarcadero. Map p 94.*

★ **kids Trattoria Contadina** NORTH BEACH *ITALIAN* Escape the North Beach crowds at this ma-and-pa trattoria serving no-nonsense dishes like linguine with homemade meatballs. *1800 Mason St. (at Union St.)* ☎ *415/982-5728. Entrees $12–$24. AE, DC, DISC, MC, V. Dinner daily. Bus: 30, 41. Cable car: Powell-Mason. Map p 98.*

Ton Kiang, way off the tourist track in the Richmond district, is SF's #1 joint for Dim Sum.

★ **Universal Café** POTRERO HILL *CALIFORNIA* Glorious New American dishes in a cool, intimate locale. An out-of-the way treasure worth the detour. *2814 19th St. (between Byrant & Florida sts.)* ☎ *415/821-4608. Entrees $14–$27. AE, DC, DISC, MC, V. Lunch Fri, dinner daily, brunch Sat–Sun 9am–2:30pm. Bus: 9, 27. Map p 93.*

★ **Vicolo Pizzeria** HAYES VALLEY *PIZZA* Delish cornmeal-crust pizzas and inventive salads in a cozy, corrugated building. *150 Ivy Alley. (off Gough St., between Hayes & Grove sts.)* ☎ *415/863-2382. Entrees $8–$8.50. MC, V. Dinner daily, lunch only during symphony & opera matinees. 11:30am–2pm. Bus: 21. Map p 94.*

★ **Yank Sing** FINANCIAL DISTRICT *CHINESE/DIM SUM* Serves 60 varieties of excellent dim sum daily, from stuffed crab claws to steamed pork buns. *101 Spear St. (in Rincon Center, at Mission St.)* ☎ *415/957-9300. $3.50–$7.50. AE, DC, DISC, MC, V. Lunch daily. Streetcar: All Market St. lines. Map p 94. 49 Stevenson St. (between 1st & 2nd sts.).* ☎ *415/541-4949. AE, DC, DISC, MC, V. Lunch daily. BART/Muni: Embarcadero. Map p 96.*

kids Zao Noodle Bar MARINA *ASIAN* An SF family favorite, serving coconut–lemon-grass soup, yellow-curry prawns, and kids' noodles. *2031 Chestnut St. (between Fillmore & Steiner sts.)* ☎ *415/928-3088. Entrees $8–$10. AE, MC, V. Lunch & dinner daily. Bus: 22, 30. 2406 California St. (at Fillmore St.).* ☎ *415/345-8088. Bus: 1, 22. Map p 94.*

San Francisco's beloved Zuni Café is hip, chic, and never fails to serve up delectable Mediterranean cookery.

★ **kids ZA Pizza** RUSSIAN HILL *PIZZA* Thin-crust pizza with sun-dried tomatoes, pesto, or more classic toppings. A good stop en route to Fisherman's Wharf. *1919 Hyde St. (between Green & Union sts.)* ☎ *415/771-3100. Slices $3.30–$4.35. AE, DC, MC, V. Lunch & dinner daily. Bus: 41, 45. Cable car: Powell-Hyde. Map p 94.*

★★ **Zuni Cafe** HAYES VALLEY *MEDITERRANEAN/CALIFORNIA* After 2 decades, acclaimed chef Judy Rodgers still creates masterpieces like her signature roast chicken with bread salad. *1658 Market St. (between Gough & Franklin sts.)* ☎ *415/552-2522. Entrees $15–$38. AE, MC, V. Lunch & dinner daily. Bus: 6, 7, 66, 71. Muni: Van Ness. Map p 94.* ●

The Best **Nightlife**

Nightlife Best Bets

Best **Irish Coffee**
★ The Buena Vista Café, *2765 Hyde St.* *(p 121)*

Best **Singles Scene**
Matrix Fillmore, *3138 Fillmore St.* *(p 123)*

Best **Happy Hour Food**
★ The Tonga Room & Hurricane Bar, Fairmont Hotel, *950 Mason St.* *(p 122)*

Best Place to **Spot a Local Celebrity**
★ Tosca, *242 Columbus Ave.* *(p 122)*

Best **Beer Selection**
★ Toronado Pub, *547 Haight St.* *(p 127)*

Best **View**
★★ The Top of the Mark, Inter-Continental Mark Hopkins, *1 Nob Hill* *(p 124)*

Best **Cabaret Lounge**
★★ Empire Plush Room, *940 Sutter St.* *(p 125)*

Best **Place to Watch European Soccer**
★★ Mad Dog in the Fog, *530 Haight St.* *(p 127)*

Best **Old-Time Bar**
Perry's, *1944 Union St.* *(p 121)*

Best **Neighborhood for Barhopping**
The Mission, various venues (see *p 128* for minitour)

Best **Karaoke**
★ The Mint Karaoke Lounge, *1942 Market St.* *(p 126)*

Best **Blues Bar**
★★ The Boom Boom Room, *1601 Fillmore St.* *(p 122)*

Best **Sports Bar**
★ Greens Sports Bar, *2239 Polk St.* *(p 126)*

Best **Champagne Bar**
★ The Bubble Lounge, *714 Montgomery St.* *(p 123)*

Best **Martini**
★ Blondie's, *540 Valencia St.* *(p 128)*

Best **Rock Club**
★★★ Fillmore Auditorium, *1805 Geary Blvd.* *(p 127)*

Best **Beatnik Bar**
★ Vesuvio, *225 Columbus Ave.* *(p 122)*

Best **Dive Bar**
★ Hemlock, *1131 Polk St.* *(p 121);* and 500 Club, *500 Guerrero* *(p 128)*

Best **Gay Bar**
★ Moby Dick, *4049 18th St.* *(p 125)*

Best **Dance Club**
★★ The EndUp, *401 6th St.* *(p 124)*

Best **SF Jazz Club**
★★ Rasselas, *1534 Fillmore St.* *(p 126)*

Vesuvio, City Lights Bookstore's neighbor and Jack Kerouac's old haunt, attracts a diverse clientele.

Nightlife: East of Van Ness Ave.

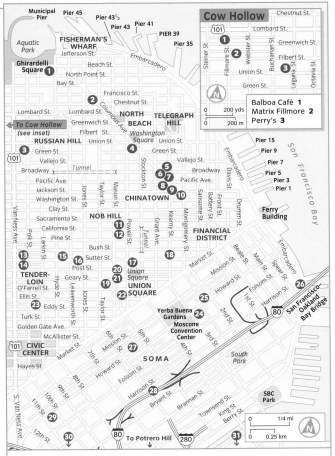

Cow Hollow

Balboa Café **1**
Matrix Fillmore **2**
Perry's **3**

Bambuddha Lounge **23**
Bimbo's 365 Club **2**
Biscuits & Blues **21**
Blur **14**
Bottom of the Hill **30**
The Bubble Lounge **10**
The Buena Vista Café **1**
Empire Plush Room **15**
The EndUp **28**
Enrico's Sidewalk Café **5**
Ginger's Trois **18**
Gold Club **25**
Gordon Biersch **26**

Greens Sports Bar **3**
Harry Denton's
 Starlight Lounge **17**
Hemlock **13**
Jazz at Pearl's **6**
Johnny Foley's
 Irish House **22**
Mezzanine **27**
O'Reilly's Irish Pub
 & Restaurant **4**
The Ramp **31**
Red Room **16**
Redwood Room **19**

Ruby Skye **20**
San Francisco
 Brewing Co. **9**
Slim's **29**
Thirsty Bear
 Brewing Co. **24**
The Tonga Room
 & Hurricane Bar **11**
The Top of the Mark **12**
Tosca **7**
Vesuvio **8**

Nightlife: West of Van Ness Ave.

Post St.
Geary Blvd.
① Japan Center
② ③
O'Farrell St.
O'Farrell St.
Ellis St.
Ellis St.
Eddy St.
Eddy St.
Turk St.
Ellis St.
Eddy St.
Jefferson Square
Golden Gate Ave.
McAllister St.
TENDERLOIN
Hyde St.
Van Ness Ave.
Franklin St.
Gough St.
Laguna St.
Buchanan St.
Webster St.
Fillmore St.
Steiner St.
Turk St.
Golden Gate Ave.
McAllister St.
CIVIC CENTER
WESTERN ADDITION
Fulton St.
Alamo Square
Grove St.
Hayes St.
HAYES VALLEY
Linden St.
Fell St.
Oak St.
Page St.
Haight St.
Waller St.
Hermann St.
Divisadero St.
Broderick St.
Scott St.
Pierce St.
④
⑤ ⑥
⑦
Octavia Blvd.
Market St.
⑧
Gough
⑨
Dubo ce **⑩** Ave.
⑪
{101}
9th St.
10th St.
11th St.
S. Van Ness Ave.
Howard St.
12th St.
SOMA
Market St.
{101}
Dubo ce Ave.
Duboce Park
Duboce Ave.
14th St.
14th St.
Castro St.
Noe St.
Corona Heights Playground
⑫
Market St.
16th St.
Church St.
15th St.
Dolores St.
Guerrero St.
Valencia St.
Mission St.
South Van Ness Ave.
Shotwell St.
Folsom St.
See Mission Bar Hop, p. 128
THE CASTRO
17th St.
Sanchez St.
17th St.
18th St.
⑬ **⑭**
18th St.
19th St.
Mission Dolores Park
THE MISSION
⑱
19th St.
Eureka St.
Diamond St.
Collingwood St.
Castro St.
Hartford St.
Noe St.
Mission Playground
Lexington St.
Mission St.
Capp St.
20th St.
Liberty St.
21st St.
Hill St.
Dolores St.
Valencia St.
20th St.
21st St.
22nd St.
⑮
⑯
⑰

0   1/4 mi
0   0.25 km
Ⓝ

The Boom Boom Room **1**	Lexington Club **18**	Pilsner Inn **12**
El Rio **16**	Mad Dog in the Fog **6**	Rasselas **3**
Fillmore Auditorium **2**	Martuni's **8**	Suppenkuche **4**
Harvey's **13**	The Mint Karaoke Lounge **9**	Toronado Pub **5**
Laszlo **17**	Moby Dick **14**	Wild Side West **15**
Levende Lounge **11**	Nickie's **7**	Zeitgeist **10**

Nightlife A to Z

Bars

Balboa Café COW HOLLOW   Filled with affluent 30- and 40-somethings from the neighborhood, this preppie bar with an old-time flair is an SF institution. *3199 Fillmore St. (at Greenwich St.)* ☎ *415/921-3944. www.plumpjack.com. Bus: 22, 30. Map p 119.*

★ **Blur** TENDERLOIN   Hidden away amongst the grittier Tenderloin bars is this sleek candlelit lounge serving up excellent cocktails and yummy sushi rolls. *1121 Polk St.(between Post & Sutter sts.)* ☎ *415/567-1918. Bus: 2, 3, 4, 19. Map p 119.*

★ **The Buena Vista Café** COW HOLLOW   Despite popular belief, the Buena Vista didn't invent Irish coffee, but it has served more of them than any other bar in the world. It's an SF tradition. *2765 Hyde St. (at Beach St.)* ☎ *415/474-5044. www.thebuenavista.com. Bus: 10, 30. Cable car: Powell-Hyde. Map p 119.*

500 Club MISSION *(p 128 for review). Map p 128.*

★ **Hemlock** TENDERLOIN   Tattooed bartenders and a laid-back vibe, plus local and national bands playing every night in the back room (a separate, small cover charge applies), make for a popular place on weekend evenings. *1131 Polk St. (at Hemlock St., between Post & Sutter sts.)* ☎ *415/923-0923. Bus: 2, 3, 4, 19. Map p 119.*

★★ **Laszlo** MISSION   This industrial-chic bar next to the hip Foreign Cinema restaurant (p 105) serves up funky cocktails like the "Heat Seeker": Absolut Peppar, Cointreau, and lime juice. *2534 Mission St. (between 21st & 22nd sts.)* ☎ *415/648-7600. Bus: 14, 49. BART to 24th St. Map p 120.*

★ **Martuni's** MISSION   This stylish piano bar attracts a cool over-30 crowd and makes a mean martini, including inventive concoctions like a chocolate martini with Godiva chocolate liqueur and vodka. *4 Valencia St. (at Market St.) 415/241-0205. martunis.citysearch.com. Bus: 26. Map p 120.*

Perry's COW HOLLOW   Immortalized in Armistead Maupin's *Tales of the City,* this bar/restaurant serving classic American fare was once the hot bar for singles from the surrounding posh neighborhoods. It's got a mellower, old-time feel about it these days. *1944 Union St. (between Buchanan & Laguna sts.)* ☎ *415/ 922-9022. Bus: 45. Map p 119.*

★**Red Room** UNION SQUARE   This crimson hot spot—sultry, sleek, and very red—serves a mean Cosmopolitan. *In the Commodore Hotel. 827 Sutter St. (between Leavenworth & Jones sts.)* ☎ *415/346-7666. Bus: 2, 3, 4, 27. Map p 119.*

The Red Room reflects no other color but ruby red.

Boogie down to the blues at the Boom Boom Room.

★★ Suppenkuche HAYES VALLEY The best selection of German beers and food in town. *(See "San Francisco Dining A to Z," p 120).*

★ The Tonga Room & Hurricane Bar NOB HILL With umbrella drinks and fake thunderstorms, it doesn't get kitschier than this. But the $7 Asian-style happy hour is a bargain. *Fairmont Hotel, 950 Mason St. (at California St.)* ☎ *415/ 772-5278. www.tongaroom.com. Bus: 1. Cable car: All. Map p 119.*

★ Tosca NORTH BEACH This relaxed North Beach institution draws local politicos and celebrities. With a dark wood bar and red leather stools, it's a true classic. *242 Columbus Ave. (between Broadway St. & Pacific Ave.)* ☎ *415/986-9651. Bus: 12, 15, 41. Map p 119.*

★ Vesuvio NORTH BEACH Once the favored beatnik watering hole, Vesuvio still draws an artsy crowd. Order the Bohemian coffee: brandy, amaretto, and lemon twist. *225 Columbus Ave. (at Pacific Ave.)* ☎ *415/362-3370. www.vesuvio.com. Bus: 12, 15, 41. Map p 119.*

★ Zeitgeist MISSION This indie-rocker Mission staple has a spacious outdoor beer garden, a long list of microbrews on tap, and many devoted customers. *199 Valencia St. (at Duboce Ave.)* ☎ *415/255-7505. zeitgeist.citysearch.com. Bus: 26. Map p 120.*

Blues Bars

★ Biscuits & Blues UNION SQUARE This basement nightclub is a nationally known blues venue. *401 Mason St. (at Geary St.).* ☎ *415/ 292-2583. www.biscuitsandblues.com. Cover during performances $5–$20. Bus: 2, 3, 4, 38. Cable car: Powell lines. Map p 119.*

★★ The Boom Boom Room WESTERN ADDITION This dark, steamy joint hosts some of the best blues bands in the country. *1601 Fillmore St. (at Geary Blvd.).* ☎ *415/673-8000. www.boomboom blues.com. Cover free–$15. Bus: 22, 38. Map p 120.*

Brewpubs

Gordon Biersch SOMA SF's largest brewery restaurant, big with the after-work crowd, serves tasty German-style brews and decent food. *2 Harrison St. (at The Embarcadero)* ☎ *415/243-8246. www. gordonbiersch.com. Bus: 12. Streetcar: N. Map p 119.*

★ San Francisco Brewing Company NORTH BEACH This old-time saloon, complete with stained-glass windows and mahogany bar, serves a complete menu and homemade brews to a usually-packed house. *155 Columbus Ave.(between Jackson St. & Pacific Ave.)* ☎ *415/434-3344. www.sfbrewing.com. Bus: 12, 14, 15. Map p 119.*

★★ **Thirsty Bear Brewing Company** SOMA   The excellent, house-made beers are complemented by a tasty menu of Spanish tapas. Pool tables and dartboards are upstairs, and there's live flamenco on Sunday, jazz on Tuesday, and a DJ Thursday nights. *661 Howard St. (between New Montgomery St. & 3rd St.)* ☎ *415/ 974-0905. www.thirstybear.com. Bus: 10, 13, 15, 45. Map p 119.*

Cocktail Lounges

★ **Bambuddha Lounge** TENDERLOIN   This swanky club in the Phoenix Hotel plays a mix of ambient, hip-hop, funk, and house tunes and serves tasty Asian cuisine. *601 Eddy St. (at Larkin St.)* ☎ *415/ 885-5088. www.bambuddhalounge. com. Bus: 19, 31. Map p 119.*

★ **The Bubble Lounge** FINAN-CIAL DISTRICT   The SF sister to the NY club is très posh. Beyond the dizzying array of champagnes, martinis, and caviars, a dress code is enforced: no sneakers, combat fatigues, or baseball caps. *714 Montgomery St. (at Washington St.)* ☎ *415/434-4204. www.bubble lounge.com. No cover. Bus: 10, 15, 41. Map p 119.*

★ **Levende Lounge** MISSION   Enjoy small plates, fancy cocktails, and DJ-spun tunes at this venue

Choose from brews like Alcatraz Stout and Oofty Goofty Barleywine (a type of ale) at the San Francisco Brewing Company.

populated by trendy 20- and 30-somethings. *1710 Mission St. (between 13th & 14th sts.)* ☎ *415/ 864-5585. www.levendesf.com. Streetcar: F. Map p 120.*

Matrix Fillmore UNION SQUARE   With expensive drinks and sleek decor, this is the center of the sin-gles universe for SF's fashionable, young yuppies. *3138 Fillmore St. (between Greenwich & Filbert sts.)* ☎ *415/563-4180. www.plumpjack. com. Bus: 22, 30. Map p 119.*

Filipino, Balinese, and Thai influences generate the feng shui at the poolside Bambuddha Lounge.

Chill out to groovy tunes at the Levende Lounge.

Redwood Room UNION SQUARE It's worth checking out the historic Redwood Room for the cool, updated decor given it by famed hotelier Ian Schrager. But the once-hip scene now includes a few too many posers. *Clift Hotel, 495 Geary St. (at Taylor St.)* ☎ *415/775-4700. Bus: 2, 3, 4, 27, 38. Map p 119.*

★★ **The Top of the Mark** NOB HILL This historic lounge, with the best view in town and a 100-martini menu, has live entertainment on weekend nights. A $49 prix-fixe sunset dinner's also a weekend option.

The Beautiful People dominate the Redwood Room.

InterContinental Mark Hopkins, 1 Nob Hill. (at Mason & California sts.) ☎ *415/616-6916. Cover $5–$10. Bus: 1. Cable car: All. Map p 119.*

Dance Clubs

★★ **The EndUp** SOMA After 30 years this is SF's most enduringly popular dance club. It's a nonstop party every weekend until the wee hours of Monday morning—despite the sketchy 'hood. *401 6th St. (at Harrison St.)* ☎ *415/646-0999. www.theendup.com. Cover varies. Bus: 12, 27. Map p 119.*

★★ **Mezzanine** SOMA This current dance hot spot is an upscale, industrial-chic nightclub and gallery in one of the grittier sections of town. *444 Jesse St. (off 6th St., between Market & Mission sts.)* ☎ *415/625-8880. www.mezzaninesf. com. Cover varies. Bus: 12, 27. Map p 119.*

Nickie's HAIGHT The crowd here depends on the music. Monday is Grateful Dead night, complete with incense. Other nights feature hip-hop, soul, and funkier beats. *460 Haight St. (between Fillmore & Webster sts.)* ☎ *415/621-6508. www.nickies.com. Bus: 22, 67. Map p 120.*

★ **The Ramp** SOMA   From May through October you can dance to live jazz, salsa, and world music Friday through Sunday evenings, with no cover charge, at this indoor/outdoor bar and restaurant. *855 China Basin. (east of Mariposa St., past 3rd St.)* ☎ *415/621-2378. www.ramprestaurant.com. No cover. Bus: 15. Map p 119.*

Ruby Skye UNION SQUARE   This former Victorian movie house is SF's biggest dance space, featuring live music and DJs from around the country on weekend nights. *420 Mason St. (between Post & Geary sts.) 415/693-0777. www.rubyskye.com. Cover free–$30. Bus: 2, 3, 4, 38. Cable car: Powell lines. Map p 119.*

Shake your tush under the strobes or on the outdoor heated deck at the EndUp.

Gay Bars

Ginger's Trois FINANCIAL DISTRICT Popular with the after-work crowd, strong drinks and a friendly ambience are the bar's main draw. *246 Kearny St. (between Bush & Sutter sts.)* ☎ *415/989-0282. Bus: 3, 4, 15. Map p 119.*

Harvey's CASTRO   A lively bar/ restaurant attracting a cross section of Castro patrons for reasonable food and plenty of drinks. *500 Castro St. (at 18th St.)* ☎ *415/431-4278. Bus: 33. Streetcar: F. Map p 120.*

★ **Moby Dick** CASTRO   A 25-year-old Castro institution, with a low-key attitude, pool table, pinball machines, and a massive fish tank above the bar. *4049 18th St. (between Castro & Noe sts.)* ☎ *415/861-1199. www. mobydicksf.com. Bus: 33. Streetcar: F. Map p 120.*

Pilsner Inn CASTRO   This mellow bar, with a good selection of on-tap beers and an outdoor garden, is more of a scene on weekend nights. *225 Castro St. (between 15th & 16th sts.)* ☎ *415/621-7058. Bus: 33. Streetcar: F. Map p 120.*

Jazz Venues

★★ **Empire Plush Room** UNION SQUARE   This former 1920s speakeasy with red velvet banquettes and round tables is a swank spot to hear nationally known jazz and cabaret singers. *940 Sutter St. (between Leavenworth & Hyde sts.).* ☎ *415/885-2800. www.plushroom. com. Tickets $20–$100. Bus: 2, 3, 4, 27. Map p 119.*

★ **Enrico's Sidewalk Café** NORTH BEACH   Tourists and locals gather on the front patio for people-watching, Italian cuisine, and excellent swing, jazz, and blues from around the country. *504 Broadway (at Kearny St.).* ☎ *415/982-6223. www.enricossidewalkcafe.com. Bus: 12, 15, 41. Map p 119.*

★ **Jazz at Pearl's** NORTH BEACH A 1930s-supper-club ambience, with white tablecloths, low lighting, and a sultry mood. Try the $10 cocktail package with two drinks and priority seating, or the $40 dinner package. *256 Columbus Ave. (at Broadway).* ☎ *415/291-8255. www.jazzatpearls. com. No cover, 2-drink minimum. Bus: 12, 15, 41. Map p 119.*

Belt out a show tune at the Mint Karaoke Lounge.

★★ **Rasselas** WESTERN ADDITION This local favorite is a casual, comfortable lounge where you can listen to jazz, Latin rhythms, R&B, or blues, or enjoy snacks from the adjacent Ethiopian restaurant. *1534 Fillmore St. (at O'Farrell St.).* ☎ *415/346-8696. www.rasselasjazzclub.com. 2-drink minimum weekdays. Cover $7 weekends after 9pm. Bus: 22, 38. Map p 120.*

Karaoke
★ **The Mint Karaoke Lounge** MISSION This once-gay destination now draws patrons of all persuasions, who, after one of the many potent cocktails, are ready to take to the stage. *1942 Market St. (between Guerrero & Dolores sts.).* ☎ *415/626-4726. www.themint.net. Bus: 22. Streetcar: F, J, N. Map p 120.*

Lesbian Bars
El Rio MISSION This eclectic club features dancing, an outdoor patio, and funky rhythms from around the world. *3158 Mission St.(south of Cesar Chavez, between Precita & Powers aves.)* ☎ *415/282-3325. Bus: 14, 26. Map p 120.*

Lexington Club MISSION A friendly crowd, pool table, and cheap beers grace this ladies club. *3464 19th St. (at Lexington St., between Valencia & Mission sts.)* ☎ *415/863-2052. www.thelexingtonclub.com. Bus: 14, 26, 49. BART: 16th St. Map p 120.*

★ **Wild Side West** BERNAL HEIGHTS This cozily cluttered, saloon-style bar and outdoor garden area is a longtime staple in the SF lesbian community. *424 Cortland Ave. (between Benington & Andover sts.)* ☎ *415/647-3099. Bus: 9, 14, or 49; transfer to bus 24. Map p 120.*

Sports Bar
★ **Greens Sports Bar** RUSSIAN HILL The best sports bar in SF boasts polished dark wood, 15 TVs, 18 beers on tap, a pool table, video games, and happy hour Monday through Friday from 4 to 7pm. *2239 Polk St. (at Green St.).* ☎ *415/775-4287. greenssportsbar.citysearch. com. Bus: 19. Cable car: Powell-Hyde. Map p 119.*

Strip Club
Gold Club SOMA They say the girls are fine and friendly here. *650 Howard St. (between 2nd & 3rd sts.).* ☎ *415/536-0300. www.goldclubsf. com. $20 Sat–Sun & Mon–Fri after 7pm. Bus: 15, 30, 45. Map p 119.*

Supper Clubs
★ **Harry Denton's Starlight Lounge** UNION SQUARE This classic 1930s penthouse lounge offers stellar city views, a lengthy appetizer menu, and dancing. The Harry Denton Starlight Orchestra plays Friday and Saturday eves. Call to reserve a table, and don't wear jeans or sneakers. *Sir Francis Drake Hotel, 450 Powell St.(between Sutter & Post sts.)* ☎ *415/395-8595. www.harrydenton. com. Cover $10 Wed after 7pm; $5 Thurs after 8pm; $10 Fri after 8pm; $15 Sat after 8pm. Bus: 2, 3, 4. Cable car: Powell lines. Map p 119.*

Smoking Laws

On January 1, 1998, smoking was officially banned in all California bars. This law is generally enforced and though San Francisco's police department has not made bar raids a priority, people caught smoking in bars can be ticketed and fined. If you must smoke, do it outside.

Pubs

★ **Johnny Foley's Irish House** UNION SQUARE   This spacious pub serves a full menu of Irish and non-Irish fare, has a large selection of Irish whiskies and single-malts and screens European soccer. *243 O'Farrell St. (between Mason & Powell sts.)* ☎ *415/954-0777. www.johnny foleys.com. Bus: 27, 38. Cable car: Powell lines. Map p 119.*

★★ **Mad Dog in the Fog** HAIGHT This quirky British pub is the best place to watch European soccer. It's also good for a pint of bitter and a game of darts. *530 Haight St. (between Steiner & Fillmore sts.)* ☎ *415/626-7279. Bus: 22, 67. Map p 120.*

★ **O'Reilly's Irish Pub & Restaurant** NORTH BEACH You'll find your pint of Guinness at this cozy joint, along with Irish lamb stew and the less traditional "Irishman's quesadilla." *622 Green St. (between Powell St. & Columbus Ave.)* ☎ *415/989-6222. www.oreillysirish. com. Bus: 15, 30, 41, 45. Cable car: Powell-Mason line. Map p 119.*

★ **Toronado Pub** HAIGHT   A boisterous Lower Haight hangout with over 40 microbrews on tap and dozens of bottled beers. Bonus: Most pints are $2.50 until 6pm every day. *547 Haight St. (between Steiner & Fillmore sts.)* ☎ *415/863-2276. www.toronado.com. Bus: 6, 7, 22. Map p 120.*

Rock/Alternative Venues

★ **Bimbo's 365 Club** NORTH BEACH   Swanky 1930s decor, complete with chandeliers and tux-clad servers belies the low-key atmosphere at this North Beach staple, which is more likely to feature rock and hip-hop than jazz or cabaret. *1025 Columbus Ave. (at Chestnut St.).* ☎ *415/474-0365. www.bimbos365 club.com. Tickets $18–$40. Bus: 30. Cable car: Powell-Mason. Map p 119.*

★★ **Bottom of the Hill** POTRERO HILL   This unpretentious rock club draws a broad cross section of rock 'n' roll fans. Happy hour takes place Friday from 3 to 7pm. *1233 17th St. (at Missouri St.).* ☎ *415/621-4455. www.bottomofthehill.com. Cover $6–$14. Bus: 22. Map p 119.*

★★★ **Fillmore Auditorium** WESTERN ADDITION   The club that featured bands like Jefferson Airplane and the Grateful Dead is once again the best rock venue in town. *1805 Geary Blvd. (at Fillmore St.).* ☎ *415/346-6000. www.thefillmore. com. Tickets $17–$35. Bus: 22, 38. Map p 120.*

★★ **Slim's** SOMA   Co-owned by musician Boz Scaggs, this bar and restaurant plays rock and hip-hop acts almost nightly. Hot acts sell out quickly. *333 11th St. (at Folsom St.). www.slims-sf.com. Cover free–$30. Bus: 9, 47. Map p 119.*

Mission Bar Hop

0   100 yds
0   100 m

N

15th St.

Spencer Alley

2

Albion St.

3

Caledonia St.
Julian Ave.
Wiese St.

16th St.

16th St.

Dolores St.

Gaiser Ct.

4

5

Valencia St.

6

Rondel Pl.

Hoff St.

Mission St.

Guerrero St.

Camp St.

Albion St.

7

17th St.

1

Dearborn St.

17th St.

Clarion Alley

8

Sycamore St.

Dolores Terr.

Dorland St.

Bird St.

Lexington St.
San Carlos St.

Mission Dolores Park

18th St.

18th St.

SF's best place to barhop is the Mission, where you'll find up to five bars on a single block. This tour leads you to a cross section of some of my favorite venues, from neighborhood dives to swinging lounges. ***Note of caution:*** Don't stray too far from the crowds, and avoid the BART station after dark. (Therefore, if you start your barhopping after dark, take a cab to and from the Mission.) START: **Bus: 26, 49. BART: 16th Street (before dark).**

1 500 Club *(500 Guerrero St.;* ☎ *415/851-2500).* The first stop is easy to find: a huge pink neon cocktail beckons you inside, where you'll discover a classic dive bar, made festive by year-round chile lights. It's a bit more upscale at **2 Elixir** *(3200 16th St.;* ☎ *415/552-1633),* the subdued site of an 1875 saloon, but you can buy a pitcher, play a rock tune on the jukebox, and sit in a weathered booth at neighborhood tavern **3 ★ Kilowatt** *(3160 16th. St.;* ☎ *415/861-2592).* Next stop is **4 Dalva** *(3121 16th St.;* ☎ *415/252-7740),* a narrow, high-walled joint abuzz with an eclectic

crowd. For a sleeker feel, hit **5 Skylark** *(3089 16th St.;* ☎ *415/621-9294),* where trendy young things come for expensive cocktails and DJ-spun tunes. Quirky **6 ★ Cassanova** *(527 Valencia St.;* ☎ *415/863-9328)* is a good mix of both Mission locals and hipsters from around town. At **7 ★ Blondie's** *(540 Valencia St.;* ☎ *415/864-2419)* you're almost done, so order their famous 16-ounce martini. Now it's time to chill out by the inviting bar at the **8 ★★ Elbo Room** *(647 Valencia St.;* ☎ *415/552-7788),* or head upstairs for excellent live music (separate cover up to $10). ●

Arts & Entertainment
Best Bets

Best **Theater Company**
★★ American Conservatory Theater (A.C.T.), *Geary Theater, 415 Geary St. (p 136)*

Longest-Running **Comedy**
★ Beach Blanket Babylon, *Club Fugazi, 678 Green St. (p 133)*

Best **Inexpensive Shows**
★★ San Francisco Conservatory of Music, *1201 Ortega St. (p 133)*

Best **Broadway Shows**
★ Curran Theatre, *445 Geary St. (p 136)*

Best **Foreign & Independent Films**
★★ Embarcadero Center Cinema, *1 Embarcadero Center (p 135)*

Wackiest Place to Watch a Film
★★ Castro Theatre, *429 Castro St. (p 135)*

Best **Comedy Club**
★ Punchline, *444 Battery St. (p 134)*

Enjoy a morning of Gospel Music at the Glide Memorial Church.

Expect the unexpected at Beach Blanket Babylon's comedy show.

Best for **Visiting Virtuosos**
San Francisco Performances, *Various locations (p 133)*

Best **Free Sports Event**
★ San Francisco Pro-Am Summer Basketball, *Kezar Pavilion, Stanyan and Waller sts. (p 136)*

Best **Seasonal Event**
★★★ San Francisco Ballet's *Nutcracker, War Memorial Opera House, 301 Van Ness Ave. (p 134)*

Best **Inexpensive Show**
★★ San Francisco Conservatory of Music, *1201 Ortega St. (p 133)*

Best **Entertainment for the Whole Family**
★ Lamplighters Music Theatre, Various locations (p 136)

Best **Gospel**
★ Glide Memorial Church, *330 Ellis St. (p 133)*

Best **Modern Dance**
★★ ODC/San Francisco, *3153 17th St. (p 134)*

San Francisco **A & E**

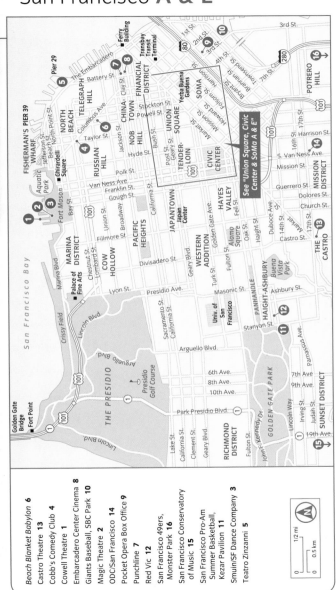

"See 'Union Square, Civic Center & SoMa A & E'"

Beach Blanket Babylon **6**
Castro Theatre **13**
Cobb's Comedy Club **4**
Cowell Theatre **1**
Embarcadero Center Cinema **8**
Giants Baseball, SBC Park **10**
Magic Theatre **2**
ODC/San Francisco **14**
Pocket Opera Box Office **9**
Punchline **7**
Red Vic **12**
San Francisco 49ers,
Monster Park **16**
San Francisco Conservatory
of Music **15**
San Francisco Pro-Am
Summer Basketball,
Kezar Pavilion **11**
Smuin/SF Dance Company **3**
Teatro Zinzanni **5**

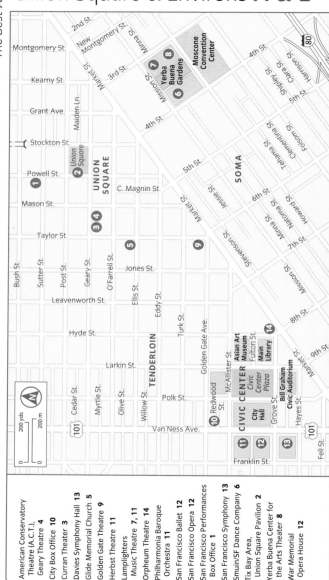

Montgomery St.

Kearny St.

Grant Ave.

Stockton St.

Powell St.

Mason St.

Taylor St.

Bush St.

Sutter St.

Post St.

Geary St.

O'Farrell St.

Leavenworth St.

Hyde St.

Larkin St.

Polk St.

Van Ness Ave.

Franklin St.

2nd St.

New Montgomery St.

Minna St.

3rd St.

Market St.

Mission St.

Maiden Ln.

4th St.

C. Magnin St.

5th St.

Jessie St.

6th St.

Stevenson St.

Mission St.

7th St.

8th St.

9th St.

4th St.

5th St.

Shipley St.

Clara St.

Harrison St.

Clementina St.

Tehama St.

Folsom St.

Natoma St.

Minna St.

Howard St.

Market St.

Moscone Convention Center

Yerba Buena Gardens

7

8

6

UNION SQUARE

Union Square

2

1

3 4

5

9

SOMA

TENDERLOIN

Ellis St.

Eddy St.

Jones St.

Turk St.

Golden Gate Ave.

McAllister St.

Redwood St.

Cedar St.

Myrtle St.

Olive St.

Willow St.

CIVIC CENTER

City Hall

Civic Center Plaza

Asian Art Museum

Fulton St.

Main Library

Bill Graham Civic Auditorium

Grove St.

Hayes St.

Fell St.

10

11 12

13

14

80

101

101

200 yds

200 m

American Conservatory Theatre (A.C.T.), Geary Theatre **4**
City Box Office **10**
Curran Theater **3**
Davies Symphony Hall **13**
Glide Memorial Church **5**
Golden Gate Theatre **9**
Herbst Theatre **11**
Lamplighters Music Theatre **7, 11**
Orpheum Theatre **14**
Philharmonia Baroque Orchestra **11**
San Francisco Ballet **12**
San Francisco Opera **12**
San Francisco Performances Box Office **1**
San Francisco Symphony **13**
Smuin/SF Dance Company **6**
Tix Bay Area, Union Square Pavilion **2**
Yerba Buena Center for the Arts Theater **8**
War Memorial Opera House **12**

Arts & Entertainment **A to Z**

Classical & Choir Music

★ **Glide Memorial Church** TENDERLOIN Nationally recognized Rev. Cecil Williams leads Sunday services, featuring rousing Gospel choir music at 9 and 11am. Arrive 30 minutes early to get seats. *330 Ellis St. (at Taylor St.)* ☎ *415/771-6300. www.glide.org. Bus: 27, 38. BART/Muni: Powell St. Cable car: Powell lines. Map p 132.*

★ **Philarmonia Baroque Orchestra** CIVIC CENTER Performs early music in SF and the Bay Area. *Herbst Theater, 401 Van Ness Ave. (at McAllister St.)* ☎ *415/759-3475. www.philharmonia.org. Tickets $28–$62. Bus: 5, 21. BART/Muni: Civic Center. Map p 132.*

★ **San Francisco Conservatory of Music** SUNSET Beyond educating young musicians, also offers inexpensive or free orchestral and opera recitals. *1201 Ortega St. (at 19th Ave.)* ☎ *415/759-3475. www.sfcm.edu. Tickets free–$15. Muni: N, then transfer to bus 28. Map p 131.*

★★ **San Francisco Performances** LOCATION VARIES Its October-through-April season includes classical music, dance, and jazz at various locations, including Herbst Theater and Yerba Buena Center for the Arts Theater. Saturday 2pm family matinees are $7 to $15. *500 Sutter St., (at Powell St.) Suite 700.* ☎ *415/392-2545. www.performances.org. Tickets $12–$60. BART/Muni: Civic Center. Map p 132.*

★★★ **San Francisco Symphony** CIVIC CENTER Founded in 1911 and directed by internationally acclaimed conductor Michael Tilson Thomas. *Davies Symphony Hall, 201 Van Ness Ave. (between Grove &*

Conductor Michael Tilson Thomas leads the San Francisco Symphony.

Hayes sts.) ☎ *415/864-6000. www.sfsymphony.org. Tickets $12–$97. Bus: 5, 21. BART/Muni: Civic Center. Map p 132.*

Comedy & Cabaret

★ **Beach Blanket Babylon** NORTH BEACH For over 30 years, BBB has spoofed popular culture with updated parodies of well-known figures. *Club Fugazi, 678 Green St. (at Columbus Ave.)* ☎ *415/421-4222. www.beachblanketbabylon.com. Tickets $33–$75. Bus: 15, 30, 45. Cable car: Powell-Mason. Map p 131.*

Cobb's Comedy Club NORTH BEACH Touring comics Thursday

Where to **Score Tickets**

Tix Bay Area sells advance and full-price tickets with a service charge of $2 to $5, plus half-price theater, dance, and music tickets on show days (Sun–Mon tickets are sold Sat–Sun). *Union Sq. Pavilion, Powell St.* ☎ 415/433-7827. www.tixbayarea.org. Try **City Box Office** for tickets to most theater and dance events. *180 Redwood St., Suite 110.* ☎ *415/392-4400. www.cityboxoffice.com.* **Ticketmaster** offers advance ticket purchases for a fee. ☎ *415/421-8497. www.ticket master.com.* **Craigslist** also connects people with tickets (especially to 49ers games). *www.craigslist.org.*

through Saturday; local comedians on Wednesday nights for $10. *915 Columbus Ave. (at Lombard St.)* ☎ *415/928-4320. www.cobbscomedy club.com. Tickets $15–$25. Bus: 30. Cable car: Powell-Mason. Map p 131.*

★ **Punchline** EMBARCADERO Largest comedy nightclub in SF; it features both locally and nationally known comedians. *444 Battery St. (at Clay St.)* ☎ *415/397-7573. punchline comedyclub.com. Tickets from $7.50. Bus: 1, 10, 15. BART/Muni: Embarcadero. Map p 131.*

Dance
★★ **ODC/San Francisco** MISSION The renowned modern dance company's last few seasons have sold out. They perform *The Velveteen Rabbit* in November and December. *ODC Theater, 3153 17th St. (at Van Ness Ave.)* ☎ *415/863-9834. www.*

odcdance.org. Tickets $15–$45. Bus: 22, 33. BART: 16th St. Map p 131.

★★★ **San Francisco Ballet** CIVIC CENTER The first and one of the finest professional ballet company in the U.S., directed by Helgi Tomasson. The season runs February through May, plus *The Nutcracker* in December. *War Memorial Opera House, 301 Van Ness Ave. (at Grove St.)* ☎ *415/865-2000. www.sfballet.org. Tickets $9–$130. Bus: 5, 21. BART/ Muni: Civic Center. Map p 132.*

★ **Smuin/SF Dance Company** SOMA Theatrical ballet performances featuring tango, rock, or other music for a modern spin. They perform at Yerba Buena and Cowell Theater in Fort Mason. *300 Brannan St. (at Mission St.)* ☎ *415/495-2234. www.smuinballet.org. Tickets $23–$50. BART/Muni: Powell St. Bus:*

Two SF Ballet Dancers leaping during a performance of Tomasson's "Criss-Cross."

A game at SBC Park comes with an unobstructed view of San Francisco Bay.

28, 30 (to Fort Mason). Map p 131 and 132.

Film

★★ Castro Theatre CASTRO
This Art Deco theater plays classic motion pictures and hosts film festivals—often accompanied by a Mighty Wurlitzer Organ. Get advance tix through Ticketweb.com. *429 Castro St. (at 17th St.)* ☎ *415/621-6120. www.castrotheatre.com. Tickets $8.50, $5.50 seniors & kids. Streetcar: F. BART/Muni: Castro. Map p 131.*

★★ Embarcadero Center Cinema EMBARCADERO
A cineplex featuring excellent foreign and indie films, plus award-winning documentaries. *1 Embarcadero Center (Battery & Clay sts.)* ☎ *415/267-4893. www.landmarktheatres.com. Tickets $10, $7 seniors & kids. Bus: 1, 10. BART/Muni: Embarcadero. Map p 131.*

Red Vic HAIGHT
This worker-owned theater screens indie films and cult classics. *1727 Haight St. (at Cole St.)* ☎ *415/668-3994. www.redvicmoviehouse.com. Tickets $7, $4 seniors & kids. Bus: 7, 66, 71. Map p 131.*

★★ San Francisco International Film Festival VARIOUS LOCATIONS
Every April, films from new and established directors hit several SF venues. ☎ *415/931-3456.*

San Francisco Film Society: www.sffs. org. Tickets to 3 films: $35; 10 films: $100. Varying ticket prices for each event; discount for members. Check website to order.

Opera

★ Pocket Opera LOCATION VARIES
Since 1978, the Pocket Opera has presented comical operas staged with a small cast, simple sets, and a chamber orchestra. *469 Bryant St. (between 2nd & 3rd sts.)* ☎ *415/972-8930. www.pocket opera.org. Tickets $15–$30. Map p 131.*

★★ San Francisco Conservatory of Music See p 133.

★★★ San Francisco Opera CIVIC CENTER
North America's second-largest opera company is among the finest. ***Tip:*** Ten-dollar standing-room tix are sold on the day of show. (Cash only; one per person.) The season runs from September through December and June and July. *War Memorial Opera House, 301 Van Ness Ave. (at Grove St.)* ☎ *415/864-3330. www.sfopera. com. Tickets $25–$195. Bus: 5, 21. BART/Muni: Civic Center. Map p 132.*

Spectator Sports

★★ Giants Baseball SOMA
Dramatic views of the Bay and Treasure Island and excellent food—from well

prepared traditional baseball fare to sushi and other ethnic cuisine—make a day at SBC Park well spent. Check the Giants website or Craigslist (www. craigslist.org) for tix. *SBC Park, 24 Willie Mays Plaza. (King & 2nd sts.)* ☎ *415/972-2000. www.giants.mlb. com. Tickets $6–$77. Bus: 10, 15, 30, 45. Muni: N. Map p 131.*

San Francisco 49ers CANDLE-STICK POINT SF's pro football team. Because there are so many season ticket holders, single tickets are hard to come by. Check Ticketmaster or Craigslist. *Monster Park, Candlestick Point.* ☎ *415/972-2000. www.sf49ers.com. Tickets $73. Map p 131.*

★ **San Francisco Pro-Am Summer Basketball** HAIGHT Current and retired college, high school, and pro basketball players mix it up in this 26-year-old league. Free to spectators. *Kezar Pavilion (Stanyan & Waller sts.) www.san franciscoproam.com. Bus: 7, 66, 71. Muni: N. Map p 131.*

Theater

★★★ **American Conservatory Theater (A.C.T.)** UNION SQUARE The Tony Award–winning theater troupe is among the top in the U.S. and performs in a world-class theater. *Geary Theater, 415 Geary St. (between Mason & Taylor sts.)* ☎ *415/749-2228. www.act-sf.org. Tickets $19–$68. Bus: 2, 3, 4, 38.*

The highly-esteemed American Conservatory Theater has been operating since 1967.

BART/Muni: Powell St. Cable car: Powell lines. Map p 132.

★ **Curran Theatre** UNION SQUARE Established in 1922 to host European and East Coast productions. Along with the **Orpheum Theater** *(1192 Market St.;* ☎ *415/551-2000; map p 132)* and the **Golden Gate Theater** *(1 Taylor St.;* ☎ *415/551-2000; map p 132)*, its "Best of Broadway" series brings NY hit plays and musicals to SF for 2- to 6-week runs. *445 Geary St. (between Mason & Taylor sts.)* ☎ *415/551-2000. www.curran theatre.com. Tickets $30–$85. Bus: 2, 3, 4, 38. BART/Muni: Powell St. Cable car: Powell lines. Map p 132.*

★ **Lamplighters Music Theatre** LOCATION VARIES Brings the works of Gilbert & Sullivan plus other comic operas to Bay Area stages. Good family fun staged at Yerba Buena Gardens or Herbst Theatre. ☎ *415/227-4797. www.lamplighters.org. Tix through Yerba Buena Center for the Arts* ☎ *415/978-2787. Tickets $30–$42, $10–$17 kids. Bus/streetcar: Market St. lines (to Yerba Buena or Civic Center). Map p 132.*

★ **Magic Theatre** MARINA This prominent national theater is dedicated to developing and producing new playwrights' works. *Building D, Fort Mason Center, Marina Blvd. (at Gough St.)* ☎ *415/441-8822. www.magictheater.org. Tickets $20-$38. Bus: 28, 30. Map p 131.*

Teatro Zinzanni EMBARCADERO Circus artists, a five-piece band, and a five-course meal come together for a 3-hour show/dinner extravaganza. *Pier 29, The Embarcadero (at Battery St.)* ☎ *415/438-2668. www.teatro zinzanni.org. Tickets $125. Bus: 10. Streetcar: F. Map p 131.* ●

Lodging Best Bets

Most **Luxurious**
★★★ The Four Seasons $$$$
757 Market St. (p 143)

Best **Business Hotel**
★★★ Mandarin Oriental *$$$$*
222 Sansome St. (p 148)

Best **Views**
★★★ InterContinental Mark Hopkins $$$$ *Number One Nob Hill (p 147)*; and ★★★ Mandarin Oriental $$$$ *222 Sansome St. (p 147)*

Most **Exclusive Hotel**
★★★ Campton Place $$$$
340 Stockton St. (p 142)

Most Historic
★★ The Palace $$$$ *2 New Montgomery St. (p 148)*

Hippest Hotel
★★ Clift Hotel $$$$ *495 Geary St. (p 142)*

Best **Fisherman's Wharf Hotel**
★★ **kids** The Argonaut $$$
495 Jefferson St. (p 142)

Best **Moderately Priced Hotel**
★★ Nob Hill Lambourne $$
725 Pine St. (p 148)

Best **Family Hotel**
★★ The Laurel Inn $$ *444 Presidio Ave. (p 147)*

Best **Bathrooms**
★★★ Ritz-Carlton $$$$ *600 Stockton St. (p 149)*

Best **Cheap Bed**
★ Hostelling International—Fisherman's Wharf $ *Fort Mason, Building 240 (p 144)*

Most **Romantic**
★★ The Archbishop's Mansion $$$ *1000 Fulton St. (p 142)*

Best **Boutique Hotel**
★★★ Harbor Court $$$$
165 Steuart St. (p 144)

The ultra-hip Triton comes with Friday-night freebies like wine parties and chair massages.

Best **Rock 'n' Roll Hotel**
★★ Hotel Triton $$ *342 Grant Ave. (p 146)*

Best **Spa**
★★★ The Huntington Hotel $$$$
1075 California St. (p 146)

Best **Under $100**
★ Marina Inn $ *3110 Octavia St. (p 148)*

Best **Hidden Gem**
★★ Hotel Drisco $$$ *2901 Pacific Ave. (p 145)*

Best **Bed & Breakfast**
★ The Golden Gate Hotel $
775 Bush St. (p 143)

Best **Place to Pretend the Summer of Love Never Ended**
★ Red Victorian B&B $$
1665 Haight St. (p 149)

Union Square & Nob Hill **Lodging**

The Argent **32**

Campton Place Hotel **15**

Cartwright Hotel **11**

Chancellor Hotel **12**

Clift Hotel **23**

Fairmont Hotel **2**

Four Seasons **31**

Galleria Park Hotel **16**

Golden Gate Hotel **7**

Grant Plaza **6**

The Handlery
  Union Square **25**

Hotel Adagio **21**

Hotel Bijou **28**

Hotel Monaco **22**

Hotel Nikko **27**

Hotel Palomar **30**

Hotel Rex **10**

Hotel Triton **8**

The Huntington Hotel **1**

The Inn at
  Union Square **18**

InterContinental
  Mark Hopkins **3**

King George Hotel **26**

Monticello Inn **29**

Nob Hill Lambourne **5**

Orchard Hotel **14**

Pan Pacific Hotel **17**

Ritz-Carlton **4**

The Savoy **20**

Serrano Hotel **24**

The Sheehan **9**

Sir Francis Drake **13**

Westin St. Francis **19**

San Francisco **Lodging**

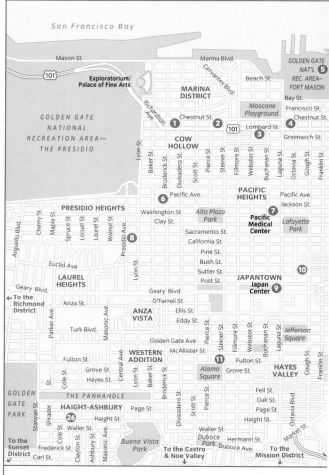

San Francisco Bay

Mason St.

Exploratorium/
Palace of Fine Arts

GOLDEN GATE
NATIONAL
RECREATION AREA—
THE PRESIDIO

Marina Blvd.

Cervantes Blvd.

Beach St.

GOLDEN GATE
NAT'L ❺
REC. AREA—
FORT MASON

MARINA
DISTRICT

Moscone
Playground

Francisco St.

Bay St.

Chestnut St. ❹

❶ Chestnut St. ❷

Lombard St. ❸

Greenwich St.

COW
HOLLOW

Lyon St. Baker St. Broderick St. Divisadero St. Scott St. Pierce St. Steiner St. Fillmore St. Webster St. Buchanan St. Laguna St. Octavia St. Gough St. Franklin St.

❻ Pacific Ave.

PACIFIC
HEIGHTS

Pacific Ave.

Jackson St.

PRESIDIO HEIGHTS

Washington St.

Alta Plaza
Park

❼ Pacific
Medical
Center

Lafayette
Park

Arguello Blvd. Cherry St. Maple St. Spruce St. Locust St. Laurel St. Walnut St. Presidio Ave.

Clay St.

Sacramento St.

California St.

Pine St.

Bush St.

Sutter St.

Post St.

JAPANTOWN ❿

Japan
Center ❾

❽

Lyon St.

Euclid Ave.

LAUREL
HEIGHTS

← To the
Richmond
District

Geary Blvd.

Anza St.

Geary Blvd.

O'Farrell St.

Ellis St.

Parker Ave. Masonic Ave.

Turk Blvd.

ANZA
VISTA

Eddy St.

Golden Gate Ave.

Jefferson
Square

Fulton St.

Central Ave.

McAllister St.

WESTERN
ADDITION

Steiner St. Pierce St. Fillmore St. Webster St. Buchanan St. Laguna St. Gough St. Franklin St.

❶❶

Fulton St.

HAYES
VALLEY

GOLDEN
GATE
PARK

Stanyan St. Shrader St. Cole St. Clayton St. Ashbury St. Masonic Ave.

THE PANHANDLE

HAIGHT-ASHBURY

❷❻

Grove St.

Hayes St.

Page St.

Haight St.

Waller St.

Frederick St.

Carl St.

Lyon St. Baker St. Broderick St. Divisadero St. Scott St. Pierce St.

Alamo
Square

Grove St

Fell St.

Oak St.

Page St.

Haight St.

Waller St.

Duboce
Park

Hermann St.

Duboce Ave.

Octavia Blvd. Market St. Gough St.

To the
Sunset
District ↙

Buena Vista
Park

To the Castro
& Noe Valley ↓

To the
Mission District ↓

101

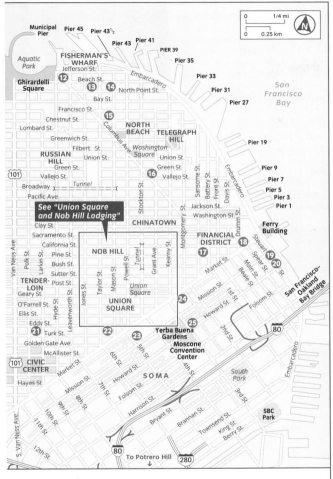

Hyatt at Fisherman's Wharf **13**
Hyatt Regency San Francisco **18**
Jackson Court **7**
The Laurel Inn **8**
Mandarin Oriental **17**
The Marina Inn **4**
Marina Motel **1**

The Palace Hotel **24**
The Phoenix Hotel **21**
Radisson Miyako Hotel **9**
Red Victorian B & B **26**
San Remo Hotel **15**
Tuscan Inn **14**
W Hotel **25**

Hotels **A to Z**

★★ The Archbishop's Mansion
CIVIC CENTER   Built in 1904 for SF's archbishop, this flamboyantly decorated mansion is the most romantic B&B in town. *1000 Fulton St. (at Steiner St.)* ☎ *800/543-5820 or 415/563-7872. www.thearchbishops mansion.com. 15 units. Doubles $145–$355 w/breakfast. AE, DC, DISC, MC, V. Bus: 5, 22. Map p 140.*

★ The Argent SOMA   This corporate hotel often has weekend and holiday deals. Deluxe rooms above the 15th floor are bigger and many have great views. *50 3rd St. (at Market St.)* ☎ *877/222-6699 or 415/974-6400. www.argenthotel.com. 667 units. Doubles $179–$349. AE, DC, DISC, MC, V. Bus: 5. BART/Muni: Montgomery St. Map p 139.*

★★ kids The Argonaut FISHERMAN'S WHARF   The beautifully restored 1907 building has vibrant decor, a great location, and some bay views. Best choice at the wharf. *495 Jefferson St. (at Hyde St.)* ☎ *866/415-0704 or 415/563-0800. www. argonauthotel.com. 252 units. Doubles $199–$229. AE, DC, DISC, MC, V. Bus: 10, 30. Cable car: Powell-Hyde. Map p 140.*

★★★ Campton Place Hotel
UNION SQUARE   The epitome of refined opulence and exclusivity. Bathrooms, with Portuguese limestone and deep soaking tubs, are a dream. *340 Stockton St. (between Post & Sutter sts.)* ☎ *800/234-4300 or 415/781-5555. www.campton place.com. 110 units. Doubles $345–$475. AE, DC, DISC, MC, V. Bus: 2, 3, 4. BART/Muni: Montgomery St. Cable car: Powell lines. Map p 139.*

★ Cartwright Hotel UNION SQUARE   This old-time hotel redid its cozy rooms in 2004. Bathrooms

The Nautical feel of the Argonaut is fitting for this wharf-adjacent hotel.

are wee, but rates include a hearty breakfast and evening wine hour. *524 Sutter St. (between Mason & Powell sts.)* ☎ *800/227-3844 or 415/421-2865. www.cartwrighthotel. com. 114 units. Doubles $119–$189. AE, DC, DISC, MC, V. Bus: 2, 3, 4. BART/Muni: Powell St. Cable car: Powell lines. Map p 139.*

★ Chancellor Hotel UNION SQUARE   A prime location makes up for the plain decor, as do nice touches like free coffee, apples, and cookies, plus a menu of 12 pillows. *433 Powell St. (between Sutter & Post sts.)* ☎ *800/428-4748 or 415/362-2004. www.chancellorhotel.com. 137 units. Doubles $175. AE, DC, DISC, MC, V. Bus: 2, 3, 4. BART/Muni: Montgomery St. Cable car: Powell lines. Map p 139.*

★★ Clift Hotel UNION SQUARE   Hotelier Ian Schrager and designer Philippe Starck created this über-hip hotel with very modern furnishings and a cool attitude. Most rooms scream minimalism, and bathrooms are stylish but small. The in-house Redwood Room is a hopping lounge. The staff is friendly and efficient. *495 Geary St. (at Taylor St.)* ☎ *800/652-5438 or 415/775-4700. www.clifthotel.com. 389 units. Doubles $295–$355. AE, DC, DISC, MC, V. Bus: 2, 3, 4, 27, 38. Map p 139.*

★ kids **Cow Hollow Motor Inn & Suites** MARINA   The motel has spacious rooms, but avoid those on noisy Lombard Street. The suites on quieter Chestnut Street are like well-furnished apartments—ideal for longer stays. *2190 Lombard St. (at Steiner St.)* ☎ *415/921-5800. www.cowhollowsuites.com. 129 units. Doubles $86–$135; suites $225–$275. AE, DC, MC, V. Bus: 22, 30, 76. Map p 140.*

★★ **Fairmont Hotel** NOB HILL This 1907 landmark's exterior and lobby impress. Historic Building rooms and closets are very large. For great bathrooms and views, opt for the Tower Building. *950 Mason St. (at California St.)* ☎ *800/441-1414 or*

Muted, pale colors infuse a tranquil vibe at in the ultra-trendy Clift hotel.

415/772-5000. www.fairmont.com. 591 units. Doubles $269–$499. AE, DC, DISC, MC, V. Bus: 1. Cable cars: All. Map p 139.

★★★ **Four Seasons** SOMA SF's most luxurious hotel has top furnishings and large marble bathrooms. The impeccable service and access to the massive Sports Club/LA add to the wonders. *757 Market St. (at 3rd St.)* ☎ *415/633-3000. www.fourseasons.com. 277 units. Doubles $439–$600. AE, DC, DISC, MC, V. BART/Muni: Montgomery St. Map p 139.*

★ **Galleria Park Hotel** FINAN-CIAL DISTRICT   Unique features here are a rooftop jogging track/garden, an easy-access garage, and a shopping center next door. *191 Sutter St. (at Kearny St.)* ☎ *800/792-9639 or 415/781-3060. www.galleriapark.com. 177 units. Doubles $179–$299. AE, DC, DISC, MC, V. Bus: 15, 30, 45. BART/Muni: Montgomery St. Map p 139.*

★ **Golden Gate Hotel** UNION SQUARE   This B&B's petite rooms have wicker furniture and floral prints. Nice touches: an antique bird-cage elevator and afternoon cookies. *775 Bush St. (between Powell & Mason sts.)* ☎ *800/835-1118 or 415/392-3702. www.goldengatehotel.com. 23 units, some with shared bathrooms. Doubles $85–$130 w/breakfast. AE, DC, MC, V. Bus: 2, 3, 4. BART/Muni: Powell St. Cable car: Powell lines. Map p 139.*

Grant Plaza CHINATOWN   This no-frills bargain has clean, compact rooms and bathrooms. Sixth-floor rooms are newer and a bit quieter. The hotel does not have a kitchen. *465 Grant Ave. (at Pine St.)* ☎ *415/434-3883. www.grantplaza.com. 72 units. Doubles $89–$99. AE, DC, DISC, MC, V. Bus: 30, 45. Map p 139.*

The Best Lodging

★ The Handlery Union Square

UNION SQUARE   The central location and outdoor pool are the draws. Poolside club rooms are nice, but the dark lobby and long hallways detract. *351 Geary St. (between Powell & Mason sts.)* ☎ *800/843-4343 or 415/781-7800. www.handley.com. 377 units. Doubles $149–$289. AE, DC, DISC, MC, V. Bus: 2, 3, 4, 38. BART/Muni: Powell St. Cable car: Powell lines. Map p 139.*

★★★ Harbor Court Hotel

FINANCIAL DISTRICT   Boutique hotel with chic decor and fine bay views. A YMCA fitness center and pool are next door, and its slick restaurant, Ozumo (p 111) is downstairs. *165 Steuart St. (between Mission & Howard sts.)* ☎ *800/346-0555 or 415/882-1300. www.harborcourthotel. com. 131 units. Doubles $139–$209. Bus: 12. Muni: Folsom & Embarcadero. Map p 140.*

★ Hostelling International— Fisherman's Wharf

FISHERMAN'S WHARF/MARINA   Free breakfast, woodsy location, bay views, free parking, and cheap rates make up for the bunk beds and shared showers. *Fort Mason, Building 240. (N. on Franklin St. past Bay St. Franklin St. ends at the hostel).*

☎ *415/771-7277. www.sfhostel.org. 164 beds (8–12 beds per room). Singles $22–$29 w/breakfast. MC, V. Bus: 10, 28. Map p 140.*

★★ Hotel Adagio

UNION SQUARE   New in 2004, the Adagio offers sleek charm for a good price. Double queen rooms are a great deal for families. The in-house Cortez restaurant shines. *550 Geary St. (between Jones & Taylor sts.)* ☎ *800/228-8830 or 415/775-5000. www.thehotel adagio.com. 173 units. Doubles from $185. AE, DC, DISC, MC, V. Bus: 2, 3, 4, 38. BART/Muni: Powell St. Map p 139.*

★ Hotel Bijou

UNION SQUARE   This 1911 building has vibrantly hued, cozy rooms and screens made-in-SF movies nightly in the lobby. On the sketchier side of Union Square. *111 Mason St. (at Eddy St.)* ☎ *800/771-1022 or 415/ 771-1200. www.hotelbijou.com. 65 units. Doubles $109–$159. AE, DC, DISC, MC, V. BART/Muni: Powell St. Map p 139.*

★ The Hotel Boheme

NORTH BEACH   This inn has an intimate feel and extras like afternoon sherry, but the tiny bathrooms have showers only. Get a room at the back, off noisy Columbus Street.

The Harbor Court Hotel is situated inside the historic Embarcadero YMCA spa building.

444 Columbus Ave. (between Vallejo & Green sts.) ☎ 415/433-9111. www.hotelboheme.com. 16 units. Doubles $164–$184. AE, DC, DISC, MC, V. Bus: 15, 30, 41. Map p 140.

★ kids **Hotel Del Sol** COW HOLLOW   A 1960s motel livened up with paint and palm trees. Rooms are compact, but it's quiet, has a small pool, and parking is free. 3100 Webster St. (at Greenwich St.) ☎ 877/433-5765 or 415/921-5520. www.thehoteldelsol.com. 57 units. Doubles $145–$165 w/breakfast. AE, DC, DISC, MC, V. Bus: 30. Map p 140.

★★ **Hotel Drisco** PACIFIC HEIGHTS   Stylish exclusivity in an elegant neighborhood. The 1903 building has all the amenities of a top-tier hotel, except parking. 2901 Pacific Ave. (at Broderick St.) ☎ 800/634-7277 or 415/346-2880. www.hoteldrisco.com. 48 units. Doubles $245 w/breakfast. AE, DC, DISC, MC, V. Bus: 1, 3, 41, 45. Map p 140.

★★ **The Hotel Griffon** FINANCIAL DISTRICT   Highlights at this boutique inn include mahogany headboards, marble vanities, whitewashed exposed brick walls, and some stellar views. 155 Steuart St. (between Mission & Howard sts.) ☎ 800/321-2201 or 415/495-2100. www.hotelgriffon.com. 62 units. Doubles $175–$375. AE, DC, DISC, MC, V. Bus: 12. BART/Muni: Embarcadero. Map p 140.

★ **The Hotel Majestic** PACIFIC HEIGHTS Ornately furnished in European antiques, the Majestic is an escape from the rough edges of modern living. 1500 Sutter St. (between Octavia & Gough sts.)

☎ 800/869-8966 or 415/922-3200. www.thehotelmajestic.com. 58 units. Doubles $200 w/breakfast. AE, DC, DISC, MC, V. Bus: 2, 3, 4. Map p 140.

kids **Hotel Metropolis** UNION SQUARE   The family suite has a special kids' room with bunk bed and toys. Decor is nice, but rooms are small and the location iffy. 25 Mason St. (at Turk St.) ☎ 800/ 553-1900 or 415/775-4600. www. hotelmetropolis.com. 105 units. Doubles $75–$125. AE, DC, DISC, MC, V. BART/Muni: Powell St. Map p 140.

Hotel Milano SOMA   Location is the top draw at this small, modern hotel. The upholstery is fading, but rates are attractive. Room sizes vary. 55 5th St. (between Market & Mission sts.) ☎ 800/398-7555. www. hotelmilano.citysearch.com. 108 units. Doubles $109–$299. AE, DC, DISC, MC, V. BART/Muni: Powell St. Map p 140.

★★ **Hotel Monaco** UNION SQUARE   Vivid Art Deco design and many amenities, like a renovated spa, Aveda products, and evening wine tasting. Pets welcome. The popular Grand Café (p 106) is downstairs. 501 Geary St. (at Taylor St.) ☎ 800/214-4220 or 415/292-0100. www.monaco-sf.com. 201 units. Doubles $199–$299. AE, DC, DISC, MC, V. Bus: 2, 3, 4, 27, 38. BART/ Muni: Powell St. Cable car: Powell lines. Map p 139.

★★ **Hotel Nikko** UNION SQUARE Rooms are large, light, and well furnished. The atrium houses a large pool, fitness center,

Guppy Love: at the Hotel Monaco, you can order a companion goldfish for your room.

The Best Lodging

and hot tubs. Good weekend rates at this biz hotel. *222 Mason St. (between Ellis & O'Farrell sts.)* ☎ 415/394-1111. www.hotelnikko sf.com. 532 units. Doubles from $350. AE, DC, DISC, MC, V. Bus: 27, 38. Cable car: Powell lines. Map p 139.

★★ **Hotel Palomar** SOMA   On the top five floors of a historic building, Palomar is luxurious but lacks the grand common areas and superlative service of SF's most elite hotels. *12 4th St. (at Market St.)* ☎ 877/294-9711 or 415/348-1111. www.hotelpalomar.com. 198 units. Doubles from $329. AE, DC, DISC, MC, V. BART/Muni: Powell St. Map p 139.

★★ **Hotel Rex** UNION SQUARE Plush 1930s decor in the lobby and rooms. Request a room overlooking the courtyard; it will be quieter than the Sutter-side rooms. *562 Sutter St. (between Powell & Mason sts.)* ☎ 800/433-4434 or 415/433-4434. www.thehotelrex.com. 94 units. Doubles $245–$255. AE, DC, DISC, MC, V. Bus: 2, 3, 4. BART/Muni: Powell St. Map p 139.

★★ **Hotel Triton** UNION SQUARE A rock 'n' roll–themed hotel with suites designed by famous musicians, eco-friendly floors, complimentary Friday-night wine parties (with DJ, tarot-card readings, and chair massages!). Rooms are tiny. (at Bush St.) Free Wi-Fi. *342 Grant Ave.* ☎ 800/433-6611 or 415/394-0500. www.hoteltriton.com. 140 units. Doubles $149–$189. AE, DC, DISC, MC, V. Bus: 2, 3, 4, 15, 30. BART/Muni: Montgomery St. Map p 139.

★★★ **The Huntington Hotel** NOB HILL   A discreet but very upscale Nob Hill choice. Rooms are sizable and seven suites have kitchens. The hotel's spa is magnificent. *1075 California St. (at Powell St.)* ☎ 800/227-4683 or 415/474-5400. www.huntingtonhotel.com.

135 units. Doubles $315–$375. AE, DC, DISC, MC, V. Bus: 1. Cable cars: All. Map p 139.

★ **kids Hyatt at Fisherman's Wharf** FISHERMAN'S WHARF Best of the wharf chain hotels. Nice outdoor pool, but, with 28 TVs, the restaurant is like a sports bar. *555 N. Point St. (between Jones & Taylor sts.)* ☎ 800/233-1234 or 415/563-1234. www.fishermanswharf.hyatt. com. 313 units. Doubles $168–$268. AE, DC, DISC, MC, V. Bus: 10, 30. Streetcar: F. Map p 140.

★ **Hyatt Regency San Francisco** FINANCIAL DISTRICT   This corporate hotel has a 17-story atrium, spacious rooms, some fine views, and the Embarcadero Center next door. *5 Embarcadero Center. (at Market St. by The Embarcadero.)* ☎ 800/233-1234 or 415/788-1234. www.sanfrancisco.regency.hyatt. com. 805 units. Doubles $179–$320. AE, DC, DISC, MC, V. BART/Muni: Embarcadero. Map p 140.

The Mark Hopkins Hotel sits on the site of the former mansion (destroyed in the 1906 earthquake) of Mark Hopkins, one of the founders the Southern Pacific Railroad.

Kitchens are included in some of the Laurel Inn's affordable units.

★★ The Inn at Union Square

UNION SQUARE   An intimate inn with airy rooms, attentive staff, snacks throughout the day, and many repeat customers. *440 Post St. (between Mason & Powell sts.)* ☎ *800/288-4346 or 415/397-3510. 30 units. Doubles $159–$189 w/breakfast. AE, DC, DISC, MC, V. Bus: 2, 3, 4. Cable car: Powell lines. BART/Muni: Powell St. Map p 139.*

★★★ InterContinental Mark Hopkins

NOB HILL   The plush rooms have stellar views and the Top of Mark is a stunning place to dine. An extra $50 per day grants access to the club lounge and free food. *Number One Nob Hill. (at Mason & California sts.)* ☎ *800/327-0200 or 415/392-3434. www.markhopkins.net. 380 units. Doubles $355–$485. AE, DC, DISC, MC, V. Bus: 1. Cable cars: All. Map p 139.*

★ Jackson Court

PACIFIC HEIGHTS   Rooms in this brown-stone mansion, set in SF's most posh neighborhood, are furnished with antique pieces, and four rooms have fireplaces. *2198 Jackson St. (at Buchanan St.)* ☎ *415/929-7670. www.jacksoncourt.com. 10 units. Doubles $150–$225 w/breakfast. AE, DC, DISC, MC, V. Bus: 12, 22. Map p 140.*

★ King George Hotel

UNION SQUARE   Popular with European tourists, this 1912 hotel offers modern amenities and handsome, albeit petite, rooms. On weekends and holidays English afternoon tea is served in the hotel's Windsor Tea Room. *334 Mason St. (between Geary & O'Farrell sts.) 800/288-6005 or 415/781-5050. www.kinggeorge. com. 152 units. Doubles $140. AE, DC, DISC, MC, V. Bus: 2, 3, 4, 38. Cable car: Powell lines. BART/Muni: Powell St. Map p 139.*

★★ kids The Laurel Inn

PACIFIC HEIGHTS   This inn is great for families and longer stays. Many rooms have kitchens, and bus lines are convenient. *444 Presidio Ave. (at California St.)* ☎ *800/555-8735 or 415/567-8467. www.thelaurelinn. com. 49 units. Doubles $155–$180 w/breakfast. AE, DC, DISC, MC, V. Bus: 1, 3, 4, 43. Map p 140.*

The affordable Marina Motel was built in the 1930s to celebrate the opening of the Golden Gate Bridge.

★★★ Mandarin Oriental FINANCIAL DISTRICT

Atop one of SF's tallest buildings, the Mandarin affords jaw-dropping views from every room and regal service. *222 Sansome St. (between Pine & California sts.)* ☎ *800/622-0404 or 415/276-9600. www.mandarinoriental.com. 158 units. Doubles $260–$475. AE, DC, DISC, MC, V. BART/Muni: Montgomery St. Cable car: California. Map p 140.*

★ The Marina Inn MARINA

Personal feel and friendly staff make this the best low-priced option. Inside rooms are quieter than Lombard Street rooms. *3110 Octavia St. (at Lombard St.)* ☎ *800/274-1420 or 415/928-1000. www.marinainn.com. 40 units. Doubles $65–$135 w/breakfast. AE, DC, DISC, MC, V. Bus: 28, 30, 43. Map p 140.*

★ Marina Motel MARINA

The updated rooms have pleasant decor and fridges and coffeemakers. Kitchenette units are rented by the week. Avoid rooms facing noisy Lombard St. *2576 Lombard St.* ☎ *800/346-6118 or 415/921-9406. www.marinamotel.com. 38 units. Doubles $69–$109. AE, DISC, MC, V. Bus: 28, 30, 43. Map p 140.*

★★ Monticello Inn UNION SQUARE

A literary-themed hotel with an inviting lobby, tasteful rooms, central location, and decent (for SF) rates. Check the Web for hot deals. *127 Ellis St. (between Powell & Mason sts.)* ☎ *800/669-7777 or 415/392-8800. www.monticelloinn.com. 91 units. Doubles $109–$289. AE, DC, DISC, MC, V. BART/Muni: Powell St. Cable car: Powell lines. Map p 139.*

★★ Nob Hill Lambourne NOB HILL

Each large room has a deep tub, kitchenette, and minibar snacks (most are organic). This true find fills up quickly and offers a complimentary wine (organic) and cheese (not organic) reception daily from 6 to 7 pm. *725 Pine St. (between Powell & Stockton sts.)* ☎ *800/274-8466 or 415/433-2287. www.nobhilllambourne.com. 20 units. Doubles $139–$189 w/breakfast. AE, DC, DISC, MC, V. Bus: 30, 45. Cable car: All. Map p 139.*

★★ Orchard Hotel UNION SQUARE

Basic business hotel in a central location with perks like free internet (in-room), loaner DVD's, and CD's, plus plush robes and Aveda toiletries. *665 Bush St (between Powell & Stockton sts.),* ☎ *415/362-8878. www.theorchardhotel.com. Doubles $139–$419 w/breakfast. AE, DC, DISC, MC, V. BART/Muni: Powell St. Cable car: All. Map p 139.*

★★ The Palace Hotel SOMA

The over-the-top decor includes the landmark Garden Court Restaurant (p 105). The large rooms have 14-foot ceilings and marble bathrooms. *2 New Montgomery St. (at Market St.)* ☎ *415/512-1111. www.sfpalace.com. 552 units. Doubles $499–$539. AE, DC, DISC, MC, V. BART/Muni: Montgomery St. Map p 140.*

★★ Pan Pacific Hotel UNION SQUARE

This luxury Asian chain has a massive atrium and sizable rooms. Corporate guests like the superlative

Kick back and relive Flower Power in the Flower Child Room of the Red Victorian B&B.

service and LCD TVs. *500 Post St. (at Mason St.)* ☎ *415/771-8600. www.panpacific.com. 329 units. Doubles $360–$420. AE, DC, DISC, MC, V. Bus: 2, 3, 4. Cable car: Powell lines. BART/Muni: Powell St. Map p 139.*

The Phoenix Hotel CIVIC CENTER   A So Cal rocker hotel with palm trees and a pool. Its Bambuddha Lounge is great for a party, but not a quiet sleep. Iffy neighborhood. *602 Eddy St. (at Larkin St.)* ☎ *800/248-9466 or 415/776-1380. www.thephoenixhotel.com. 44 units. Doubles $165–$195. AE, DC, DISC, MC, V. Bus: 19, 31. Map p 141.*

★ **Radisson Miyako Hotel** JAPANTOWN   Renovated in 2002, this serene Eastern hotel overlooking Japan Center offers Western-style rooms or Eastern rooms with tatami mats and futons. *1625 Post St. (at Laguna St.)* ☎ *800/533-4557 or 415/922-3200. www.radisson.com. 218 units. Doubles $149–$229. AE, DC, DISC, MC, V. Bus: 2, 3, 4, 38. Map p 140.*

★ **Red Victorian B&B** HAIGHT There should be a sign in front of this lovely and eccentric Haight-Ashbury

inn that reads WELCOME BACK TO 1967. Each room has its own theme, such as the Flower Child Room. *1665 Haight St. (at Belvedere St.)* ☎ *415/864-1978 or 415/296-7465. www.redvic.com. 19 units (6 w/private bath). Doubles $86–$200. AE, DC, DISC, MC, V. Bus: 6, 7, 43, 66, 71. Muni: Carl & Cole. Map p 140.*

★★★ **Ritz-Carlton** NOB HILL The Ritz has impeccable service, regal decor, and prices to match. Even by local standards, the $50 valet parking fee is high. *600 Stockton St. (at California St.)* ☎ *800/241-3333 or 415/296-7465. www.ritz-carlton.com. 336 units. Doubles $500 & up. AE, DC, DISC, MC, V. Cable car: All. Map p 139.*

San Remo Hotel FISHERMAN'S WHARF   A budget European-style *pensione* with period furnishings and beveled glass. No phones, TVs, or en suite bathrooms. *2237 Mason St. (between Chestnut & Francisco sts.)* ☎ *800/352-7366 or 415/776-8688. www.sanremohotel.com. 62 units. Doubles $75–$85. AE, DC, MC, V. Bus: 10, 15, 30. Streetcar: F. Cable car: Powell-Mason. Map p 140.*

★ **The Savoy** UNION SQUARE
The well-priced Savoy offers French ambience and pluses like feather beds and down pillows. Minuses are tiny rooms and Sutter Street noise. *580 Geary Blvd. (between Taylor & Jones sts.)* ☎ *800/227-4223 or 415/ 441-0124. www.thesavoyhotel.com. 83 units. Doubles $119–$139. AE, DC, DISC, MC, V. Bus: 2, 3, 4, 27, 38. BART/Muni: Powell St. Map p 139.*

★★ **Serrano Hotel** UNION SQUARE   The 1920s building has small, lushly designed rooms and well-stocked bathrooms. A tarot-card reader drops by the evening wine reception. *405 Taylor St. (at O'Farrell St.)* ☎ *415/885-2500 or 877/294-9709. www.serranohotel. com. 236 units. Doubles $139–$299. AE, DC, DISC, MC, V. Bus: 2, 3, 4, 27, 38. BART/Muni: Powell St. Cable car: Powell lines. Map p 139.*

★ **The Sheehan** UNION SQUARE
This former YMCA has the largest heated indoor pool in town. Despite rug stains and old fixtures, the big rooms and central locale are a bargain. *620 Sutter St. (at*

The stylish doormen at the Sir Francis Drake bring an air of nostalgia to this European Renaissance-style landmark.

Mason St.) ☎ *415/775-6500 or 800/ 848-1529. www.sheehanhotel.com. 65 units. Doubles $85–$115 w/breakfast. AE, DC, DISC, MC, V. Bus: 2, 3, 4. BART/Muni: Powell St. Cable car: Powell lines. Map p 139.*

Sir Francis Drake UNION SQUARE   Despite the grandiose lobby and beefeater-clad doormen, stay here only if you get a great deal. The tiny rooms are not as well maintained as the lobby. *450 Powell St. (at Sutter St.)* 800/227-5490 or 415/392-7755. www.sirfrancisdrake. com. 417 units. Doubles $239–$259. AE, DC, DISC, MC, V. Bus: 2, 3, 4. BART/Muni: Powell St. Cable car: Powell lines. Map p 139.*

★★ **Tuscan Inn** FISHERMAN'S WHARF   A pleasant wharf option with nicely furnished guest rooms, lots of amenities, free morning coffee and evening wine, and a friendly staff. *425 N. Point St. (at Mason St.)* ☎ *800/648-4626 or 415/561-1100. www.tuscaninn.com. 221 units. Doubles $139–$189. AE, DC, DISC, MC, V. Bus: 10, 15. Streetcar: F. Map p 140.*

★★ **W Hotel** SOMA   This ultrahip hotel next door to the SFMOMA has sleek rooms, great views, and 24-hour concierge services dubbed "whatever/whenever." *181 3rd St. (at Howard St.)* ☎ *415/777-5300. www.whotels.com. 423 units. Doubles $179–$509. AE, DC, DISC, MC, V. Bus: 15, 30, 45. BART/Muni: Montgomery St. Map p 140.*

Westin St. Francis UNION SQUARE   Despite its vast size, the hotel's historic feel and location right on Union Square make it popular. Room sizes vary, so phone in-house reservations. *335 Powell St. (at Geary St.)* ☎ *800/WESTIN-1 or 415/397-7000. www.westin.com. 1,195 units. Doubles $129–$569. AE, DC, DISC, MC, V. Bus: 2, 3, 4, 30, 45. BART/Muni: Powell St. Cable car: Powell lines. Map p 139.* ●

Sausalito

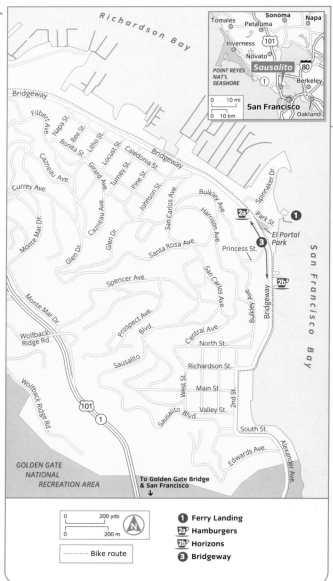

Richardson Bay

Bridgeway

Filbert Ave.
Napa St.
Bee St.
Bonita St.
Litho St.
Locust St.
Caledonia St.
Cazneau Ave.
Currey Ave.
Girard Ave.
Turney St.
Pine St.
Johnson St.
Bridgeway

Bulkley Ave.
Spinnaker Dr.
Park St.
1

2a
El Portal Park
3
Princess St.

San Carlos Ave.
Harrison Ave.
Bulkley Ave.
Bridgeway
2b

Monte Mar Dr.
Glen Dr.
Cazneau Ave.
Glen Dr.
Santa Rosa Ave.

Spencer Ave.

San Carlos Ave.

Monte Mar Dr.
Prospect Ave.
Blvd.
Central Ave.
North St.

Wolfback Ridge Rd.
Sausalito
Richardson St.
West St.
Main St.
2nd St.
Valley St.

Wolfback Ridge Rd.
101
1
Sausalito Blvd.
South St.

Edwards Ave.
Alexander Ave.

GOLDEN GATE
NATIONAL
RECREATION AREA

To Golden Gate Bridge
& San Francisco
↓

San Francisco Bay

Inset map:
Tomales
Sonoma
Napa
Petaluma
Inverness
101
Novato
POINT REYES
NAT'L
SEASHORE
Sausalito
80
Berkeley
1
San Francisco
Oakland
0   10 mi
0   10 km

0   200 yds
0   200 m

.... Bike route

1 Ferry Landing
2a Hamburgers
2b Horizons
3 Bridgeway

Eclectic Sausalito, a slightly bohemian, nonchalant, quaint adjunct to San Francisco, contains fewer than 8,000 residents. Although this is a town with a fair quota of paper millionaires, they rub their permanently suntanned shoulders with a good number of hard-up artists, struggling authors, shipyard workers, and fishermen. This is a great excursion to admire the view of the lofty hills of Marin County that so stunningly frame the San Francisco Bay and to stroll Bridgeway, the offbeat, boutique-lined main drag in town. 🕐 **3 to 4 hours. START: SF Ferry Building Downtown at the Embarcadero & Mission St. or Pier 41. Streetcar: F. BART/MUNI: Embarcadero or Pier 41 (Fisherman's Wharf). Bus: 30.**

1 kids ★★ FERRY FROM SAN FRANCISCO. Bundle up and skim across the bay from SF on the delightful and scenic ferry. Grab your camera and snap a perfect shot of **Alcatraz** (p 10), the Golden Gate Bridge, and downtown San Francisco. 🕐 *30 min., one-way. From Downtown (at the SF Ferry Building, p 15, bullet* **2***), take the Golden Gate Ferry Service (☎ 415/ 923-2000; www.goldengateferry.org). Streetcar: F. BART/Muni: Embarcadero. Bus: 30. One-way $6.15, $3.05 seniors, $4.60 kids 6–12, free for children under 6. Daily schedule varies. From Pier 41 (Fisherman's Wharf),*

Sunny Sausalito's steep, picturesque hills flank the sparkling San Francisco Bay.

take the Blue & Gold Fleet (☎ 415/ 705-5555; www.blueandgoldfleet. com). One-way $7.25, $4 kids 5–11, free for kids under 5. Daily schedule varies. Note: To reach Sausalito by bus, bike, or car (via the Golden Gate Bridge), see p 38.

2A Pick up lunch at tiny eatery **Hamburgers** *(737 Bridgeway, near the Marina;* ☎ *415/332-9471; $)* and enjoy it in the park by the Marina. Besides the popular burgers, chicken sandwiches and vegetarian burritos are on offer, as well as to-die-for fries. Alternatively, head to **2B** **Horizons** *(558 Bridgeway;* ☎ *415/331-3232; $$)* and grab a bite (or a leisurely cocktail) at this seafood-oriented fave. Try to sit on the alfresco waterside terrace, which boasts stellar views of the SF skyline and the bay.

3 Bridgeway. Stroll along Bridgeway and pop into some of the dozens of fine galleries and boutiques. My favorites are **Sausalito Art Collection**, specializing in California artists *(589 Bridgeway;* ☎ *415/339-9250),* and **Petri's Gallery** *(675 Bridgeway;* ☎ *415/332-2225),* featuring hand-blown glass and delicate jewelry.

Point Reyes National Seashore

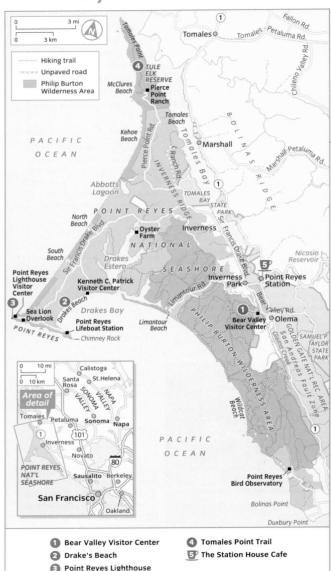

0   3 mi
0   3 km

······· Hiking trail
━━━━━ Unpaved road
▨ Philip Burton Wilderness Area

Fallon Rd.
Tomales
Tomales - Petaluma Rd.
Chileno Valley Rd.

Tomales Point
④ TULE ELK RESERVE
McClures Beach
Pierce Point Ranch
Tomales Beach

B O L I N A S   R I D G E

PACIFIC OCEAN

Kehoe Beach
Marshall

Pierce Point Rd.
INVERNESS RIDGE
Ranch Rd.

Abbotts Lagoon

TOMALES BAY STATE PARK

P O I N T   R E Y E S

North Beach
Oyster Farm
Inverness

N A T I O N A L

Sir Francis Drake Blvd.

Drakes Estero

South Beach

S E A S H O R E

Nicasio Reservoir

Point Reyes Lighthouse Visitor Center
Kenneth C. Patrick Visitor Center

Inverness Park
⑤ Point Reyes Station

③ Sea Lion Overlook
② Drakes Beach
Point Reyes Lifeboat Station
— Chimney Rock

Drakes Bay

Limantour Rd.

P H I L I P   B U R T O N

① Bear Valley Visitor Center
Olema

POINT REYES

Limantour Beach

W I L D E R N E S S   A R E A

Bear Valley Rd.

San Andreas Fault Zone
Olema Creek
GOLDEN GATE NAT'L REC AREA
SAMUEL P. TAYLOR STATE PARK

Wildcat Beach

PACIFIC OCEAN

Point Reyes Bird Observatory

Bolinas Point

Duxbury Point

0   10 mi
0   10 km

Area of detail

Calistoga
St. Helena
Santa Rosa
SONOMA VALLEY
NAPA VALLEY
Petaluma
Sonoma
Napa
① Tomales
101
Inverness
Novato
80
Sausalito
Berkeley
POINT REYES NAT'L SEASHORE
San Francisco
Oakland

① Bear Valley Visitor Center
② Drake's Beach
③ Point Reyes Lighthouse
④ Tomales Point Trail
⑤ The Station House Cafe

Point Reyes National Seashore was created to protect rural and undeveloped stretches of the coast and is part of the National Park system. It's a rugged mix of wild coastline and forest of unequivocal appeal to hikers, nature lovers, and wildlife enthusiasts. The rocky shore is a direct result of earthquake activity—the San Andreas Fault separates Point Reyes, the northernmost landmass on the Pacific Plate, from the rest of California, which rests on the North American Plate. In fact, Point Reyes is moving towards Alaska at the rate of 2 inches a year—during the 1906 earthquake, it jumped north 20 feet! This tour takes all day. START: **Rent a car (p 163), cross the Golden Gate Bridge, and head north on US 101. Exit onto Sir Francis Drake Boulevard and take Highway 1 north to Olema. Driving time is around 90 minutes.**

1 The **Bear Valley Visitor Center,** a visitor center for Point Reyes National Seashore, has ecological and historical exhibits, as well as a seismograph and weather station. Pick up a detailed trail map and chat with the helpful, friendly park rangers. You can take a ranger-led guided tour (call ahead) or inquire about activities like biking, horseback riding, and wildlife viewing. *Bear Valley Rd. (look for the sign north of Olema on Hwy 1).* ☎ *415/464-5100. www.nps.gov/pore. Weekdays 9am–5pm; weekends 8am–5pm. Free admission. Best time: weekdays.*

2 **Drake's Beach.** Take a walk along this sublime beach backed by white sandstone cliffs. Just don't swim—the water is frigid and the undertow dangerous. Don't turn your back on the sea, as occasional powerful "sneaker waves" can suddenly come to shore.

3 **Point Reyes Lighthouse.** You'll drive by dairy farms and pastures to reach this dramatic vista point—look for the sea lions and harbor seals. In winter, you may catch sight of gray whales on their 5,000-mile journey north from Mexico. *Open Thurs–Mon 10am–4:30pm.* ☎ *415/669-1534. Stairs to lighthouse closed when winds exceed 40 mph. (Lighthouse is 300 steps down from center; no wheelchair*

ramp.) *Free admission. On busy winter weekends a shuttle ($5, kids 16 & under free) takes visitors from Drake's beach to the lighthouse. Call* ☎ *415/464-5100 for details.*

4 **Tomales Point Trail.** The northern tip of Point Reyes boasts sweeping views of the rocky coast; in spring, it also contains a breathtaking array of wildflowers, and July to October offer the best viewing of the 500 elk living on a protected reserve on this peninsula. Bring binoculars.

5 **The Station House Cafe** is a, low-key favorite where the daily specials draw on organic, local ingredients with a selection of fine California wines and beer. *11180 State Rte. 1.* ☎ *415/663-1515. $.*

The Point Reyes lighthouse is the top lookout point for whales and sea lions.

A **Wine Country** Detour

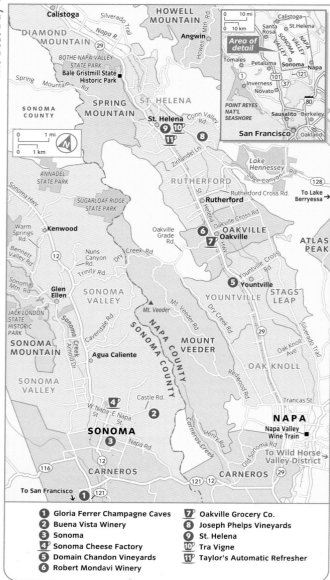

1. Gloria Ferrer Champagne Caves
2. Buena Vista Winery
3. Sonoma
4. Sonoma Cheese Factory
5. Domain Chandon Vineyards
6. Robert Mondavi Winery
7. Oakville Grocery Co.
8. Joseph Phelps Vineyards
9. St. Helena
10. Tra Vigne
11. Taylor's Automatic Refresher

Napa and Sonoma valleys are home to over 400 wineries and two of the finest, most productive winegrowing regions in the world. But remember, those sips add up; drinking-and-driving rules still apply. My recommendation is this: Choose no more than three to four wineries to visit (I've listed five of my favorites), pick up a gourmet picnic lunch along the way (many wineries boast delightful picnic areas), and indulge in a sit-down meal at the end of the day. This is a full-day tour and includes dinner—you'll need to leave SF in the morning, and you won't return until the late evening. START: **Rent a car (p 163), cross the Golden Gate Bridge, and head north on US 101. Exit at Hwy. 37; after 10 miles (16km) turn north onto Calif. 121. Driving time is just over an hour.**

❶ ★★ **Gloria Ferrer Champagne Caves.** Gloria Ferrer is the wife of José Ferrer (d. 1992), whose family is the world's largest producer of sparkling wine. This regal estate offers sweeping views of the verdant Carneros District. Take the free tour of the fermenting tanks, bottling line, and caves brimming with racks of yeast-laden bottles. Unless you are averse to sipping bubbly before lunch, arrive by 11am for the first free tour of the day. The winery will be least crowded then. *2355 Carneros Hwy. (Calif. 121), Sonoma.* ☎ *707/ 996-7256. www.gloriaferrer.com. Daily 10am–5:30pm. Tours (free) daily 11am–4pm. Tastings: $2–$7.50. Hwy. 101N. Exit at Hwy. 37, then north on Calif. 121.*

❷ ★ **Buena Vista Winery.** Hungarian Count Agoston Haraszthy established this winery in 1857. In 1861 he brought 100,000 of the finest vine cuttings from European wine regions and made them available to all local growers—essentially founding California's wine industry. Although Buena Vista's winemaking now takes place at another facility, their tasting room is located within this restored 1862 press house. *1800 Old Winery Rd., Sonoma.* ☎ *800/ 926-1266 or 707/938-1266. www. buenavistawinery.com. Daily 10am– 5pm. Free self-guided tours all day;*

Visiting a tasting room in Napa & Sonoma is decadent, fun, and educational.

$15 guide "heritage tours" daily at 11am & 2pm. Tastings: $5. Calif. 121N to Napa St. & turn right. Take Napa St. to Old Winery Rd.

❸ ★ **Sonoma.** This charming town was designed after a typical Mexican village and includes charming duck ponds, a central plaza framed by adobe buildings, and a monument marking where the Bear Flag was raised in 1846, signaling the end of Mexican rule. The bear symbol was later adopted into California's state flag. **Note:** *The plaza contains picnic tables—perfect if you prefer to pick up food and eat in town rather than picnic at a vineyard. Plaza located at Broadway (Hwy. 12) & Napa St.*

4 Sonoma Cheese Factory. Pick up a snack or picnic lunch at this venerable local favorite; options include caviar, homemade cheese, gourmet salads, and sandwiches. *2 Spain St.* ☎ *707/996-1000. $$.*

5 ★★ Domain Chandon Vineyards. The grounds of the valley's most renowned sparkling-wine maker, founded by French champagne house Moët et Chandon, are predictably grand. Take the free winery tour, or simply enjoy the tastings ($9–$14). *1 California Dr. (at Hwy. 29), Yountville.* ☎ *707/944-2280. www.chandon.com. Call ahead; hours vary by season.*

6 ★ Robert Mondavi Winery. Forget notions of mass-market wines. Mondavi's reserve reds are excellent. Moreover, the tours at this winery are among the most extensive in Napa. The basic, free tour includes an excursion into the vineyards. Reservations for it and other, more detailed tours are recommended. *7801 St. Helena Hwy. (Hwy. 29), Oakville.* ☎ *800/MONDAVI or 707/226-1395. www.robertmondaviwinery.com. Tastings: $5–$8. Daily 10am–4pm.*

7 ★★★ Oakville Grocery Co. One of the finest gourmet-food spots in the area, here you can pick up an array of top-quality fare like fresh foie gras, bread, cheese, sandwiches, salads, and California wines, plus coffee drinks from the in-store espresso bar. (The staff can also prepare a picnic basket for you—call 24 hr. in advance.) *7856 St. Helena Hwy. (at Oakville Cross Rd), Oakville.* ☎ *707/944-8802. www. oakvillegrocery.com. $.*

8 ★★ Joseph Phelps Vineyards. This modern, state-of-the-art winery with a big-city vibe is a

Special tours at the Mondavi winery include a stroll through their barrel rooms.

favorite stop for serious wine lovers. The tours are intimate and comprehensive, and the wines are a knock-out. *Taplin Rd. (off the Silverado Trail), St. Helena.* ☎ *800/707-5789. www.jpvwines.com. Tastings: $6–$12. Mon–Sat 9am–5pm; Sun 9am–4pm.*

9 St. Helena. This quiet, attractive little town with an Old West feel has expensive boutiques, beautiful old homes, and first-rate restaurants. *Located 6 miles north of Oakville on Calif. 121.*

10 Tra Vigne. Dine at one of the valley's favorite haunts, which features Italian-style California cuisine *(1050 Charter Oak Ave., St. Helena;* ☎ *707/963-4444. www. travignerestaurant.com. $$)* or for a more casual option, try the best diner you'll ever visit: **11 Taylor's Automatic Refresher,** established in 1949, serves naturally raised beef burgers, ahi tuna burgers, tacos, and incredible milkshakes *(933 Main St., St. Helena.* ☎ *707/963-3486. www.taylorsrefresher.com. $).* ●

The
Savvy Traveler

Before You Go

Tourist Office

Contact the **SAN FRANCISCO CON-VENTION AND VISITORS BUREAU,** 900 Market St., Lower Level, Hallidie Plaza, San Francisco, CA 94142-2809 ☎ *415/391-2000,* for a visitors information kit by mail, or through the website at *www.sfvisitor.org.*

The Best Times to Go

September and October are "Indian summer" months and are a great time to visit the city—the weather is warm and the fog disappears. The summer months from June to August are busy with fun fairs and festivals, but it's cold and foggy. Winter is beautiful and mild, plus, the city is decked out between November and January for Thanksgiving, Christmas, and the New Year's holiday. Spring is pleasant but can be rainy.

Festivals & Special Events

SPRING. Mid- to late April is the time for the **Cherry Blossom Festival** in Japantown. Watch traditional drumming, flower arranging, origami making, or a parade celebrating the cherry blossom and Japanese culture. ☎ *415/563-2313.* Mid-April to early May is when the **San Francisco International Film Festival** takes place around San Francisco, with screenings at the AMC Kabuki 8 Cinemas (Fillmore and Post sts.), and at many other locations. Started in 1957, this is America's oldest film festival. ☎ *415/931-FILM, www. sffs.org.* The Sunday before May 5 brings the **Cinco de Mayo Celebration** in the Mission District. This is when the Latino community celebrates the victory of the Mexicans over the French at Puebla in 1862; mariachi bands, dancers, food, and a parade fill the streets of the Mission.

The parade starts at 10am at 24th and Bryant streets and ends at the Civic Center. The **Bay to Breakers Foot Race** (third Sun of May) runs from the Embarcadero through Golden Gate Park to Ocean Beach. More than 60,000 entrants gather— many dressed in wacky, innovative, and sometimes X-rated costumes— for the approximately 7½-mile (12 km) run. The *San Francisco Examiner* ☎ *415/359-2800; www.examiner. com* sponsors the event. The Mission District's largest annual event, **Carnaval,** is a day of festivities that culminates in a parade on Mission Street. More than half a million spectators line the route, and samba musicians and dancers continue to entertain on 14th Street, near Harrison, at the end of the march. It takes place the Sunday of Memorial Day (last Monday in May) weekend. ☎ *415/920-0125.*

SUMMER. During the first weekend each June, the outdoor **Union Street Art Festival** celebrates San Francisco with gourmet -food booths, music, entertainment, and a juried art show featuring works by more than 350 artists. Contact the Union Street Association. ☎ *415/ 441-7055, www.unionstreetfestival. com.* A far cry from the chic Union Street Fair, the grittier **Haight Street Fair** features alternative crafts, ethnic foods, rock bands, and a healthy number of hippies and street kids whooping it up and slamming beers in front of the blaring rock-'n'-roll stage. ☎ *415/661-8025.* Organizers claim the **North Beach Festival** is the oldest urban street fair in the country. Close to 100,000 city folk meander along Grant Avenue, between Vallejo and Union streets, to eat, drink, and enjoy the arts and crafts booths, poetry readings, swing-dancing venue, and *arte di gesso* (sidewalk chalk art). It usually takes place on Father's Day weekend in mid-June, but call to confirm. ☎ *415/989-2220.* Free concerts take place every Sunday at 2pm between mid-June and late August at the annual **Stern Grove Midsummer Music Festival,** in the Sunset District. Head out early to join the thousands who come here to lie in the grass and enjoy classical, jazz, and ethnic music and dance. Bring warm clothes—the Sunset District can be one of the coldest parts of the city. ☎ *415/252-6252.* Usually the third or last weekend of June, the **San Francisco Lesbian, Gay, Bisexual, Transgender Pride Parade & Celebration** draws up to half a million participants who celebrate all of the above—and then some. The parade proceeds west on Market Street to Market and 8th streets. ☎ *415/864-3733, www.sfpride.org.* The first weekend in July starts with a bang, when the upscale portion of Fillmore closes to traffic and several blocks of arts and crafts, gourmet food, and live jazz fill the street for the **Fillmore Street Jazz Festival** in Pacific Heights. Call for more information. ☎ *510/970-3217.* The **Fourth of July Celebration & Fireworks** at Fisherman's Wharf can be something of a joke—more often than not, fog rolls into the city. Sometimes it's almost impossible to view the million-dollar pyrotechnics from PIER 39 on the northern waterfront. Still, it's a party, and if the skies are clear, it's a darn good show. The **San Francisco Marathon** (usually the second or third weekend in July) is one of the largest marathons in the world. For entry information, contact West End Management, the event organizer. ☎ *800/698-8699 or 415/284-9653; www.runsfm.com.* AUTUMN. You probably won't get to visit all the restaurants you'd like to, but you can get a good sampling at the annual Labor Day weekend (first Monday in Sept) **A La Carte, A La Park,** at Sharon Meadow in Golden Gate Park. Restaurants, microbreweries, and wineries offer tastings. Call for prices. ☎ *415/458-1988.* Also on Labor Day weekend is the **Sausalito Art Festival,** a juried exhibit of more than 180 artists which includes music and international cuisine, enhanced by local wine. Parking is impossible; take the Blue & Gold Fleet ferry ☎ *415/705-5555; www.blueandgoldfleet.com* from Fisherman's Wharf or the Golden Gate Ferry Service ☎ *415/923-2000; www.goldengateferry.org* from downtown at the SF Ferry Building to the festival site. ☎ *415/332-3555, www.sausalitoartfestival.org.* Each year in early September, the San Francisco Opera launches its season with **Opera in the Park** (usually in Sharon Meadow, Golden Gate Park), a free concert featuring a selection of arias. ☎ *415/861-4008.* The largest outdoor blues music event on the West Coast is the late-September **San Francisco Blues Festival** (on the grounds of Fort Mason, the Marina) featuring local and national musicians performing back-to-back during the 3-day extravaganza. ☎ *415/826-6837, www.sfblues.com.* At the end of September, the **Folsom Street Fair** in SoMa is a local favorite for its kinky, outrageous, leather-and-skin gay-centric blowout celebration. It's hard-core, so only open-minded and adventurous types need head this way. ☎ *415/861-3247, www.folsomstreetfair.com.* During **Fleet Week** in October, residents gather along the bay front to watch aerial performances by the Blue Angels, flown in tribute to the U.S. Marines. ☎ *415/705-5500, www.fleetweek.com.* On the first Sunday in October, the **Castro Street Fair** celebrates life in the city's most famous gay neighborhood. ☎ *415/841-1824,* www.castrostreetfair.org. On the first weekend in October, **Reggae in the Park** (Sharon Meadow, Golden Gate Park) draws thousands to dance and celebrate the soulful sounds of reggae. ☎ 415/458-1988. On a Sunday near October 12, the **Italian Heritage Parade** celebrates Columbus's landing in the Americas. The festival includes a parade along Columbus Avenue and sporting events, but mainly, it's a great excuse to hang out in North Beach and people-watch. ☎ 415/434-1492, www.sfcolumbusday.org. **Halloween** (Oct 31) is a huge night in San Francisco. A fantastical parade is organized at Market and Castro streets, and a mixed gay/straight crowd revels in costumes of extraordinary imagination.

WINTER. Late October and early November, the two-week **San Francisco Jazz Festival** presents eclectic programming in an array of fabulous jazz venues throughout the city. ☎ 800/850-SFJF or 415/788-7353, www.sfjazz.org. Each December, the **San Francisco Ballet** performs the holiday classic *The Nutcracker.* Order tickets to this Tchaikovsky tradition well in advance. ☎ 415/865-2000. **Chinese New Year** celebrations spill onto every street in Chinatown, including parades of marching bands, rolling floats, barrages of fireworks, and a block-long dragon writhing in and out of the crowds. The revelry runs for several weeks and wraps up with a memorable parade through Chinatown that starts at Market and 2nd streets and ends at Kearny Street. Chinese New Year begins with the New Moon on the first day of the new calendar year and ends on the full moon 15 days later—thus, dates vary between January and February each year. ☎ 415/982-3000, www.chineseparade.com. On the Sunday before March 17, everyone's an honorary Irish person at the **St. Patrick's Day Parade,** which starts at 12:45pm at Market and 2nd streets and continues to City Hall.

The Weather

San Francisco has a temperate, marine climate, which means relatively mild weather all year round. Summers bring dense fog and low temperatures with highs only in the 70s (20s Celsius). The "Indian summer" of September and October bring temperatures up to the 90s (30s Celsius) but can drop down significantly. Always bring layers as it could be warm in one neighborhood and cold in the next. For up-to-the-minute weather reports, log on to www.sfgate.com/weather.

Useful **Websites**

- SF Gate (local newspapers *Chronicle* and *Examiner* website): www.sfgate.com
- *The Bay Guardian* (local free weekly): www.sfbg.com
- Citysearch: sanfrancisco.citysearch.com
- San Francisco Reservations: www.hotelres.com
- PlanetOut (Gay & Lesbian travel guide): www.planetout.com
- Opentable (Restaurant reservations): www.opentable.com
- Travel guides for families: www.gocitykids.com, www.gokid.org
- Up-to-the-minute worldwide weather reports: www.weather.com

SAN FRANCISCO'S HIGH & LOW DAILY TEMPERATURE & MONTHLY RAINFALL					
	JAN	FEB	MAR	APR	MAY	JUNE
High °F/°C	56/13	59/15	60/16	61/16	63/17	64/18
Low °F/°C	46/8	48/19	49/9	49/9	51/11	53/12
Rain in./cm	4.5/11.5	2.8/7	2.6/6.5	1.5/4	0.4/1	0.2/0.5

	JULY	AUG	SEPT	OCT	NOV	DEC
High °F/°C	64/18	65/18	69/21	68/20	63/17	57/14
Low °F/°C	53/12	54/12	56/13	55/13	52/11	47/8
Rain in./cm	0.1/0.25	0.1/0.25	0.2/0.5	1.1/3	2.5/6.5	3.5/9

Cell (Mobile) Phones

One good wireless rental company is **INTOUCH USA** ☎ *800/872-7626 or 703/222-7161*. In downtown San Francisco, **TRIPTEL MOBILE RENTAL PHONES** ☎ *415/474-3330; 1525 Van Ness Ave., between California and Pine sts.* rents cellular phones at $3 per day, or $15 per week. Airtime rates are 95¢ per minute for domestic calls, with an additional $1.25 per minute for international calls. Triptel also sells SIM cards for foreign travelers bringing their own phones.

Cell phones (mobiles) with triband GSM capabilities work in the U.S.; call your service provider before departing your home country to ensure that the international call bar has been switched off and to check call charges, which can be extremely high. Also remember that you are charged for calls you *receive* on a U.K.

mobile used abroad. U.K. visitors can rent a U.S. phone before leaving home. Contact **CELLHIRE** ☎ *0800/ 610-610; www.cellhire.co.uk.*

Car Rentals

For booking rental cars online, the best deals are usually found at rental-car company websites. U.K. visitors should check **HOLIDAYAUTOS** *(online only; www.holidayautos.co.uk).*

Major car rental companies operating in San Francisco include **AVIS,** ☎ *800/331-1212; 415/929-4555; www.avis.com;* **BUDGET,** ☎ *800/527-0700; 415/928-7864; www.budget.com;* **ENTERPRISE,** ☎ *800/325-8007; 415/837-1700; www.enterprise.com;* **HERTZ,** ☎ *800/654-3131; 415/771-2200; www.hertz.com;* and **THRIFTY,** ☎ *800/367-2277; 415/788-6906; www.thrifty.com.*

Getting **There**

By Plane

Two major airports serve San Francisco: San Francisco International (SFO) and Oakland International Airport, which is across the Bay Bridge off Interstate 880. SFO is closer and more airlines fly into this major hub—most international flights arrive here. Oakland is smaller and easier to navigate, but fares for

cabs and shuttle buses into the city will be about 50% higher. It's worth checking your options flying into either airport, as you'll sometimes find a cheaper or more convenient flight arriving in Oakland; it also often enjoys better weather than San Francisco, where flights can be delayed due to foggy conditions. *For a list of airlines, see p 176.*

Getting to & from the Airport

TAXIS: Rates are around $2.85 for the first mile and $2.25 for each additional mile. From SFO, the approximate fare is $25 to $37 for the 20- to 25- min. trip. From Oakland the fare costs approx $50 and takes 30 to 40 min.

AIRPORT SHUTTLES   SFO: SUPER-SHUTTLE ☎ *800/558-8500 or 415/558-8500*, **BAY SHUTTLE** ☎ *800/564-3400 or 415/564-3400*, and **QUAKE CITY SHUTTLE** ☎ *415/255-4899* charge average rates of $14 per adult and $8 per child. **OAKLAND INTERNATIONAL AIRPORT: BAY-PORTER EXPRESS** ☎ *877/467-1800 or 415/467-1800* charges $26 for the first person and $12 for each additional person; $7 per child.

PUBLIC TRANSPORT (BART, A COMMUTER TRAIN)   FROM SFO: From any terminal, take the free, 5 to 10 min. AIRTRAIN to the BART SF Int'l Airport station, and transfer to the BART train. A one-way ticket from the airport to downtown San Francisco is $4.95 and takes about 35 min. This is the cheapest option of getting into the city.

FROM OAKLAND INTERNATIONAL AIRPORT: Catch the **AIRBART SHUTTLE** ☎ *510/465-2278,* which runs every 15 minutes in front of either terminal. The fare is $2 for adults and 50¢ for children and seniors for the 15-minute ride to the Oakland Coliseum BART station. From there, you'll transfer to a BART train San Francisco. The trip to downtown takes about 20 min.; the fare is $3.15.

By Car

You can get to San Francisco along three major highways. Interstate 5 runs through the center of the state and intersects with Interstate 80, which goes to the Bay Bridge. The drive from Los Angeles to San Francisco on I-5 is about 6 hours. The drive from Los Angeles to San Francisco on 101, a slower option, takes 7 hours.

Drivers arriving from the east will cross the Bay Bridge ($3 toll) and head toward downtown on 5th Street or toward North Beach and Fisherman's Wharf on Fremont Street. Cars coming from the south on Highway 101 will see the city skyline on their left a few miles past Monster Park (the former Candlestick Park). Downtown exits here are either 7th or 4th streets. If you're driving from the coast heading south, you'll enter San Francisco by the Golden Gate Bridge. Once you pass the tollbooth ($5 toll!), exit along the bay to Van Ness Avenue.

By Train & Bus

AMTRAK ☎ *800/872-7245 or 800/USA-RAIL; www.amtrak.com* doesn't stop in San Francisco proper, but lands in Emeryville, just south of Berkeley in the East Bay. From the station, an Amtrak bus takes passengers into downtown San Francisco. The buses stop at the Ferry Building at the foot of Market Street, and at the Cal Train station, where you can catch the streetcar to Embarcadero Station and thus into town. The Ferry Building is more convenient to most of the hotels listed in this book, as long as you manage to hail a cab. The **GREYHOUND LINES** ☎ *415/495-1569; www.greyhound.com* terminal is located at 425 Mission St. (3rd floor) in the Transbay Terminal and is open from 4:45am to 12:15am daily.

Getting **Around**

By Car
Driving in San Francisco can be frustrating. Along with aggressive local drivers, one-way streets, no right/left turns when you really need one, and dead ends, there's a lack of parking, period. Fortunately, it isn't necessary to drive to most of the places you'll want to go. When driving is imperative, rent a car for the day. For those of you who are driving to SF, park at your hotel and use public transportation.

By Taxi
You have to call for cab in San Francisco unless you are boarding one from your hotel. **TAXI COMPANIES: DESOTO CAB** ☎ *415/970-1300*, **LUXOR CABS** ☎ *415/282-4141*, **PACIFIC CAB** ☎ *415/986-7220*, **VETERAN'S CAB** ☎ *415/552-1300*, and **YELLOW CAB** ☎ *415/626-2345*. Rates are around $2.85 for the first mile and $2.25 for each additional mile.

By Muni (Bus, Streetcar, Cable Car & Subway)
The Bay Area has a hodgepodge of transit systems that are all managed by the county. San Francisco's Municipal Railway, known simply as "Muni," operates the city's buses, streetcars, and cable cars. For detailed route information, call Muni or visit its website ☎ *415/673-6864; www.sfmuni. com.* Most routes run from 6am to midnight and some busy routes have night-owl services. Another helpful website is *http://transit.511.org*, which also lists schedules and route maps for all Bay Area transit systems.

Muni Passports can be a bargain for visitors who plan to take buses,

streetcars, or cable cars often. A 1-day Passport is $9, a 3-day Passport is $15, and a 7-day Passport is $20. Special Passports for kids and seniors don't exist, but Muni sells monthly Youth/Discount Passes for $10. Passports and $2 Muni maps (a necessary item) can be purchased at the Visitor Information Center on Hallidie Plaza, at Tix Bay Area on Union Square, and at the baggage-level information booths at SFO. Passes and passports can be found at the cable car ticket booths at Powell and Market or Beach and Hyde streets. Single-day Passports are available onboard the cable cars as well. See also "Passes" on p 170.

By BART
BART, an acronym for **BAY AREA RAPID TRANSIT** ☎ *415/989-2278; www.bart.gov,* connect San Francisco with the East Bay—Oakland, Richmond, Concord, and Fremont. Fares range from $1.25 to $7.10, depending on how far you go. Machines in the stations dispense tickets that are magnetically encoded with a dollar amount. Computerized exits automatically deduct the correct fare. Children 4 and under ride free. Trains run every 15 to 20 minutes, Monday through Friday from 4am to midnight, Saturday from 6am to midnight, and Sunday from 8am to midnight.

On Foot
Seeing the city on foot is a fantastic way to get around—but remember, the hills can kill you.

Fast **Facts**

APARTMENT RENTALS For short-term rentals, your best bet is *www.craigslist.org*. You'll most likely negotiate a rental directly from the unit's owner (or the person subletting). **American Marketing Systems** *www.amsires.com* and **Executive Suites** *www.executivesuites-sf.com* offer furnished apartments for rentals of a few days or more, although rates can be high. To research house exchanges, check out **Homelink International** *www.homelink.org*, which has over 14,000 listings in several countries, and **Homebase Holidays** *www.homebase-hols.com*.

ATMS/CASHPOINTS As in most cities these days, obtaining money is a simple matter of lining up at the nearest ATM and plugging in your bankcard. Unless you go to an ATM from your bank, they all charge fees of $1.50 to $3. The **Cirrus** ☎ *800/424-7787; www.mastercard.com* and **PLUS** ☎ *800/843-7587; www.visa.com* networks span the globe; look at the back of your bankcard to see which network you're on, then call or check online for ATM locations at your destination. Find out your daily withdrawal limit before you depart.

BABYSITTING Most hotel concierges will simply provide referrals to a babysitting service, which guests must then call on their own. Local companies supplying short-term sitters are: **American Child Care Service** ☎ *415/285-2300; www.americanchildcare.com,* **Bay Area 2nd Mom** ☎ *888/926-3666; www.2ndmom.com,* and **Town & Country Resources** ☎ *800/398-8810 or 415/567-0956; www.tandcr.com.* For $100 per child, you can give kids a memorable night out through the **Explorer's Club** ☎ *415/902-7014; www.eckidsclub.com.*

BANKING HOURS Most banks are open Monday through Friday from 9am to 5pm. Many banks also have ATMs for 24-hour banking.

B&BS Go to **Bed & Breakfast Inns Online** ☎ *615/868-1946; www.bbonline.com* or **Pamela Lanier's Bed & Breakfasts** *www.lanierbb.com.*

BIKE RENTALS If you want to bike along the Golden Gate Promenade over the Golden Gate Bridge over to Sausalito, your best bet is **Blazing Saddles,** 1095 Columbus Ave. and Pier 41, Fisherman's Wharf ☎ *415/202-8888.* Rental prices ($7 per hour, $28 per day) include helmets, locks, front packs, rear racks, maps, and advice. Tandems, kids' trailers, and baby seats are available. **Avenue Cyclery,** 756 Stanyan St. ☎ *415/387-3155,* offers bike sales and rentals and is convenient to Golden Gate Park. Rental rates are $7 per hour or $28 per day, and they do stock children's bikes and tandems.

CLIMATE See "The Weather," earlier in this chapter.

CONCERTS See "Tickets," below.

CONSULATES & EMBASSIES All embassies are located in the nation's capital, Washington, D.C. Some consulates are located in major U.S. cities, and most nations have a mission to the United Nations in New York City. For a directory of embassies in Washington, D.C. call ☎ *202/555-1212* or log on to *www.embassy.org/embassies.* The following are SF consulate addresses for a selection of countries: The **consulate of Australia** is at 625 Market Street, Suite 200, San Francisco ☎ *415/536-1970.* The **embassy of Australia** is at 1601 Massachusetts Ave. NW, Washington, DC 20036 ☎ *202/797-3000; www.austemb.org.*

There is no Canadian consulate in SF. The **embassy of Canada** is at 501 Pennsylvania Ave. NW, Washington, DC 20001 ☎ 202/682-1740; www.canadianembassy.org. The **consulate of Ireland** is at 100 Pine Street, San Francisco ☎ 415/392-4214. The **embassy of Ireland** is at 2234 Massachusetts Ave. NW, Washington, DC 20008 ☎ 202/462-3939; www.irelandemb.org. The **consulate of Japan** is at 50 Fremont Street, Suite 2300, San Francisco ☎ 415/777-3533. The **embassy of Japan** is at 2520 Massachusetts Ave. NW, Washington, DC 20008 ☎ 202/238-6700; www.embjapan.org. The **consulate of New Zealand** is at One Maritime Plaza, Suite 700, San Francisco ☎ 415/399-1255. The **embassy of New Zealand** is at 37 Observatory Circle NW, Washington, DC 20008 ☎ 202/328-4800; www.nzemb.org. The **consulate of the U.K.** is at One Sansome Street, Suite 850, San Francisco ☎ 415/617-1300. The **embassy of the U.K.** is at 3100 Massachusetts Ave. NW, Washington, DC 20008 ☎ 202/462-1340; www.britainusa.com.

CREDIT CARDS Credit cards are a safe way to "carry" money, they provide a convenient record of all your expenses, and they generally offer good exchange rates. You can also withdraw cash advances from your credit cards at banks or ATMs, provided you know your PIN.

CUSTOMS Visitors arriving by air, no matter what the port of entry, should cultivate patience and resignation before setting foot on U.S. soil. Getting through immigration control can take as long as 2 hours on some days, especially on summer weekends. People traveling by air from Canada, Bermuda, and certain countries in the Caribbean can sometimes clear Customs and Immigration at the point of departure, which is much quicker.

DENTISTS If you have dental problems, a nationwide referral service known as *1-800-DENTIST* ☎ 800/336-8478 will provide the name of a nearby dentist or clinic.

DINING Dining in SF, as in most of California, is generally casual and a jacket is rarely required, unless you are at one of the most upscale restaurants in town. **Restaurant reservations:** Call the restaurant directly or try the website www.opentable.com, a free and convenient way to make reservations online.

DOCTORS See "Emergencies," below.

ELECTRICITY Like Canada, the United States uses 110 to120 volts AC (60 cycles), compared to 220 to 240 volts AC (50 cycles) in most of Europe, Australia, and New Zealand. If your small appliances use 220 to 240 volts, you'll need a 110-volt transformer and a plug adapter with two flat parallel pins to operate them here. Downward converters that change 220 to 240 volts to 110 to120 volts are difficult to find in the United States, so bring one with you.

EMBASSIES See "Consulates & Embassies," above.

EMERGENCIES Dial ☎ 911 for fire, police, and ambulance. The **Poison Control Center** can be reached at ☎ 800/222-1222 toll-free from any phone. If you encounter serious problems, contact **Traveler's Aid International** ☎ 202/546-1127; www.travelersaid.org.

EVENT LISTINGS See "Useful Websites" box p 162.

HOLIDAYS Banks, government offices, post offices, and many stores, restaurants, and museums are closed on the following legal national holidays: January 1 (New Year's Day), the third Monday in January (Martin Luther King Jr. Day), the third Monday in February (Presidents' Day, Washington's Birthday), the last Monday in May (Memorial Day), July 4 (Independence Day), the first Monday in September (Labor Day), the second Monday in October (Columbus Day), November 11 (Veterans' Day/Armistice Day), the fourth Thursday in November (Thanksgiving Day), and December 25 (Christmas). Also, the Tuesday following the first Monday in November is Election Day and is a federal government holiday in presidential-election years held every 4 years (the next is in 2008).

INSURANCE **For Domestic Visitors:** Trip-cancellation insurance helps you get your money back if you have to back out of a trip, if you have to go home early, or if your travel supplier goes bankrupt. Allowed reasons for cancellation can range from sickness to natural disasters to the State Department declaring your destination unsafe for travel. (Insurers usually won't cover vague fears, though, as many travelers discovered who tried to cancel their trips in Oct 2001 because they were wary of flying.) In this unstable world, trip-cancellation insurance is a good buy if you're getting tickets well in advance—who knows what the state of the world, or of your airline, will be in 9 months! Insurance policy details vary, so read the fine print—and make sure that your airline or cruise line is on the list of carriers covered in case of bankruptcy. For information, contact one of the following insurers: **Access America** ☎ 866/807-3982; www.accessamerica.com, **Travel Guard International** ☎ 800/826-4919; www.travelguard.com, **Travel Insured International** ☎ 800/243-3174; www.travelinsured.com, or **Travelex Insurance Services** ☎ 888/457-4602; www.travelex-insurance.com. **Medical Insurance:** Insurance policies can cover everything from the loss or theft of your baggage to trip cancellation to the guarantee of bail in case you're arrested. Good policies will also cover the costs of an accident, repatriation, or death. Packages such as **Europ Assistance's "Worldwide Healthcare Plan"** are sold by European automobile clubs and travel agencies at attractive rates. **Worldwide Assistance Services, Inc.** ☎ 800/821-2828; www.worldwideassistance.com is the agent for Europ Assistance in the United States. Although it's not required of travelers, health insurance is highly recommended. Unlike many European countries, the United States does not usually offer free or low-cost medical care to its citizens or visitors. Doctors and hospitals are expensive, and in most cases will require advance payment or proof of coverage before they render their services. Though lack of health insurance may prevent you from being admitted to a hospital in nonemergencies, don't worry about being left on a street corner to die: The American way is to fix you now and bill the living daylights out of you later.

INSURANCE **For British Travelers:** Most big travel agents offer their own insurance and will probably try to sell you their package when you book a holiday. Think before you sign. **The Consumers' Association** recommends that you insist on seeing the policy and reading the fine print before buying travel insurance. **The Association of British Insurers** ☎ 020/7600-3333; www.abi.org.uk gives advice by phone and publishes *Holiday Insurance*, a free guide to policy provisions and prices. You might also shop around for better deals: **Insurance for Canadian Travelers:** Canadians should check with their provincial health plan offices or call **Health Canada** ☎ 613/957-2991; www.hc-sc.gc.ca to find out the extent of your coverage and what documentation and receipts you must take home in case you are treated in the United States. **Insurance for**

Australian Travelers: Online Travel Insurance ☎ *02/6262-8754; www.travelinsuranceaustralia.com. au* offers a variety of policies for U.S. travel.

    Lost-Luggage Insurance: On domestic flights, checked baggage is covered up to $2,500 per ticketed passenger. On international flights (including U.S. portions of international trips), baggage is limited to approximately $9 per pound, up to approximately $635 per checked bag. If you plan to check items more valuable than the standard liability, see if your valuables are covered by your homeowner's policy, get baggage insurance as part of your comprehensive travel-insurance package, or buy Travel Guard's "BagTrak" product. Don't buy insurance at the airport, as it's usually overpriced. Be sure to take any valuables or irreplaceable items with you in your carry-on luggage, since many valuables (including books, money, and electronics) aren't covered by airline policies.

    If your luggage is lost, immediately file a lost-luggage claim at the airport, detailing the luggage contents. For most airlines, you must report delayed, damaged, or lost baggage within 4 hours of arrival. The airlines are required to deliver luggage, once found, directly to your house or destination free of charge.

INTERNET   San Francisco has few Internet cafes. The closest one to Union Square is **Cafe.com,** 120 Mason St., near Eddy Street ☎ *415/433-4001,* open Monday through Saturday. Other options include **Copy Central,** 110 Sutter St., at Montgomery Street ☎ *415/392-6470,* and **Fedex Kinko's,** 1967 Market St., near Gough ☎ *415/252-0864.* If you are staying in the Marina, the Kinko's there is at 3225 Fillmore St., near Lombard Street ☎ *415/441-2995.*

LIMOS   Try **Allstate** ☎ *800/453-4099* or **San Francisco Limo Service** ☎ *415/440-6666.*

MAIL & POSTAGE   Dozens of post offices are located around the city. The closest to Union Square is inside Macy's department store, 170 O'Farrell St. ☎ *800/275-8777.* Another convenient location is Sutter Street Postal Store at 150 Sutter. You can pick up mail addressed to you and marked "General Delivery" (Poste Restante) at the Civic Center Post Office Box Unit, P.O. Box 429991, San Francisco, CA 94142-9991 ☎ *800/275-8777.* The street address is 101 Hyde St.

MONEY   **Traveler's checks:** You can get traveler's checks at almost any bank. **American Express** offers denominations of $20, $50, $100, $500, and (for cardholders only) $1,000. You'll pay a service charge ranging from 1% to 4%. You can also get American Express traveler's checks over the phone by calling ☎ *800/221-7282;* ☎ *0870/600-1060* in the U.K.; visit *www.american express.com.au* in Australia; Amex gold and platinum cardholders who use this number are exempt from the 1% fee. **American Automobile Association** members can obtain checks without a fee at most AAA offices. In the U.S., **Visa** offers traveler's checks at Citibank locations nationwide, as well as at several other banks. The service charge ranges between 1.5% and 2%; checks come in denominations of $20, $50, $100, $500, and $1,000. ☎ *800/732-1322.* **MasterCard** also offers traveler's checks. ☎ *800/223-9920.* Outside the U.S. contact your bank, who will be able to advise you on buying U.S. dollar traveler's checks. If you choose to carry traveler's checks, be sure to keep a record of their serial numbers separate from your checks in the event that the checks are stolen or lost. You'll get a refund faster if you know the numbers. **Credit Cards:** See Credit Cards, p 167.

PARKING   Most city parking meters take nickels, dimes, and quarters and have time limits of anywhere from 15 minutes to 4 hours. Legal street-parking spaces do exist; they are next to unpainted curbs and usually are accompanied by meters. Yellow, white, green, and red curbs are all off-limits; the exceptions are commercial zones (the yellow curbs), which are open to cars after delivery hours. If you return to your parking space but your car isn't there, phone ☎ 415/553-1239 to see if it's been towed, as opposed to stolen.

The best parking rates are at city-owned garages, some of which are listed here: **Union Square Garage,** 333 Post St.; $2/first hour, $12/4 hours. **Fifth and Mission Garage,** 833 Mission St. (SoMa); $2/first hour, $8/4 hours. **Ports-mouth Square Garage,** 733 Kearny, at Clay (Chinatown); $2/first hour, $8/4 hours. **North Beach Garage,** 735 Vallejo near Powell; $2/first hour, $8/4 hours.

PASSES   The **San Francisco City-Pass** is the best way to experience all the color and culture of the city. The CityPass features a book of admission tickets to a variety of attractions. You also get 7 days of unlimited transportation on the cable cars, new Embarcadero streetcars, and all Muni services. City-Passes can be purchased online or throughout SF—ask at your hotel or visit *www.citypass.com.*

PASSPORTS   Always keep a photocopy of your passport with you when you're traveling. If your passport is lost or stolen, having a copy significantly facilitates the reissuing process at a local consulate or embassy. Keep your passport and other valuables in your room's safe or in the hotel safe. See "Consulates & Embassies," above, for more information.

PHARMACIES   **Walgreens,** the Starbucks of drugstores, has stores just about everywhere. Phone ☎ 800/WALGREEN for the address and phone number of the nearest store.

SAFETY   Don't walk alone at night, stay in well-lighted areas, and carry a minimum of cash and jewels Although San Francisco isn't crime-ridden, it is not a 24-hour town and you are putting yourself at risk if you venture out at 2am. We have some dodgy neighborhoods you might consider avoiding: The Tenderloin isn't great, although it is home to a huge immigrant population that manages to live side by side with the drug addicts, hookers, and vagrants. Evenings are particularly rough; daytime is okay. Parts of Van Ness Avenue, from Civic Center to Broadway, are grimy. Sixth and Seventh streets from Market east to Harrison are home to an assortment of folk that are iffy; this is another area to avoid any time day or night.

SENIOR TRAVELERS   The **Senior Citizen Information Line** ☎ 415/626-1033 offers advice, referrals, and information on city services. The **Friendship Line for the Elderly** ☎ 415/752-3778 is a support, referral, and crisis-intervention service. Members of **AARP** (formerly known as the American Association of Retired Persons), 601 E St. NW, Washington, DC 20049 ☎ 800/424-3410 or 202/434-2277; www.aarp.org, get discounts on hotels, airfares, and car rentals. U.K. seniors can contact **Saga** ☎ 0800/414-525; www.saga.co.uk for a range of products and services, including holidays and insurance. Australians over 50 should contact the **National Seniors Association** ☎ 1300/76-5050; www.nationalseniors.com.au.

SMOKING   California law prohibits smoking in public buildings, restaurants, and bars. Many hotels are completely nonsmoking, and others have limited floors for smokers.

SPECTATOR SPORTS   **Giants Baseball,** 24 Willie Mays Plaza, 2nd and

King sts. 📞 *415/972-2000; www. giants.mlb.com.*

San Francisco 49ers (American Football), Candlestick Point 📞 *415/656-4900; www.sf49ers.com.*

TAXES   Sales tax of 8.5% is added to all purchases except snack foods. The hotel tax is 14%.

TAXIS   See "Getting Around" earlier in this chapter.

TELEPHONES   For directory assistance, dial 📞 411. Pay phones (which are getting difficult to find) cost 35¢ to 50¢ for local calls.

TICKETS   **Theater tickets:** Ticket Web *(www.ticketweb.com)* is a popular online box office with an easy-to-use interface and relationships with most clubs and entertainment venues. Other resources include **City Box Office** 180 Redwood St., Suite 100, San Francisco, CA 94102; 📞 *415/392-4400; www.cityboxoffice. com* and box offices at the individual theaters and concert halls. **TIX Bay Area** *(tixbayarea.com)* is a walk-up box office selling half-price tickets on the day of performance and full-price tickets in advance to select events. Tuesday to Thursday 11am to 6pm, Friday 11am to 7pm, Saturday 10am to 7pm, and Sunday 10am to 3pm. Closed Mondays. The TIX Pavilion is located in Union Square on Powell Street, between Geary and Post.

TIPPING   In hotels, tip **bellhops** at least $1 per bag and tip the **chamber staff** $2 to $3 per day (more if you've left a disaster area); the **doorman** or **concierge** $1-$5 only if he or she has provided you with some specific service (for example, calling a cab for you or obtaining difficult-to-get theater tickets). Tip the **valet-parking attendant** $1 every time you get your car. In restaurants, bars, and nightclubs, **service staff** expect 15% to 20% of the check, **bartenders** 10% to 15%, **checkroom attendants** $1 per garment, and **valet-parking attendants** $1 per vehicle. Tip **cab drivers** 15%, **skycaps** at airports at least $1 per bag and **hairdressers** and **barbers** 15% to 20%.

TOILETS   Public toilets can be hard to find in San Francisco. A handful of fancy new French stalls have been strategically placed on high-volume streets, and a few small stores may allow you access to their facilities. Large hotels and fast-food restaurants are probably the best bet for good, clean facilities. Museums, department stores, shopping malls and, in a pinch, gas stations all have public toilets. If possible, avoid the toilets at parks and beaches, which tend to be dirty and may even be unsafe.

TOURIST INFORMATION   **San Francisco Convention and Visitors Bureau,** 900 Market St., Lower Level, Hallidie Plaza, San Francisco, CA 94142-2809 📞 *415/391-2000; www.sfvisitor.org.*

TOURIST TRAPS   Around Fisherman's Wharf and elsewhere, you may see manned booths with signs proclaiming themselves tourist information centers. These booths are operated by private businesses such as tour companies, boat lines, or other attractions, and, as such, are not the best sources of unbiased advice.

TOURS   **Gray Line** 📞 *888/428-69371; www.sfsightseeing.com* is SF's largest bus-tour operator.

TRAVELERS WITH DISABILITIES   Travelers in wheelchairs can request special ramped taxis by calling **Yellow Cab** 📞 *415/626-2345,* which charges regular rates for the service. Travelers with disabilities can also get a free copy of the *Muni Access Guide,* published by the San Francisco Municipal Railway, Accessible Services Program, 949 Presidio Ave. 📞 *415/923-6142,* which is staffed weekdays from 8am to 5pm. Many travel agencies offer customized tours and itineraries for travelers with disabilities. Two of them are **Flying Wheels Travel** ☎ 507/451-5005; www.flyingwheels travel.com and **Accessible Journeys** ☎ 800/846-4537 or 610/521-0339; www.disabilitytravel.com. From the U.K. **Access Travel** ☎ 01942/888844; www.access-travel.co.uk offers a variety of holidays for persons with disabilities. The U.S. National Park Service offers a **Golden Access Passport** that gives free lifetime entrance to all properties administered by the National Park Service—national parks, monuments, historic sites, recreation areas, and national wildlife refuges—for persons who are visually impaired or permanently disabled, regardless of age ☎ 888/467-2757; www.nps.gov/fees_passes.htm.

San Francisco: **A Brief History**

1542 Juan Rodriguez Cabrillo sails up the California coast.

1579 Sir Francis Drake lands near San Francisco, missing the entrance to the bay.

1769 The Spanish expedition led by Gaspar de Portolá become the first Europeans to see San Francisco Bay.

1775 The *San Carlos* is the first European ship to sail into San Francisco Bay.

1776 Captain Juan Bautista de Anza establishes a presidio (military fort); San Francisco de Asis Mission opens.

1821 Mexico wins independence from Spain and annexes California.

1835 The town of Yerba Buena develops around the port; the United States tries unsuccessfully to purchase San Francisco Bay from Mexico.

1846–48 War between the United States and Mexico.

1847 Americans annex Yerba Buena and rename it San Francisco.

1848 Gold is discovered near Sacramento. San Francisco's population swells from about 900 to 26,000.

1851 Lawlessness becomes acute before attempts to curb it.

1869 The transcontinental railroad reaches San Francisco.

1873 Andrew S. Hallidie invents the cable car.

1906 The Great Earthquake strikes; the resulting fire levels the city.

1915 The Panama-Pacific International Exposition celebrates San Francisco's restoration and the completion of the Panama Canal.

1936 The Bay Bridge is completed.

1937 The Golden Gate Bridge is completed.

1945 The United Nations Charter is drafted in San Francisco and adopted by the representatives of 50 countries.

1950 The Beat Generation moves into North Beach.

1967 A free concert in Golden Gate Park attracts 20,000 people, ushering in the Summer of Love and the hippie era.

1974 BART's high-speed transit system opens the tunnel linking San Francisco with the East Bay.

1978 Harvey Milk (a city supervisor and America's first openly gay politician) and Mayor George Moscone are both assassinated, by political rival Dan White.

1989 An earthquake registering 7.1 on the Richter scale hits San Francisco just before a World Series baseball game (100 million watch it on TV).

1991 Fire rages through the Berkeley and Oakland hills, destroying 2,800 homes.

1993 Yerba Buena Center for the Arts opens.

1995 The new SF MOMA opens.

1996 Former assembly speaker Willie Brown is elected mayor of San Francisco.

1998 El Niño deluges San Francisco with its second-highest rainfall in recorded history.

2000 Pacific Bell Park opens as the new home of the San Francisco Giants baseball team.

2003 Gavin Newsome is elected mayor of San Francisco.

2004 San Francisco Mayor Gavin Newsom issues over 4,000 same-sex marriage licenses, which are later annulled by the state's Supreme Court.

A Quick Guide to **Wine Varietals**
by Erika Lenkert & Matthew Poole

Major Grape Varietals
Below is a list of some of the most prevalent grape varietals found in California Wine Country.

CABERNET SAUVIGNON This transplant from Bordeaux has become California's most well known varietal. The small, deep-colored, thick-skinned berry is a complex grape, yielding medium- to full-bodied red wines that are highly tannic when young and usually require a long aging period to achieve their greatest potential. Cabernet is often blended with other related red varietals, such as merlot and cabernet franc (see below), into full-flavored red table wines. Cabernet is often matched with red-meat dishes and strong cheeses. If you're looking to invest in several cases of wine, cabernet sauvignon is always a good long-term bet.

CHARDONNAY Chardonnay is the most widely planted grape variety in the Wine Country, and it produces exceptional medium- to full-bodied dry white wines. In fact, it was a California chardonnay that revolutionized the world of wine when it won the legendary Paris tasting test of 1976. You'll find a range of chardonnays in the Wine Country, from delicate, crisp wines that are clear and light in color to buttery, fruity, and oaky (no other wine benefits more from the oak aging process) wines that tend to have deeper golden hues as they increase in richness. This highly complex and aromatic grape is one of the few grapes in the world that doesn't require blending; it's also the principal grape for making sparkling wine. Chardonnay goes well with a variety of dishes, from seafood to poultry, pork, veal, and pastas made with cream and/or butter.

MERLOT Traditionally used as a blending wine to smooth out the rough edges of other grapes, merlot has gained popularity in California since the early 1970s—enough so that wineries such as Sonoma's St.

Francis are best known for producing masterful merlots. The merlot grape is a relative of cabernet sauvignon, but it's fruitier and softer, with a pleasant black-cherry bouquet. Merlots tend to be simpler and less tannic than most cabernets, and they are drinkable at an earlier age, though these wines, too, gain complexity with age. Serve this medium- to full-bodied red with any dish you'd normally pair with a cabernet. (It's great with pizza.)

PINOT NOIR   It has taken California vintners decades to make relatively few great wines from pinot noir grapes, which are difficult to grow and vinify. Even in their native Burgundy, the wines are excellent only a few years out of every decade, and they are a challenge for winemakers to master. Recent attempts to grow the finicky grape in the cooler climes of the Carneros District have met with promising results. During banner harvest years, California's pinot grapes produce complex, light- to medium-bodied red wines with such low tannins and such silky textures that they're comparable to the finest reds in the world. Pinots are fuller and softer than cabernets and can be drinkable at 2 to 5 years of age, though the best improve with additional aging. Pinot noir is versatile at the dinner table, but it goes best with lamb, duck, turkey, game birds, semisoft cheeses, and even fish.

RIESLING   Also called Johannisberg Riesling or white riesling, this is the grape from which most of the great wines of Germany are made. It was introduced to California in the mid–19th century by immigrant vintners and is now used mainly to produce floral and fruity white wines of light to medium body, ranging from dry to very sweet. (It's often used to make late-harvest dessert wine.) Well-made rieslings, of which California has produced few, have a vivid fruitiness and lively balancing acidity, as well as a potential to age for many years. Suggested food pairings include crab, pork, sweet-and-sour foods, and anything with a strong citrus flavor. Asian-influenced foods also pair well with riesling.

SAUVIGNON BLANC   Also labeled as fumé blanc, sauvignon blanc grapes are used to make crisp, dry whites of medium to light body that vary in flavor from slightly grassy to tart or fruity. The grape grows very well in the Wine Country and has become increasingly popular due to its distinctive character and pleasant acidity; indeed, it has recently become a contender to the almighty chardonnay. Because of their acidity, sauvignon blancs pair well with shellfish, seafood, and salads.

ZINFANDEL   Zinfandel is often called the "mystery" grape because its origins are uncertain. "Zinfandel" first appeared on California labels in the late 1800s; hence, it has come to be known as California's grape. In fact, most of the world's zinfandel acreage is planted in Northern California, and some of the best zinfandel grapes grow in cool coastal locations and on century-old vines up in California's Gold Country. Zinfandel is by far the Wine Country's most versatile grape, popular as blush wine (the ever-quaffable white zinfandel: a light, fruity wine, usually served chilled); as dark, spicy, and fruity red wines; and even as a port. Premium zins, such as those crafted by Ravenswood winery in Sonoma (the Wine Country's Zeus of zins), are rich and peppery, with a lush texture and nuances of raspberries, licorice, and spice. Food-wise it's a free-for-all, although premium zins go well with beef, lamb, venison, hearty pastas, pizza, and stews.

Lesser-Known Grape Varietals

CABERNET FRANC   A French black grape variety that's often blended with and overshadowed by the more widely planted cabernet sauvignon, cabernet franc was actually recently discovered to be one of the parent grape species that gave rise to cabernet sauvignon. The grape grows best in cool, damp climatic conditions and tends to be lighter in color and tannins than cabernet sauvignon; therefore, it matures earlier in the bottle. These wines have a deep purple color with an herbaceous aroma.

CHENIN BLANC Planted mainly in France, chenin blanc runs the gamut from cheap, dry whites with little discernible character to some of the most subtle, fragrant, and complex whites in the world. In the Wine Country the grape is mostly used to create fruity, light- to medium-bodied, and slightly sweet wines. Chenin blanc lags far behind chardonnay and sauvignon blanc in popularity in the Wine Country, though in good years it's known for developing a lovely and complex bouquet, particularly when aged in oak. It's often served with pork and poultry, Asian dishes with soy-based sauces, mild cheeses, and vegetable and fruit salads.

GEWÜRZTRAMINER The gewürztraminer grape produces white wines with a strong floral aroma and litchi-nut-like flavor. Slightly sweet yet spicy, it's somewhat similar in style to Johannisberg Riesling, and it is occasionally used to make late-harvest, dessert-style wine. The grape grows well in the cooler coastal regions of California, particularly Mendocino County. The varietal is particularly appreciated for its ability to complement Asian foods; its sweet character stands up to flavors that would diminish a drier wine's flavors and make it seem more tart.

PETITE SIRAH Widely grown throughout the warmer regions of California, petite sirah's origins are a mystery. The grape, which produces rich red wines that are high in tannins, serves mainly as the backbone for Central Valley "jug" wines. Very old vines still exist in cooler northern regions, where the grapes are often made into a robust and well-balanced red wine of considerable popularity.

PINOT BLANC A mutation of the pinot gris vine, the pinot blanc grape is generally grown in France's Alsace region to make dry, crisp white wines. In California, pinot blanc is used to make a fruity wine similar to the simpler versions of chardonnay. It's also blended with champagne-style sparkling wines, thanks to its acid content and clean flavor.

SANGIOVESE The primary grape used in Italy's Tuscany region and northern and central Italy is used to make everything from chianti and Brunello di Montalcino to "Super Tuscan" blends. As of late, it's also making a name for itself in California. Its style varies depending on where it's grown, but it's commonly described as anything from "fruity," "smooth," "spicy," "good acidity," and "medium-bodied" to "structured" and "full-bodied."

SYRAH This red varietal is best known for producing France's noble and age-worthy Rhône Valley reds such as côte-rôtie and hermitage. Syrah vines produce dark, blackish berries with thick skins, resulting in typically dark, rich, dense, medium- to full-bodied wines with distinctive pepper, spice, and fruit flavors (particularly cherry, black currant, and blackberry).

Toll-Free Numbers and Websites

Airlines

AER LINGUS
☎ 800/474-7424
☎ 01/886-8844 in Ireland
www.aerlingus.com

AIR CANADA
☎ 888/247-2262
www.aircanada.ca

AIR FRANCE
☎ 800/237-2747
☎ 0820-820-820 in France
www.airfrance.com

ALASKA AIRLINES
☎ 800/252-7522
www.alaskaair.com

AIR NEW ZEALAND
☎ 800/262-1234 or -2468
☎ 0800/737-000 in New Zealand
www.airnewzealand.com

AIRTRAN AIRLINES
☎ 800/247-8726
www.airtran.com

ALITALIA
☎ 800/223-5730
☎ 8488-65641 in Italy
www.alitalia.it

AMERICAN AIRLINES
☎ 800/433-7300
www.aa.com

AMERICAN TRANS AIR
☎ 800/225-2995
www.ata.com

AMERICA WEST
☎ 800/327-7810
www.americawest.com

AUSTRIAN AIRLINES
☎ 800/843-0002
☎ 43/(0)5-1789 in Austria
www.aua.com

BRITISH AIRWAYS
☎ 800/247-9297
☎ 0870/850-9-850 in the U.K.
www.british-airways.com

CONTINENTAL AIRLINES
☎ 800/525-0280
www.continental.com

DELTA AIR LINES
☎ 800/221-1212
www.delta.com

HAWAIIAN AIR LINES
☎ 800/367-5320
www.hawaiianair.com

IBERIA
☎ 800/772-4642
☎ 902/400-500 in Spain
www.iberia.com

INDEPENDENCE AIR
☎ 800/FLY-FLYi
www.flyi.com

JET BLUE AIRLINES
☎ 800/538-2583
www.jetblue.com

KLM
☎ 800/374-7747
☎ 020/4-747-747 in the Netherlands
www.klm.nl

LUFTHANSA
☎ 800/645-3880
☎ 49/(0)- 180-5-838426 in Germany
www.lufthansa.com

NORTHWEST AIRLINES
☎ 800/225-2525
www.nwa.com

QANTAS
☎ 800/227-4500
☎ 612/131313 in Australia
www.qantas.com

SCANDINAVIAN AIRLINES
☎ 800/221-2350
☎ 0070/727-727 in Sweden
☎ 70/10-20-00 in Denmark
☎ 358/(0)20-386-000 in Finland
☎ 815/200-400 in Norway
www.scandinavian.net

SINGAPORE AIRLINES
☎ 800/742-3333
☎ 65/6223-8888 in Singapore
www.singaporeair.com

SONG
☎ 800/359-7664
www.flysong.com

SOUTHWEST AIRLINES
☎ 800/I-FLY-SWA
www.southwest.com

SWISS INTERNATIONAL AIRLINES
☎ 877/359-7947
☎ 0848/85-2000 in Switzerland
www.swiss.com

TAP AIR PORTUGAL
☎ 800/221-7370
☎ 351/21-841-66-00 in Portugal
www.tap-airportugal.com

THAI AIRWAYS INTERNATIONAL
☎ 800/426-5204
☎ (66-2)-535-2081-2 in Thailand
www.thaiair.com

TURKISH AIRLINES
☎ 800/874-8875
☎ 90-212-663-63-00 in Turkey
www.flyturkish.com

UNITED AIRLINES
☎ 800/241-6522
www.united.com

US AIRWAYS
☎ 800/428-4322
www.usairways.com

VIRGIN ATLANTIC AIRWAYS
☎ 800/862-8621
☎ 0870/380-2007 in the U.K.
www.virgin-atlantic.com

Index

Photo **Credits**

p. viii: © Daniel McGarrah/Index Stock; p. 3, top: © Omni Photo Communications, Inc./Index Stock Imagery; p. 3, bottom: © David Wasserman/Index Stock Imagery; p. 4, top: © Mark Gibson/Index Stock Imagery; p. 4, bottom: © Thomas Winz/Index Stock Imagery; p. 5: © ML Sinibaldi/Corbis; p. 7, bottom: © Phil Schermeister/Corbis; p. 9, top: © Mark Newman/Index Stock; p. 9, bottom: © Allenn Russell/Index Stock Imagery; p. 11, bottom: © San Francisco CVB; p. 12, bottom: © Ed Young/AGStockUSA, Inc./Alamy; p. 13, top: © Thomas Winz/Index Stock Imagery; p. 15, bottom: © David Wasserman/Index Stock Imagery; p. 16, bottom: